RV and Car Camping

VACATIONS IN EUROPE

RV and Car Camping Tours
To Europe's Top Vacation
Destinations

Mike and Terri
Church

ROLLING HOMES PRESS

Published by
Rolling Homes Press
161 Rainbow Dr., #6157
Livingston, TX 77399-1061

www.rollinghomes.com

Printed in the United States of America
First Printing 2004

Publisher's Cataloging in Publication

Church, Mike.
RV and car camping vacations in Europe : RV and car camping
    tours to Europe's top vacation destinations / Mike and Terri Church
    p.cm.
    Includes index.
    Library of Congress Control Number: 2004090396
    ISBN 0-9652968-9-X

1. Europe–Tours. 2. Camp sites, facilities, etc.–Europe–Guidebooks.
3. Camping–Europe–Guidebooks. 4. Automobile travel–Europe–Guidebooks.
I. Church, Terri. II. Title.

D909.C48 2004
914.04/561–dc22

ACKNOWLEDGMENTS

We highly value the information that comes from conversations, letters, e-mails, and tips passed along by other European RV travelers. Many thanks to all of you. The following is a partial list of the people who have taken the time to share their knowledge. Please forgive us if we've inadvertently left your name off the list.

Julia and Volker Biebesheimer, Bob Bulwa, Don and Halina Clifton, Judy and Jeremy Coleman, Donna Dawick, Alfred Ditterich, William Hall, Bob and Marcia Hanbury, Gloria and Ed Helmuth, Graeme and Gill Hodgson, Tina and Dennis Jaffe, Joe and Vicki Kieva, René Kluver, Monte and Walt Lloyd, Brodie Nimmo, Rich Peterson, George and Marcia Pollitt, Ramon Van Reine, Judee and Tom Stalmack, Deb and Jon Stoner, Felicia Uhden, Gaby and Dieter Weigelt, Richard Woudenberg, and Mick and Chris Young.

Other Books by Mike and Terri Church
and
Rolling Homes Press

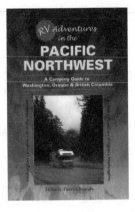

Traveler's Guide To
Mexican Camping

Traveler's Guide To
Camping Mexico's Baja

RV Adventures in the
Pacific Northwest

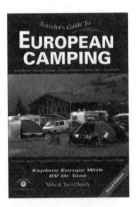

Traveler's Guide To
Alaskan Camping

Traveler's Guide To
European Camping

A brief summary of the above books is provided on pages 318-319

www.rollinghomes.com

When traveling by RV the most complete and up-to-date information is always important. To provide our readers with the most current and accurate information available we maintain a website which lists all known updates and changes to information listed in our books. Just go to our website at www.rollinghomes.com and click on the *Book Additions and Corrections* button to review the most current information.

Warning, Disclosure, and Communication With The Authors and Publishers

Half the fun of travel is the unexpected, and self-guided camping travel can produce much in the way of unexpected pleasures, and also complications and problems. This book is designed to increase the pleasures of European camping and reduce the number of unexpected problems you may encounter. You can help ensure a smooth trip by doing additional advance research, planning ahead, and exercising caution when appropriate. There can be no guarantee that your trip will be trouble free.

Although the authors and publisher have done their best to ensure that the information presented in this book was correct at the time of publication they do not assume and hereby disclaim any liability to any party for any loss or damage caused by errors, omissions, or any other cause.

In a book like this it is inevitable that there will be omissions or mistakes, especially as things do change over time. If you find inaccuracies we would like to hear about them so that they can be corrected in future editions. We would also like to hear about your enjoyable experiences. If you come upon an outstanding campground or destination please let us know, those kinds of things may also find their way to future versions of the guide or to our website. You can reach us by mail at:

Rolling Homes Press
161 Rainbow Dr., #6157
Livingston, TX 77399-1061

You can also communicate with us by sending an e-mail through our website at:

www.rollinghomes.com

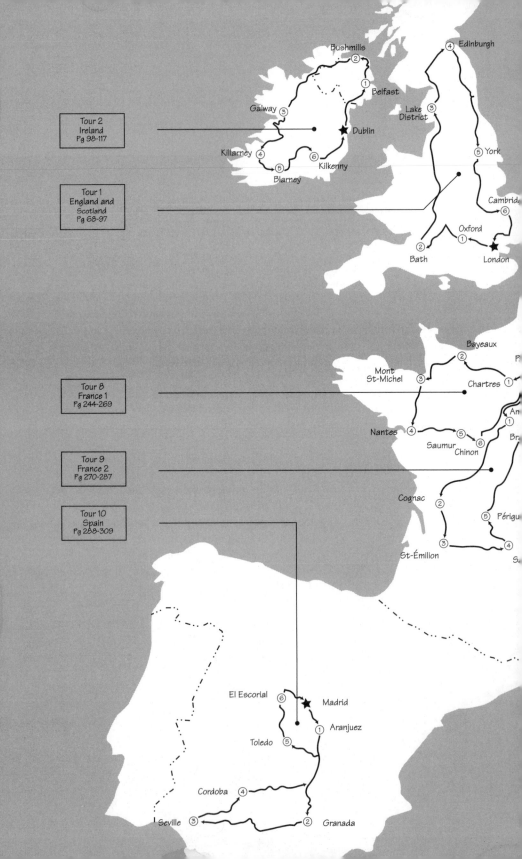

Bushmills

Edinburgh

Belfast

Lake
District

Galway

York

Dublin

Cambrid

Killarney

Oxford

Blarney

Kilkenny

Bath

London

Bayeaux

P.

Mont
St-Michel

Chartres

An

Nantes

Saumur

Br.

Chinon

Cognac

Périgu

St-Émilion

S.

El Escorial

Madrid

Aranjuez

Toledo

Cordoba

Seville

Granada

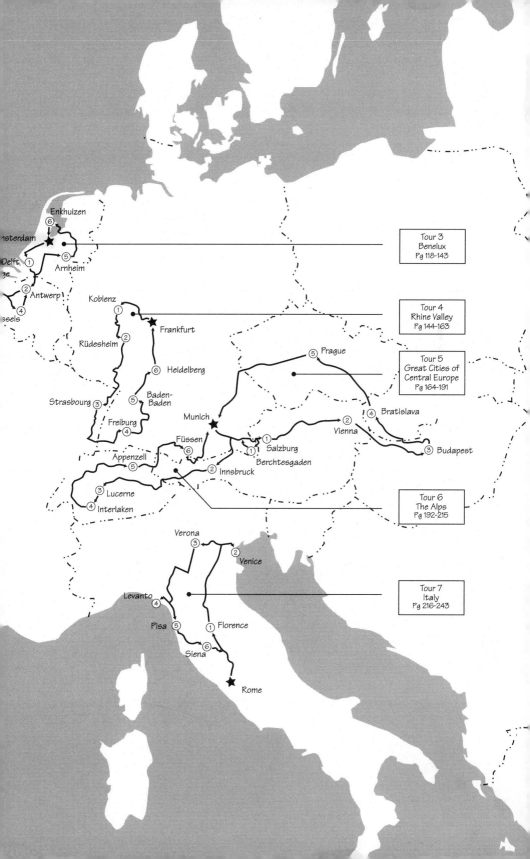

Enkhuizen

Amsterdam ⑥

Delft ① ⑤ Arnheim

ge ② Antwerp

ssels ④

Tour 3
Benelux
Pg 118-143

Koblenz ①

② ★ Frankfurt

Rüdesheim

⑥ Heidelberg

Strasbourg ③ ⑤ Baden-Baden

Freiburg ④

Tour 4
Rhine Valley
Pg 144-163

⑤ Prague

Tour 5
Great Cities of
Central Europe
Pg 164-191

④ Bratislava

Munich ★ ② Vienna

Füssen ⑥ ③ Budapest

① Salzburg

① Berchtesgaden

Appenzell ② Innsbruck

⑤

③ Lucerne

④ Interlaken

Tour 6
The Alps
Pg 192-215

Verona

③ ② Venice

Levanto ④

Tour 7
Italy
Pg 216-243

Pisa ⑤ ① Florence

⑥

Siena

★ Rome

TABLE OF CONTENTS

CHAPTER 11

TOUR 8 – FRANCE 1 244

CHAPTER 12

TOUR 9 – FRANCE 2 270

CHAPTER 13
TOUR 10 – SPAIN **288**

Preface

We're proud to introduce the first edition of our new vacation camping guide to Europe – *RV and Car Camping Vacations in Europe*. We've been writing and publishing a European camping guide for ten years now, but this one is different. It is specifically designed for people with a limited amount of time to spend touring Europe. We want to introduce European camping to people who have only a week or two of vacation time to spend traveling. With the low airfares now available European camping has become a viable vacation option. Rental automobiles and RVs make it easy. Once you give it a try we're sure that you'll return to do it again.

We haven't given up on those with more time, however. We will continue to publish our other European camping guide titled *Traveler's Guide to European Camping*. It's now in its third edition. This is a much larger and more complete guide with information about shipping, buying, and renting a camping vehicle. It also has extensive information about over 350 campgrounds throughout Europe.

The book you are holding in your hands starts with an introduction to the concept of European camping. It points out that this is a popular way for Europeans to travel the Continent, just as camping in the U.S. has always been an economical and fun way for American and Canadian families, young people, and seniors to travel at home. It reminds you that traveling by vehicle has always been the best way to see North America. It only makes sense that it's a great way to see Europe too. Then the chapter explains how you can easily procure your European camping vehicle: a car or RV. Renting one of these is easy, you can arrange everything from home and have it waiting for you when your flight lands in Europe. We give the company names and contact information you will need and tell you how to do it.

The second chapter goes into the details of camping in Europe. European camping is a little different, but it's popular, probably more popular than in North America. European campgrounds are set up to accommodate lots of tent campers. They have facilities to make it easy to camp with a minimum of equipment, they even have facilities for washing dishes and of course they offer showers and laundries. RVs are used in Europe too. If you want to travel in a rental RV you'll find that European campgrounds are built to accommodate them too with electrical hookups and comfortable parking sites.

The remainder of the book is devoted to setting down ten different touring routes that you can follow after you arrive in Europe. The tours start in towns that have good airline access and offer rental automobiles and RVs. Then they visit interesting destinations. For each destination there is a description of the camping facilities and maps and descriptions making them easy to find. There is also a description of the attractions of the area. It's not meant to be a full guidebook, but it's an easy overview that will get you started.

Most 0f the tours outlined offer seven destinations including the gateway city. That means that you could make the tour in seven days, but you really need at least two weeks to enjoy a European camping holiday. If you have more time there's no reason you can't combine several of these tours, or you can travel more slowly.

We travel to Europe for a camping tour almost every year. We love the way that we can travel at our own pace and go anywhere we want. Since camping travel by North Americans in Europe is still relatively uncommon the people we spend time with in the campgrounds are Europeans. They seldom meet other folks from North America and love to talk about their way of life and how it compares with the way things are done in North America. This is real traveling, not being a tourist. It's an adventure. We hope that with the information in this book you can join us in Europe.

RV and Car Camping Vacations in Europe is one of six guidebooks we have written. These books are all designed to be travel and campground guides for camping travelers. The others are *Traveler's Guide to European Camping, Traveler's Guide to Alaskan Camping, Traveler's Guide to Mexican Camping, Traveler's Guide to Camping Mexico's Baja*, and *RV and Car Camping Vacations in the Pacific Northwest* (formerly *RV Adventures in the Pacific Northwest*). The six volumes are the key to a world of travel fun!

E U R O P E

RV CAMPING FOR THE NIGHT AT MONT-ST-MICHEL
TENT CAMPING FROM A RENTAL RENAULT

Chapter 1

Introduction

At first most people are surprised by the idea of a camping vacation to Europe. We think of camping as something to do in the summer in a national park in the United States or Canada. It's a way to take a vacation with the kids, one that won't break the bank.

The truth is that camping is a very popular way to travel in Europe, at least among Europeans. Europe has thousands of campgrounds. In fact, Europe has many more campgrounds than the U.S. does! During the summer these campgrounds are full of travelers and vacationers. They provide a great way to see Europe, but strangely, your travel agent probably will never mention this to you.

Most of us would never think of traveling in the U.S. the way we do in Europe. Who can afford to stay in expensive hotel rooms? Who wants to travel from city center to city center on crowded airplanes or trains? How much can you learn about a foreign culture from a hotel desk clerk or a waiter? What about the countryside? Where are the real people?

One popular and well-known alternative to a first class hotel vacation is to travel by train and stay in hostels, rooms, or bed-and-breakfasts. This is better, but it's still not great. Do you want to pack everything you own on your back? If you rent a car and stay in bed-and-breakfasts you can spend a lot of money.

There are many advantages to a European camping vacation. You can do it inexpensively or you can do it first class. Some people rent a car and stay in a tent, others rent a beautiful European RV and spend the nights in style. Both ways work well, we'll talk about the pros and cons later in the chapter.

An interesting thing about European campgrounds is that many are located in places that visitors from North America want to visit. The truth is that we publish another book titled *Traveler's Guide to European Camping* that provides information similar to that in this book about over 350 campgrounds in Europe, every one in a location convenient to a destination that North American travelers want to see.

The book you have in your hands has a more limited purpose. It's aimed at the thousands of travelers who would enjoy a European camping vacation but who just don't have the time to figure it all out for themselves. It contains the information you need to easily arrange the necessary transportation, either a rental automobile or a rental RV. It gives you the necessary background information so that you take along what you need but not a lot else. It explains how to deal with the things that will come up along the way. And finally, it lays out ten different tours with great destinations and campgrounds conveniently located for a visit to the sights in the area.

Camping Travel – The Right Vehicle

The big question here is the kind of vehicle you should select. From the beginning we'll rule out train and bicycle travel. We'll also rule out motorcycles, not because they won't work but because renting a motorcycle in Europe is expensive and probably not something most people would consider. That leaves two choices, renting an automobile or renting an RV.

Camping out of an automobile is a very attractive option. This assumes that you will be traveling at a time of year when the weather is decent. Automobiles are available as normal rentals and also on short-term lease plans and you can carry enough camping gear in the trunk to be comfortable at night. Especially important is a large tent, one that has a high ceiling allowing you to stand. A small collection of folding furniture (chairs, folding cots, maybe a table), a stove with two burners (or two one-burner stoves), and maybe an ice chest will give you a comfortable home-away-from-home. European campgrounds are set up for tent campers, they have dishwashing areas, showers, lounge areas, and sometimes even cooking facilities.

Camping in a tent does have some disadvantages. Probably the worst is that you must pitch the tent and set up camp when you arrive and reverse the process when you depart. We often travel this way and find that we soon become really proficient at setting up and tearing down our camp. It takes the two of us about 20 minutes to set up and 30 minutes to hit the road. That isn't much longer than it takes with an RV.

One big attraction of automobile camping may not be readily apparent. That is flexibility. Automobile renting is easy. You can fly into any airport and pick up the vehicle right at the airport or nearby. You can do this any time of the day or any day of the week. You'll understand the automobile with cursory introduction, no need to go over the systems or get accustomed to driving a big rig as you must with an RV.

There are other advantages. You'll spend little on gas, European cars sip gas so you'll probably spend less for fuel than you would on a similar trip in North America.

Last but not least, you'll spend from a fifth to a tenth as much renting an automobile rather than an RV.

On the other hand, the RV option is pretty good too. It's really nice to have all the conveniences of home right in your rig. Rental RVs come with beds, tables, stoves, refrigerators, and even heaters. You can stop along the way and eat lunch or even take a nap. You even have your own bathroom along, sometimes with its own shower.

The major problem with RVs however, in addition to the cost, is a certain amount of scheduling inconvenience. It is hard to rent an RV for anything other than a seven day period, it's also tough to pick one up or drop it off on weekends.

Whichever way you decide to do it though, it's not hard to camp. After a discussion of the routes covered in this book we'll talk about the details of renting a vehicle. In chapter two we'll cover the details of traveling and camping in Europe.

Tour Routes

The tours in this book are laid out so that they could be done in a week. All are much better if you have two weeks to devote to them. They all start in a gateway city. These are major European cities offering lots to see and do. They also are home to both automobile and RV rental companies. Since there are a limited number of cities where RVs can be rented in two cases the tours start in the same gateway city. In each tour chapter, following the descriptions of the gateway city, there are descriptions of either five or six additional great camping destinations and the routes between them. If you have a week you can fly into the gateway city, pick up your rental, and complete the tour in time to head home. If you have more time you can spend a few days touring the gateway city, do the tour in a leisurely manner, spend extra days as you wish, and again relax in the gateway city before heading home.

Tour 1 – Great Britain – Starts in London. The first day is a short drive to Oxford. Then you spend some time in southern England in Bath before driving north to the Lake District and then Edinburgh in Scotland. Complete the tour by driving back to London and then south via York and Cambridge. Total mileage is 1,619 kilometers (1,004 miles).

Tour 2 – Ireland – Starts in Dublin. Then circles the Island counter-clockwise visiting the top attractions with overnight stops in Belfast, Bushmills, Galway, Killarney, Blarney, and Kilkenny. Total mileage is 1,252 kilometers (776 miles).

Tour 3 – The Netherlands and Belgium – Starts in Amsterdam. Then visits a choice selection of cities including Delft, Antwerp, Bruges, Brussels, Arnhem, and Enkhuizen. Total mileage is 805 kilometers (499 miles).

Tour 4 – Rhine Valley – Starts in Frankfurt. Makes a circle tour of one of the most popular regions in Europe with overnights in Koblenz, Rüdesheim, Strasbourg, Freiburg, Baden Baden, and Heidelberg. You'll drive through the Rhine gorge, along the German Wine Road and the French Route du Vin, and through the Black Forest. Total mileage is 1,075 kilometers (667 miles).

Tour 5 – Central European Cities – Starts in Munich. Then visits more of the greatest cities of Europe: Salzburg, Vienna, Budapest, Bratislava, and Prague. Total mileage is 1,613 kilometers (1,000 miles).

Tour 6 – The Alps – Starts in Munich. From there the tour takes you south to Berchtesgaden, Germany; Innsbruck, Austria; Lucerne, Interlaken and Appenzell, Switzerland; and finishes with a visit to King Ludwig's Schloss Neuschwanstein in Füssen, Germany. Total mileage is 1,307 kilometers (810 miles).

Tour 7 – Italy – Starts in Rome. Then heads north to Florence, Venice, Verona, and the Cinque Terre, before returning south through Pisa and Siena. Total mileage is 1,425 kilometers (884 miles).

Tour 8 – France 1 – Starts in Paris, of course. Then circles Normandy with visits to Chartres, Bayeux, Mont-St-Michel, Nantes, and two stops in the Loire Valley. Total mileage is 1,077 kilometers (668 miles).

Tour 9 – France 2 – Starts in Paris. Then gives you the best of France's two favorite valleys – the Loire and the Dordogne. Stops in Amboise, Cognac, St Émilion, Sarlat, Périgueux and Bracieux. If you love food and wine this is the tour for you. Total mileage is 1,291 kilometers (800 miles).

Tour 10 – Spain – Starts in Madrid. Then visits Aranjuez, Granada, Seville, Cordoba, Toledo, and El Escorial. A great introduction to Spain. Total mileage is 1,308 kilometers (811 miles).

An Important Note

In the following sections we list many firms that you may choose to use when you visit Europe. Please be aware that we do not specifically recommend any of them. Although they are the companies that are most active in their respective businesses we have not personally used many of them so we can make no guarantees. We do not receive commissions from any of them. We would love to hear from you about your experiences if you choose to use them.

Renting a Car

If your European trip is for a short time you will probably decide on a normal weekly rental. However, you should be aware that car rental rates vary considerably from country to country. Good values are usually Belgium, the United Kingdom, and Sweden. Italy and Norway are best avoided. It definitely pays to shop around. The major North American automobile rental companies all have European operations but there are some stand-out rental and short-term lease companies with good rates. They also have websites, see www.rollinghomes.com for internet links.

- **Auto France** (800 572-9655) – Peugeot short-term leases.

- **Auto-Europe** (888 223-5555) – Peugeot short-term leases and general automobile rentals.

- **Don Dooley** (800 331-9301) – Irish rental company.

- **Europe By Car** (800 223-1516) – Both rentals and Renault and Peugeot short-term leases. Wide selection, good rates.

- **Renault Eurodrive** (800 221-1052) – Renault short-term leases.

- **Rob Liddiard Travel** (800 272-3299) – Renault and Peugeot short -term leases and general automobile rental.

You'll probably get a better rental rate if you book in North America before leaving for Europe. Short-term leases are only available if booked before you travel to Europe.

Which brings us to short-term leases. These are really just of interest if you will need the car longer than 15 days. For longer terms lease-purchases are actually cheaper than most rentals. The automobile is a brand-new Renault or Peugeot which is fully insured, a great deal for long stays.

TENT CAMPING FROM A RENAULT RENTAL CAR

Here are some issues you need to ask about when booking:

1. Does the rate include Value Added Tax? VAT ranges from 7.5% to 25%, some companies include it in their quoted rates, some don't.

2. Does the rate include unlimited mileage? If not are you going to exceed the limit?

3. Can you drop the unit off in a different place than you pick it up?

4. Can you take the automobile where you want to go? For example, some U.K. companies will not let you take their units to the Continent or they charge more if you want to do this.

5. What days are the pickup stations open?

6. What kind of insurance coverage is provided? Will it cover you where you want to go? Is there a collision damage deductible, theft deductible or deposit required? Note that the collision damage waiver coverage that you normally get with your credit card may save you a considerable amount each day, check with your credit card company about this. One big advantage of short-term leases is that the collision damage deductible fee is usually included in the price.

7. Is transportation provided from and to the airport? If so, is there a charge? If not, is there an acceptable alternative?

8. Find out what documents you'll need. Do you need an International Driver's License?

Just like renting in North America make sure to check the vehicle thoroughly to make sure all damage is documented before you head out, you don't want to have to argue about it when you return the automobile.

Renting an RV

Renting an RV for a short vacation is quite practical, you can start your trip in any of the larger cities thereby limiting the amount of driving you must do. There are dozens of rental operations in Europe. Many locals rent for their own vacations. Prices will vary considerably depending upon time of year, size of rig, and country. There are basically three seasons although the months do vary from rental company to rental company: high (usually June, July, August), middle or shoulder season (usually May, September), and low (usually October through April). Typical prices are about 60 euros per day in Germany (the least expensive country for rentals) during the low season for an almost-new van conversion that sleeps two. This would go to 80 euros per day during the shoulder season and 95 euros during the high season. A larger rig that would sleep six would be about 140 euros during the summer from the same outfit. During the low season it is sometimes possible to rent for longer periods for lower rates, sometimes very low rates. If these prices seem high you should check on

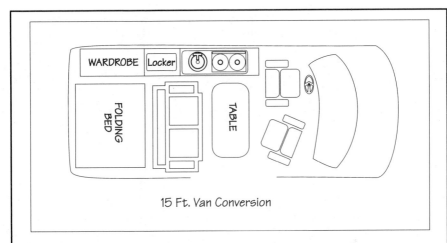

15 Ft. Van Conversion

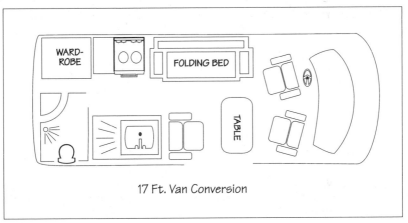

17 Ft. Van Conversion

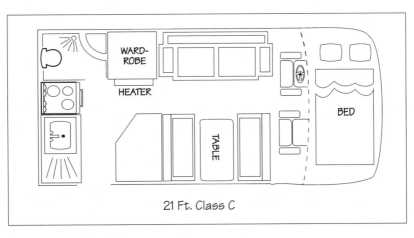

21 Ft. Class C

TYPICAL CAMPER LAYOUTS

the price of renting an RV in North America. Remember, you won't have an expensive hotel room, you have your own transportation, and you will probably save a bundle on food.

Make your reservations early, as much as six months in advance, because RV rental companies tend to get fully booked during the summer months.

Many travel agencies in North America can make motorhome reservations for your trip to Europe but it pays to work with an agency that specializes in RVs. Renting RVs is more complicated than renting automobiles and non-specialists will probably make mistakes that will inconvenience you. Here are the specialists:

- **Overseas Motorhome Tours, Inc.** (800 322-2127) – Units available in London and Glasgow in the U.K.; Amsterdam in the Netherlands; Frankfurt, Munich, Düsseldorf, and Hamburg in Germany; Madrid, Barcelona and Malaga in Spain.

- **Rob Liddiard Travel** (800 272-3299) – Will research and arrange in most countries.

- **Motorhome Rentals Worldwide** (888 519-8969) – Units available in Düsseldorf, Frankfurt, Hamburg, and Munich in Germany; London in the U.K; Madrid in Spain.

- **Owasco RV** (866 579-2267) – This Canadian company arranges RV rentals from Munich, Hamburg, Frankfurt and Düsseldorf in Germany; and Amsterdam in the Netherlands.

Australians and New Zealanders travel by RV in Europe much more than North Americans. You might want to try one of their firms that specialize in RV rentals. After all, international telephone rates are way down and the internet is almost free. To call from the U.S. or Canada dial 011, then the number listed below which includes the country code. We have links to their website from our site: www.rollinghomes.com.

- **Motorhome Holidays Worldwide** (011 800 8781 1120 toll free or 011 61 3 8781 1100 in Australia) – Units available in London, Manchester, Southend-on-Sea, Southampton, Bagshot, Preston, Golden Cross (Eastbourne), Glasgow, and Edinburgh in the U.K.; Paris, Nice, Lyon, Marseille, Blois, Digne, Toulouse, Dijon, and Ajaccio (Corsica) in France; Amsterdam in the Netherlands; Frankfurt, Munich, Hamburg, and Düsseldorf in Germany; Madrid and Barcelona in Spain; Rome, Florence, Milan, Trieste, and Venice in Italy; Dublin in Ireland; Belfast in Northern Ireland; Lisbon in Portugal; Stockholm in Sweden; Oslo in Norway; Helsinki, Rovaniemi, Ivalo and Kuopio in Finland; Tallin in Estonia; and Prague in the Czech Republic.

It is also possible but a little more difficult to deal directly with the European RV rental firms. You will probably find better prices by doing this. To call overseas from the U.S. or Canada dial 011, then the country code listed below, then the number given for the company. Many of these outfits have websites and you will find links from ours at www.rollinghomes.com.

United Kingdom *(country code 44)*

- **Sunseeker Rentals Ltd.,** 27D Stable Way, London W10 6QX, U.K. (181 960 5747).

- **Turners Motorcaravan Hire**, 11a Barry Road, East Dulwich, London SE22 OHX, U.K. (181 693 1132).

Northern Ireland and Ireland *(country code 44)*

- **Motorhome Ireland LTD**, 17 Valley Road. Banbridge, Co Down, North-

VOLKSWAGEN CAMPER READY FOR PICKUP FROM BRAITMAN & WOUDENBERG

ern Ireland BT32 (28 40621800) – Units available in Dublin and Banbridge (40 km SW of Belfast).

The Netherlands (country code 20, all firms can deal with you in English)

- **Braitman & Woudenberg,** Droogbak 4A, NL-1013 GE Amsterdam, Netherlands (20 6221168) – Units available in Amsterdam, in the Netherlands. Easy to work with, excellent off-season long-term rates. Lots of experience working with North Americans.

- **Campanje Campervans and Campers**, P.O. Box 9332, NL-3506 GH Utrecht, Netherlands (30 2447070) – Units available in Utrecht in the Netherlands.

- **Volkswagen Campercentrum Nederland**, Basicweg 5 a-c, 3821 BR Amersfoort Netherlands (33 4949944) – Units available in Amersfoort in the Netherlands.

Germany (country code 49)

- **DRM**, Stahlgruberning 30, D-81829 Munchen (89 427143-0) – Units available in Munich, Frankfurt, Düsseldorf and Hamburg in Germany. Usually the best rates in Europe.

- **Reise-Profi Service GmbH**, Offenbachstr. 6, D-Westoverledingen, Germany (55-920905) – Units available in Oslo in Norway; Stockholm in Sweden; Helsinki in Finland; Paris, Dijon, Lyon, Toulouse, and Marseille in France; Hamburg, Düsseldorf, Frankfurt, and Munich in Germany; Amsterdam in the Netherlands; and Rome in Italy. This is a German travel agency.

France (country code 33)

- **Hertz Trois Soleils**, BP-15, F-67117 Ittenheim (03 88691717) – Units available in Paris in France.

Italy (country code 39)

- **Freedom Holiday**, Via Cristoforo Colombo 2339, Rome (65 0914212) – Units available in Rome in Italy.

- **Camper Tours Italy,** Via Saragozza 225, I-40135 (3477183911) – Units available in Bologna in Italy.

Spain (country code 23)

- **Autocaravan Express**, Autovia de Burgos N-1 Km 24, I-28700 S

DRM CLASS C RENTAL MOTORHOME

Sebastioan de los Reyes, Madrid (91 6571006) – Units available in Madrid in Spain.

Switzerland *(country code 41)*

- **Moby Campers**, Postfach 20, Möslistrasse 12, Postfach 20, CH-4532 Feldbrunnen, Schweiz-Switzerland (32 6229610) – Units available near Basel in Switzerland.

Here are some of the issues you need to ask about when booking:

1. Does the rate include Value Added Tax? VAT ranges from 7.5% to 25%, some companies include it in their quoted rates, some don't.

2. Is there a minimum rental period? Usually this is a week, but during the high season it's often two weeks.

3. Does the rate include unlimited mileage? If not are you going to exceed the limit?

4. Can you drop the unit off in a different place than you pick it up?

5. Can you take the camper where you want to go? For example, some

U.K. companies will not let you take their units to the Continent or they charge more if you want to do this.

6. Some companies count the pickup and drop-off day together as one day as long as 24 hours are not exceeded, others count any part of a day as one day. Get this cleared up before renting rather than after.

7. What days are the pickup stations open? Most European companies are closed on Saturday and Sunday, some are open on Saturday if you make arrangements ahead and if you pay a fee.

8. Is there a preparation fee and what supplies are included?

9. What linens and kitchenware are included with the rig, what is not included but available for an extra price?

10. Is there a cleanup charge? If so, how can you minimize it? Can you clean the rig yourself in the company's yard when you return it?

11. What kind of insurance coverage is provided? Will it cover you where you want to go? Is there a collision damage deductible, theft deductible or deposit required? Note that the collision damage waiver coverage that you normally get with your credit card probably does not apply when renting an RV, check on this with your credit card company.

12. Is transportation provided from and to the airport? If so, is there a charge? If not, is there an acceptable alternative?

13. Find out what documents you need. Do you need an International Driver's License? If you're renting a big rig do you need something documenting that you can drive a rig over 3,500 kg at home so you can do so in Europe too?

When picking up the motorhome there are some things you should check that you might not consider:

1. Go over the rig with a fine-tooth comb looking for damage. Areas prone to have existing damage are front and rear bumpers, roof, and wheel covers. Don't forget that roof. Roof damage is common in RVs, often not covered under collision damage waivers, and often a source of contention when you return the rig. Use a ladder if possible or the ladder on the back of the rig. Look over everything, and have all dents, scratches, cracks and blemishes listed, both outside and inside. Operate everything that moves, like faucets, windows, drawers, cabinet doors and storage compartments doors.

2. You should get a pre-trip orientation. Even if you have an RV in North America some of the systems are different. Make sure you know how to lock the rig up, how to start and operate that diesel, how to operate the

transmission, how to fill the tanks with water, how to dump the holding tank and cassette toilet, how to use the cassette toilet, how to turn on the water pump, how to operate the water heater and furnace, how to get the shower to work, how to open the windows and close the cassette blinds, how to refill or replace the propane bottle. Where is the spare and the jack as well as the first-aid kit and the emergency warning triangles?

3. Check the inventory of linens, kitchenware, and reference books. Often the unit hasn't been inventoried and things are missing. Be sure there are an adequate number of plates, bowls, cups, glasses, knives, forks, spoons, pots, pans, etc. Look for spatulas, cooking spoons and forks, can opener, corkscrew, peeler, bottle opener, brush and dust pan, stove lighter, etc. If these are not present they can probably be obtained from a different unit on the lot. Many companies provide maps and camping guides. Even if you have ours go ahead and ask, they'll often let you look through and select from a box of guides that have been left behind by other renters.

4. You'll need to stop at a store first thing for paper products, cleaners, drinks and food. Don't just go look, ask at the rental agency for the nearest Lidl, Aldi, Wal-Mart or other supermarket.

LIDL - EUROPE'S ANSWER TO WAL-MART

Internet Resources

Every day there are more and more websites devoted to information about rental vehicles, destinations, campgrounds, sites, parks, and transportation. New sites appear and old ones disappear or change addresses. We've found that the only way to maintain a current listing is to set up our own site. The site is www.rollinghomes.com and has current links to a large number of websites that will be of interest to readers of this guide. Don't ignore this resource, it can make your trip much more rewarding.

When to Go

As a camper the weather is an important factor in your decision about the time of your visit. Of course, you may not have the luxury of timing your visit perfectly, other commitments tend to shape travel plans. If they do you can take comfort in the fact that off-season camping in an appropriate rig (one with a reliable heater) is entirely possible.

Northern Europe has some nasty winter weather: lots of rain (or snow in the far north) and temperatures near or below freezing. Even southern Greece, Italy and Spain, the warmest regions, are coolish during November to March.

CHRISTMAS IS BEAUTIFUL IN PARIS - BUT NOT NECESSARILY IN A MOTORHOME!

The camping season with a heated rig runs from April to October in most of Europe. Tent campers won't be comfortable in northern continental Europe until the middle of May and should be out of the high country and the north by the end of September. Northern Scotland and Scandinavia are comfortable only during June, July, and August. Southern Italy, southern Iberia, southern Greece and coastal Turkey are usually comfortable but not hot throughout the winter.

Crowded campgrounds during July and August make the months of May, June, September, and October the prime European camping months. We call this the shoulder season, it is our favorite time to be in Europe. Don't let July and August bother you however. You can deal with the crowds by traveling earlier in the day and arriving before the campgrounds fill up. Fortunately, many of the destinations that are attractive to North American travelers aren't as popular with Europeans on vacations. They generally want to go to the beach or the mountains to rest, we want to see the cultural sights and attractions.

In the introductions to each of the tours in this book we talk about the best time to travel. Some tours are limited by the dates that campgrounds in that area are open so it's important to read the tour sections carefully to determine which ones are appropriate for the time of year you want to travel.

Hooge Veluwe

Chapter 2

About Camping in Europe

EUROPEAN CAMPGROUNDS

A General Description

Europeans camp in tents and they camp in well-designed camping rigs of every description. The typical European campground is similar to the ones we are accustomed to in North America, but there are differences. Many European campers have small rigs so the facilities in campgrounds are more important than they are in North America and they tend to be more extensive. Most campgrounds have showers, clothes-washing machines, dish-washing sinks, and often even covered cooking areas. Many campgrounds also have bars, restaurants, food markets, and lounge areas.

The actual camping sites within the campgrounds are also different than the ones we are accustomed to. It is not unusual to find that individual sites are not delineated. Campgrounds are often set in an old orchard or vineyard. Campers park where they like, often in a grassy field. Electricity is often limited to an amperage suitable only for lights and refrigerators. There are usually no picnic tables, campers bring along their own folding versions. People spend a lot of time outdoors and you will find that you will meet more people than in a campground in North America. There are no fire rings, campfires are almost never a part of European camping.

Most Europeans camp during July and August. Veteran visitors to Europe know that the whole continent goes on vacation during these months, many European vacationers head for the campgrounds. Fortunately most European campers go to the seashores, the mountains, and the countryside; campgrounds near the cities are not really crowded. Outside these months, from April to early July and also in September and

October, campgrounds are half-full at best, you'll have no trouble finding a place to stay and you will not have to deal with crowds.

You will find a convenient campground near almost any destination you would want to visit in Europe. In big cities the campground is generally located away from the city center in a quiet suburb. There is almost always convenient public transportation to whisk you in to town. Using the maps provided in this guide you will have no trouble driving right to these outlying campgrounds, there is no reason to take your vehicle into the crowded city centers.

The camping lifestyle is a great way to meet Europeans. Most visitors from North America only meet people who make their livings dealing with tourists; people working as taxi drivers, desk clerks, or waiters. As a camper you'll meet Europeans who almost never see tourists, they certainly don't meet many American campers. You'll be more popular than you think!

As a camper you can eat in restaurants or you can cook your own food. This can save you lots of money, it can also be one of the best parts of the travel experience. The small restaurants at the campgrounds tend to be inexpensive, they won't break your budget. If you choose to buy groceries and cook you will be living off the local economy, not paying extortionate tourist prices. Almost all European countries have great supermarkets, small shops, and street markets full of interesting things to eat. You can try something new or cook the familiar dishes from home that other travelers miss while they are on the road. On the other hand, there is no reason that you can't join the others and visit some of the best restaurants in the world.

Camping is an excellent way to travel with children. They love it. Foreign campgrounds are interesting and the great outdoors offers lots of opportunities to use up youthful exuberance. Many campgrounds have playgrounds, bike trails, swimming pools, water slides or beaches. A family pays little more for a camping vacation than a couple does so you'll save lots of money over a hotel tour. Finally, you can cook the things that your family will eat, you won't have to deal with unfamiliar restaurant food.

A Few Problems?

It is best to be honest about some of the problems with the bathroom/shower facilities in Europe. You are going to find yourself at a few campgrounds where the toilets and showers are not up to North American standards, or European standards either for that matter.

First, there are the toilets. Pit toilets like you sometimes find in the U.S., Mexico, and Canada are unusual. Most campgrounds do have plumbing. Some of them just don't make the best use of it.

In much of southern Europe you will find that normal seat-type toilets are scarce. Instead you will find what are often indelicately called "squatters" by most North

American visitors. These consist of a ceramic fixture looking a lot like the floor of a shower stall. There is a hole in the floor with two platforms in front that are obviously places to put your feet. After you've done your business you had better stand back before you pull the flush cord, because the deluge that follows may wet your shoes. To be fair these things are common in other places around the world, some people swear by them. It must take a lifetime of use to attain proficiency.

Even if you do find a sit-down toilet your problems may not be over. The toilets in many campgrounds do not have seats. We suppose the theory here is that they are easier to clean. Your guess is as good as ours.

European toilet paper has been a joke for a long time. The quality has been poor, sometimes the proverbial Sears catalog seemed like it would be an improvement. Now you can buy good toilet paper in the stores. You had better do so because most campgrounds do not provide it for you.

The other problem area in campground bathrooms is the showers. Energy is expensive in Europe and campground designers do not want you to waste it. They have developed many ways to limit your use of hot water. Some campgrounds require that you buy a token to insert into a slot to get hot water. Others require that you push on a button on the wall the entire time you are in the shower. Many do not let you adjust the temperature of the water, you must be happy with what you get. This would be fine if the water were hot enough, but we have been in many where it was much too cool, and very few where it was too hot.

An additional shower problem is that there often is nowhere to undress or leave your clothes. You must do this in the shower, and then you must invent some way to keep everything dry while you are taking the shower.

European campers get around the shower problem just as you will. They carry their toilet articles in a plastic bag that can be hung on the shower door. They wear plastic slippers that can get wet. They don't wear a lot when they go in to take their showers. In fact, this can be a problem too. It isn't unusual to see men heading for the shower in just their underwear. We advise you to take a robe or a sweat suit if you don't want to do the same.

Don't be surprised to see references to the showers when we write about campgrounds we visit later in this book. If a campground has particularly good or bad showers we may feel compelled to mention it. After a few days camping in Europe you will come to appreciate the information.

Electrical Service in Campgrounds

European campgrounds do not provide as much electricity to campers as is usually available at North American campgrounds. You will find that most of the individual campground descriptions in this book give the amperage of electrical service offered. You'll almost never find more than 16 amps and occasionally as little as 2 amps.

You can calculate the amps required by your appliances if you know their wattage. Amps are equal to watts divided by volts. Since most countries in Europe use 220 volt current you can see that a 1,000 watt appliance draws about 4.5 amps. Here are average numbers for some frequently used appliances:

Refrigerator	0.5 amps
Microwave	5.0 amps
Battery Charger	0.1 amps
Fluorescent Lights	0.5 amps
500 Watt Heater	2.3 amps
1,000 Watt Heater	4.5 amps
2,000 Watt Heater	9.0 amps

You'll find that you become quite knowledgeable about the amount of current you need because not all campgrounds have easily-accessible breaker switches. If you trip the switch you have to find someone to reset it.

There are several types of outlets used in Europe. The newest and most common requires the European standard or CEE17 plug. In campground descriptions we call it the Euro. It is commonly used in Great Britain and at new campgrounds throughout the Continent. Usually blue in color, it has three prongs and a protective plastic collar, a hefty design. Both the Germans and French have their own older outlets styles. The plugs for them are similar, each has two round prongs (exactly the same on the two

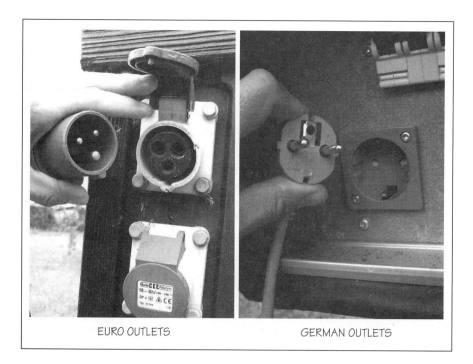

EURO OUTLETS   GERMAN OUTLETS

types) and a ground. The only difference is that the German type uses grounding strips on the outside of the plug and the French type uses a grounding prong mounted on the fixed electrical outlet. Some plugs are not interchangeable but most modern plugs can be used for both systems, they incorporate both grounding systems. Finally, the Swiss use an entirely different outlet (also used in Liechtenstein and at some Spanish sites). You'll want to have your main service cord fitted with a Euro (CEE117) plug and also carry an adapter that works for both the German and French styles. In Switzerland the campgrounds generally supply you with the adapter for their unusual outlets or you can easily find one to buy. Finally, in some small older campgrounds you'll find only old or indoor-style outlets. The management will probably have a selection of adapters to get you hooked up.

You will notice that we often mention that a long cord is required for a campground in the campground section of this book. That is because we once tried to make do with a 5-meter cord (to save storage space). If you plan to use electricity much this is not enough. Try to obtain a longer 20-meter (65-foot) cord on a convenient reel when you rent your RV. The experts say this is the longest length that is safe, it should be adequate at most locations. If you don't have one you'll have to be selective in the places you choose to park.

Cooking

One reason that camping is so much less expensive than other ways of travel is that you can do your own cooking. We like the fact that we can change our cooking and eating habits from country to country depending upon what is in the stores. One excellent example is France's great bread, wine, and cheese but each country has its specialties.

Truthfully, when you car camp the meals you cook are as much like a picnic as anything else. Complicated meals are just too much trouble. You'll devise simple things, though, that are easy to prepare and enjoyable. It's also nice to be able to prepare coffee and a simple breakfast before hitting the road in the morning.

Many, if not most, campgrounds have small stores. These are handy if you've visited a supermarket earlier in the day and forgotten something. There're also handy because they're a place to pick up cold drinks like beer and juice. Most campers in Europe don't even carry an icebox. If you shop each day and use the campground stores for cold drinks you really don't need one.

Most campgrounds also have a small restaurant of some kind. They're a great place to meet people and also very handy if you just don't feel like cooking.

Water

The water throughout Europe is usually fine to drink. You might suspect that this is not the case because Europeans drink an astonishing volume of bottled water. Unless a water source is labeled as non-potable you can feel safe in drinking it, if in doubt ask. We've not run into non-potable water in any of the areas covered in this guide. If in doubt go ahead and buy bottled water at the grocery store, those exclusive European brands are cheaper in Europe.

Laundry

Fortunately, camping allows you to wear simple clothing that is relatively easy to care for. You will probably not need to do laundry during the short period that it takes to complete the tours in this book. Campgrounds often have laundry facilities, but these are usually quite limited, consisting of one or two machines to service the whole campground. The cost of doing a load of clothes in one of these machines can be extraordinarily high compared with what we are accustomed to in North America, often well over 5 euros to wash and dry a load, sometimes over 10 euros.

The solution that most campers use is to hand wash their small, easy to wash articles. Things like underwear and socks are easily washed on a daily basis and will dry pretty quickly, even if you have to hang them on a line in the van while you drive on to the next destination. Lines of drying clothes are commonplace in European campgrounds.

Reservations

We generally find campground reservations to be a lot more trouble than they are worth. One reason for this is that many European campgrounds never fill up, they just get more and more crowded. Many of them have large grassy fields designed for campers who do not require hook-ups. If you can get along without hook-ups too you'll be able to find a place.

Another reason that reservations really are not necessary is that European campgrounds are really only crowded during the July and August school vacations. The rest of the year you'll be surprised to find one even half full. You should always be able to find a place even in July and August if you travel early in the day and arrive at the campground by three or four in the afternoon.

In most countries reservations are not easy to make. It is customary to make them by mail, usually with a substantial deposit required. Make reservations only if you want to reserve a great spot for a substantial period of time. You can make your reservation by calling the campground and checking on availability and the preferred procedure, you may get lucky and be able to make the reservation using a credit card.

Chains of campgrounds like the camping clubs in the British Isles, the Scandinavian countries, Germany and Switzerland or the commercial chains in France and Portugal often have reservation systems that are easier to work with. You might consider using them to make a few reservations if you happen to be traveling during the high season and find that it is necessary.

If you do happen to be traveling and find that the campground you want to use is full do not panic. You have many options. First, ask at the reception desk about other places to stay. They'll probably be able to suggest a less crowded alternative campground not far away. Many towns, particularly in France, Italy, and Germany have parking lots or fields devoted to campers during busy periods. A visit to the local tourist office may be useful, they know where the local campgrounds are and they also can set you up with a room as a last resort. Also, take a look at the Free Camping section below.

Free Camping

Not everyone who camps spends every night in a campground. One way to dramatically cut the costs of visiting Europe is to free camp if you are traveling in a motorhome. Many RVers visit a campground only every second or third night for a chance to take a hot shower, dump their wastewater tank, and fill tanks with water. We have met some people who almost never visit a campground.

While laws vary from country to country, even from city to city or district to district, you can safely assume that you're probably breaking some kind of law when you free camp in a spot that is not private property and sometimes even if you have permission from a landowner. Most jurisdictions have laws that they can use to control unwanted vagrants. That doesn't mean that free camping won't be allowed. If the campgrounds in the area are full free camping is often allowed when it otherwise would not be. Often free campers are tolerated if they are unobtrusive. Never camp where there are signs prohibiting it, you are likely to be socked with a fine on the spot, or worse.

You can often find a place to camp on private property, especially away from the cities. Always ask permission if you can find anyone around. You might consider offering a reasonable fee. Having permission will give you a lot of peace of mind during the night.

Freeway rest areas are often used by free campers. We recommend against this. During the last few years there have been many occasions when sleeping campers in rest areas have been put to sleep with gas introduced through vents in the campers. They wake with bad headaches and missing valuables. This really happens, and it happens often!

Safety is an important consideration if you decide to free camp. For this reason we do not recommend it unless you are in an area with other campers or help nearby.

A problem with free camping is that theft is common in Europe. If you leave a vehicle unwatched the chances are that someone will eventually break into it. We like the peace of mind we get from having our vehicle in a secure campground while we are away from it. See also the section on security later in this chapter.

BUS TRANSPORTATION FROM A CAMPGROUND INTO THE CITY

Public Transportation

Most North Americans are not accustomed to efficient and convenient public transportation. An amazing number of European cities have subway systems, all have excellent bus systems often augmented by trams or even an aerial lift of one kind or another. Don't be afraid to use any of them, you're as safe on the subways as on the streets.

Almost all of the city campgrounds in this book are serviced by public transportation. Don't even think of taking your rig into town, in most European cities a car is a liability. Why risk the traffic, narrow streets, and impossible parking to park it unprotected on the street. You can leave it safe in your campground and be whisked into town by a local specialist, the bus driver.

Pets

We get many inquiries about bringing dogs and cats to Europe. Doing so will make your travel arrangements more difficult, but we know that many campers will not travel without their pet.

Not all campgrounds will accept pets, but some do. We have included an icon in the campground section for campgrounds that will accept them. Some campground accept pets most of the year but limit them during the July-August busy season.

Your vet is probably the best place to start when researching this rather complicated area. He may have useful information. Rather than trying to distill and interpret the rules ourselves we have included several links on our Website, see ww.rollinghomes.com/elinks.htm.

Until recently Britain required dogs and cats coming into the country to go through a six-month quarantine in an approved kennel. This was unacceptable for most travelers so people just didn't bring them over. Now the U.K. has what is called the Pet Travel Scheme which does require you to jump through hoops, but they are not impossible. They involve a very specific set of steps including installation of an electronic microchip under the dog or cat's skin, vaccinations, a blood test, certification by a government authorized vet, and then treatment for ticks and tapeworms. It's all very specific, each step must be done carefully. We have links that take you to UK government Websites from our Website, www.rollinghomes.com/elinks.htm

The European Union is also putting together a unified scheme for pets, it is not scheduled to be finalized until July 2004. Again you can begin your research on how to comply by checking the links on our Website.

VISAS AND OTHER DOCUMENTS

You will have to have a passport to even get into Europe. After your arrival you are likely to never have to show it at a border again unless you leave the European Union or visit the U.K. For U.S. or Canadian citizens visas are not required unless you plan to stay over three months. Most European countries are signers of the Schengin agreement, see below. Border checks in western Europe are mostly a thing of the past. On the other hand, you will probably have to produce your passport quite often at campgrounds and hotels. They may use it to register you with the police. Some countries require that you register within three days of entering the country and campgrounds and hotels take care of this for you. Often they will want to keep your passport overnight and you have no choice but to let them. This can be inconvenient because the other place you might need it is when you are getting cash (unless you use cash machines).

For short camping trips to Europe we do not feel that a Camping Card International (also called a Camping Carnet or International Camping Card) is necessary but you may want one. People like them because campgrounds will often accept a Camping Card International instead of keeping your passport overnight. Some campgrounds give a 10% discount if you present a Camping Card. In North America you can get a Camping Card International by joining the Family Campers and RVers, Inc., 4804 Transit Road, Building 2, Depew, NY 14043 (716 668-6242). AAA (American Automobile Association) members can get one through the International Documents Department at the affiliated CAA (Canadian Automobile Association), 1145 Hunt Club

Road, Suite 200, Ottawa, Ontario K1V 0Y3 (613 247-0117). You can survive in Europe without a Camping Card but there is no reason to do so if you plan ahead.

An International Driving Licenses is just a standard form that translates the information on your national driving license into several languages. It also has a picture. They are easy to get at American Automobile Association (or CAA) offices, even if you are not a member. You should have one if you are driving in Austria, Bulgaria, the Czech Republic, Hungary, Italy, Poland, Portugal or Spain.

WHAT TO TAKE

For a camping trip to Europe it's important to take along some items that make the trip easier and more comfortable. The trips outlined in this book are short, you don't want to spend time looking for items once you are in Europe, it's easier, faster, and cheaper at home. You also don't want to take things that aren't necessary, it is definitely possible to be too well prepared.

Check with your air carrier about your luggage allowance. Most carriers allow two items of checked baggage and a carry-on or two. It's nice to check as much as possible and only carry on what you'll need on the flight and your valuables like cameras, jewelry, electronics, and this book. We've seen baggage limits of 20 kilograms per bag, that's pretty limiting so if the flight you are considering has that limit you might want to choose another carrier. We've also seen limits of 32 kg per bag, that's generous since two 32 kilogram bags would be about 140 pounds, much more than you'll want or need.

You'll want to pack your things in duffel bags that you can fold up out of the way. Suitcases are a real handicap once you've moved into your camping vehicle. Two smaller bags rather than one huge one are preferable and easier to handle.

Packing List – RV Camping

Personal:

- Clothes – See the section below.
- Towel, washcloth
- Toilet articles
- Hair dryer and converter if necessary – See Electrical Appliances below.
- Watch or clock
- Glasses, contacts and solution
- Sunglasses
- Medications and prescription drugs – Don't plan to fill prescriptions in Europe but do bring along your prescription to show that any pills you have are authorized.

Camping Items:

- Clothes line and pins
- Linens – May be supplied, check with rental company.
- First Aid Kit – Small, for minor problems.

Tourist Items:

- Passport (see Documents)
- Bank Card for cash machines (and spare)
- Traveler's checks if you don't use cash machines
- Credit cards
- International Drivers License (see Documents)
- Camping Card (see Documents)
- Knapsack for day trips
- Camera, film, and accessories
- Notebook and pen
- Guidebooks
- Something to read
- Electronics – As desired. Computers, music players, etc. But read Electrical Appliances section and Security section.
- Cheap Compass – Useful for finding direction in strange cities, small clip-on models are good.
- GPS Receiver – If you have an inexpensive one bring it along, we give GPS locations for all campgrounds in this book.
- Collapsible umbrella

Packing List – Car Camping

Most of of the RV Camping Items apply

Camping:

- Tent – We like one big enough to allow us to stand up.
- Sleeping bag for each person – Light-weight if summer.
- Inflatable Sleeping Mattress or Cot – We prefer cots, small folding ones are available. We also use small self-inflating mattresses on the cots.
- Pillow cases, pillow, or inflatable pillow – A decent pillow makes sleeping much better.
- Small folding chairs – Bulky, you could buy cheap ones in Europe, in the spring they're readily available in hypermarkets.

A TENT LARGE ENOUGH TO STAND UP IN WITH ROOM FOR COTS, CHAIRS, AND A TABLE

- Small folding table – Optional, again, you might see a cheap one in a hypermarket.
- Flashlight and batteries – Batteries in the new L.E.D. (light emitting diode) models seem to last forever.
- Reading Light – Again, L.E.D. models are great.
- Whisk or tent broom

Cooking (Not necessary if you plan to always eat out):

- Stove – If you bring from North America the best is a multi-fuel model that can burn white gas, unleaded gasoline, and kerosene. In Europe stoves that use the blue CampingGaz butane cylinders are popular but since they are inexpensive it might be better to buy one when you arrive because the cylinders sold in Europe are sometimes different than the ones sold in North America.
- Matches or stove lighter
- Plastic tablecloth
- Sauté or frying pan
- 2 Pots with lids for boiling water and cooking

- Bowl for mixing and cooking
- Bowls for eating soup or salads (plastic)
- Plates (plastic)
- Cups
- Wine Glasses – Cheap glass ones but pack carefully, also work for juice or beer. There's nothing worse than drinking wine out of a plastic glass.
- Silverware (inexpensive, perhaps durable plastic)
- Cooking spoon
- Spatula
- Can opener
- Corkscrew
- Cooking knife
- Paring knife
- Plastic storage containers
- Plastic dishpan
- Dishwashing items – sponge, scrubber

Clothes

The key to a good camping wardrobe is to keep it simple. Europe is not at all formal these days. Jeans and T-shirts will do for some people, you may be accustomed to dressing a little more formally than that even in North America. You can plan on wearing about the same thing you would at home. One set of more formal clothes for visits to nice restaurants, shows, or casinos is about all you'll want, hanging space is scarce in an automobile or RV. Don't forget a swimming suit.

You'll probably want something to wear to the shower. A robe or sweat suit works well, you'll see Europeans with even less. A pair of plastic shower sandals will also come in handy. You will appreciate some kind of hanging bag to hold your toilet articles, shelf space in bathrooms is usually nonexistent.

Outdoor clothing will be necessary since you'll be spending a lot of time outdoors. Bring some light rain gear including rain pants, they're very useful in a heavy rainstorm. Make sure your rain gear is as light and compact as possible so you don't leave it at home when you plan an all-day expedition. Synthetic fleece sweaters and coats are a good choice for staying warm, they'll continue to do their job when wet and they dry almost immediately when you wash them. You will probably want a hat of some kind and you will also really appreciate a collapsible umbrella.

Electrical Appliances

Almost all European countries use 220 to 250 volt current rather than the 110 volt we are accustomed to in the US, Canada, and Mexico. They also use different plug shapes than we do, and these vary from country to country.

As a camper the plug shape dilemma is not too much of a problem. Inside your RV or in the campground bathrooms you will have outlets like those of the country that manufactured your RV.   You can buy plug adaptors at travel stores in North America. But that may not be enough.

Some appliances, particularly hair dryers, do not work too well using adapters because the current throughout Europe cycles at 50 cycles per second rather than the 60 cycles our North American appliances are designed for. Any motors in your appliances will run too slowly. For longer trips we find that purchasing inexpensive European appliances is well worth the money, but for short trips like the ones outlined in this book you should probably just suffer along with the ones you use at home and a converter.

Much campground electrical service is limited to about 1,000 watts. This means that most heating appliances will not work. If you bring a hair dryer make sure that it draws no more than 1,000 watts.

We have had very good luck with portable computers in Europe. Most of these have power packs that adapt automatically to the 220 volt current, take a look at the information plate on yours to see if it does before plugging it in. We have never used surge protectors on our portables, even in campgrounds, where power surges must be quite common. You may not feel comfortable doing this, we certainly don't know enough about the technical details to guarantee that you won't have any problems. Also, computers can get stolen, see the section about security below.

SHOPPING

Groceries

One of the pleasures of camping in Europe is that you get to shop for your groceries in European grocery stores. It's lots of fun. Stores vary from country to country and you will enjoy the differences. Here are a few hints that will make the introduction easier.

European supermarkets usually have grocery carts that require a coin for use. They're chained together using clever latches and chains, you insert a coin to free a cart and get it back when you return your cart. It discourages theft and also keeps people from abandoning their carts all over the parking lot. Most now seem to require a one-euro coin.

When you visit the produce section of many supermarkets you are required to weight the produce and put a sticker on it with the price. There are machines to do this, you put your bag of produce on the scale and punch a button with the picture of the fruit or vegetable on it, a sticker is printed that you put on the bag. Sometimes

A FEW OF THE LARGE GROCERY CHAINS IN EUROPE

there is a store employee stationed in the department to help take care of this.

In addition to the larger supermarkets special mention must be made of some chains of smaller stores that are favorites with campers. These are Lidl, Aldi, Plus and a few similar chains. They're called "hard discounters" and are a fairly new phenomenon that is taking Europe by storm, they're even starting to show up in North America. They have a very limited selection of the things that most people want, only about 700 different items vs. probably 20,000 in a small modern supermarket. Things like beer, wine, cheese, sausages, canned goods, a few meats, and some fruits and vegetables. Their prices are the best around. You'll find that you do the bulk of your purchasing in these little stores and only stop at the bigger stores for the few items they don't carry. The exceptions to this are France, Great Britain, and a few other countries where the big supermarkets have great selections and excellent prices. See the introductory sections of each tour chapter for more about this.

Camping Supplies

We have found that good quality camping equipment is more expensive in Europe than in North America. For that reason we like to bring our camping equipment with us when we come over. It saves money and also shopping time. There are specialized outdoor stores throughout the continent, however, and all of the gateway cities should have them. About the only thing we buy in them is our camping stoves. Since the cartridges used by European butane stoves may be different than the ones you get in North America, and since you can't legally carry the cartridges with you in the air anyway, it is best to just wait until you get to Europe to buy your stove. The exception to this would be a multi-fuel stove if you already happen to have it, one that can burn a variety of fuels like white gas, gasoline, or even diesel. These are expensive, however, we wouldn't buy one for one trip.

We have also found that in the spring and summer the larger supermarkets (hypermarches), particularly in France, Germany, Italy, Spain, and England usually have car-camping supplies at inexpensive prices. This can be a good place to get inexpensive camping chairs, tables, tents, sleeping bags, stoves, iceboxes and many other items. They're not great quality but they are fine for camping out of a vehicle. They only have to last a limited period of time for our purposes and weight isn't really important.

MONEY

Money Exchange

The euro went into circulation on January 1, 2002. It made travel in Euroland (Austria, Belgium, Finland, France, Germany, Greece, Ireland, Italy, Luxembourg, The Netherlands, Portugal and Spain) much easier. All other countries in Europe have their own currency. When traveling in those countries a traveler never really gets

CASH MACHINES ARE COMMON ALL THROUGHOUT EUROPE

away from the frustrations of changing money. Just when you start to feel like you're on top of the situation you cross a border and suddenly you're penniless.

The most common way to exchange money these days is the cash machine. With a credit or debit card and pin number you'll probably never have to visit a currency exchange booth again. Cash machines are everywhere, we used them without any problems in every country covered in this book. The exchange rate you get will be better than what you could get at any exchange booth and the machine is a lot easier to deal with than most exchange booth or bank tellers.

Not all cards will work with all machines. We have cards that will work with both the Plus network and the Cirrus network. We use the Cirrus card most of the time and found that if a machine wouldn't take it (very unusual) we could use the Plus card. If we were willing to look around a little we could usually find a Cirrus machine. Our

U.S. pin number worked without a hitch, you might check with your bank to make sure that you don't need an international number with yours. You will need a pin number if you want to use your card in automated tellers so check to see if you can get one with your Visa or Master Card. Generally it must be a four digit number to work in Europe.

You should be aware that most cards have a daily limit on cash withdrawals of about $300 to $400 dollars. This isn't enough for the occasional emergency. See if you can get that daily limit raised before leaving home.

If your magnetic strip stops working or if your bank decides to cut you off for no good reason you should have a back-up plan, perhaps several. Always have two unrelated cards to use in the cash machines, perhaps a debit card on a checking account and a credit card with pin number. A few hundred dollars of traveler's checks is good insurance but they're really just good as a backup, they're very unhandy. Another possibility is American Express, if you have one of their cards they will cash your personal check (if you happen to have brought along your checkbook).

When it's time to leave a country a good way to get rid of small amounts of cash is to stop at a service station and purchase the exact amount of fuel that you have as change remaining.

Credit Cards

Credit cards really are widely used in Europe. Most countries in Western Europe are moving more and more towards their use. The cards you will find most useful are Visa, Master Card, American Express, and Diners Club. American Express and Diners Club are used much more than in the U.S., and American Express offers some services at their offices in Europe that can be quite handy. One example is the check-cashing policy noted above.

Probably the best thing about using a credit or debit card is that you don't have to worry about getting the best exchange rate. The exchange rate you get with a card will probably be better than any you can get with traveler's checks at a European bank or money exchange counter.

DRIVING IN EUROPE

Traffic Rules

Driving in Europe is really no more difficult than driving in North America. Each year the traffic rules seem to get more like ours (or ours like theirs). There are a few differences but they should give you no real problems.

Traffic signs are fairly uniform throughout Europe. The many languages spoken on the Continent have forced the use of international pictorial signs. You'll find representations of them in many guidebooks, they are largely self-explanatory and you'll soon become accustomed to them.

Safety regulations similar to those in place in North America are now also effective in most European countries. Seat belts are required and there is no tolerance for drinking and driving. Children 12 and under must not ride in the front seat unless there is no other seat available. Child safety seats are required for infants. On freeways you must never pass on the right.

There are also some differences from what we are accustomed to. In most countries the police can issue tickets and collect fines on the spot. There is usually no provision for making a right turn at a red light after a stop. You must have a green light or a dedicated turn sign with an arrow. You'll often come to intersections that have no stop or yield signs. Just as in North America the person on the right has the right-of-way, and in Europe he is much more likely to assume that you know he has it. You must be alert.

Road Systems

European roads are generally very good. Almost all countries now have extensive expressway systems, some free and others toll systems. In the introduction to each of our country chapters we have described the driving situation in the individual countries including idiosyncrasies like driving on the left in the British Isles. Large

CIRCLES LIKE THIS ONE IN EDINBURGH ARE MORE COMMON IN EUROPE THAN IN THE US

trucks use these roads just as they do at home, most major roads have plenty of room for even the largest RV.

Fuel

As you've probably heard fuel is quite expensive in Europe, it is heavily taxed. Here are some representative prices from the spring of 2004. Prices are in euros per liter. You'll also find links to information about European fuel prices in our website at www.rollinghomes.com.

FUEL PRICES BY COUNTRY
EURO PRICE PER LITRE
3.79 liters = 1 gallon

Country	Unleaded	Diesel	Country	Unleaded	Diesel
Austria	.88	.74	Netherlands	1.19	.81
Belgium	1.05	.79	Norway	.99	.94
Czech Republic	.76	.70	Poland	.72	.60
Denmark	1.10	.89	Portugal	.95	.70
Finland	1.01	.88	Republic of Ireland	.91	.84
France	1.01	.82	Slovakia	.82	.76
Germany	1.07	.87	Slovenia	.79	.69
Gibraltar	.64	.56	Spain	.81	.69
Greece	.81	.69	Sweden	1.00	.85
Hungary	.88	.79	Switzerland	.83	.85
Italy	1.06	.88	Turkey	.98	.79
Luxembourg	.85	.62	United Kingdom	1.14	1.15

Unleaded has different names in different countries. Here are some of them:

Austria	Bleifrei
Belgium	Normale sans plomb or ongelood
Czech Republic	Natural
Denmark	Blyfri benzin
Finland	Lyijyton polttoaine
France	Essence sans plomb
Germany	Bleifrei normal
Greece	Amoliwdi wensina
Italy	Benzina sensa plombo
The Netherlands	Loodvrije benzine
Norway	Blyfritt kraftstoff
Portugal	Gasolina sin plomo
Spain	Gasolina sin plombo
Sweden	Blyfri
Switzerland	Same as Germany, France or Italy
Turkey	Kursunsuz benzin

You will note that diesel is often a much better deal than gasoline. The fact that diesel yields about 25% better mileage than gas makes it an even better buy. The diesel pump is not normally hard to identify, it will probably be marked Diesel or Gasoil. When in doubt ask, attendants will recognize either the word Diesel or the word Gasoil in any country.

If you examine the chart closely you'll see that it often makes sense to plan your fuel purchases carefully. Note the bargains in Central Europe, Austria, Luxembourg and Gibraltar.

Some vehicles, especially in the Netherlands, Belgium, France, Italy and now the U.K. run on propane. Often you can run them on either gasoline or propane with the flip of a switch. Propane yields only about 80% of the mileage that gasoline does, but it is a great deal in some countries.

Maps

While this book does have quite a few maps you will need additional good commercial maps to navigate. After all, most likely you won't always be in the limited areas covered by our maps, particularly if you happen to get lost. The highest standard is probably the Michelin series which covers almost all of Europe, but there are many other companies offering similar products.

European maps, except those in Great Britain, use the metric system. This works quite well when measuring distances on the map. On a 1:200,000 scale map, our favorite scale for detailed navigation, 1 centimeter is equal to 2 kilometers. On a 1:400,000 scale 1 centimeter would equal 4 kilometers.

You should consider buying the beautiful small-scale motoring atlases that Michelin and others offer. These are easy to handle in a vehicle where sheet maps are difficult to manipulate. They seem expensive at first but the individual sheet maps you'll accumulate can add up to even more. Michelin prints atlases covering France (1:200,000, their best), Germany, Spain and Portugal, Great Britain and Ireland, Italy, and one for all of Europe.

When you are evaluating a map take a look to see if it shows campgrounds. None of them show all campgrounds but some show quite a few. This can be very useful.

Keep your eyes peeled for discount prices on last year's atlases in bookstores. Roads don't change much in a year and prices are often much lower for these out-of-date-maps.

In Britain you can find inexpensive small scale road atlases in the big supermarkets. These work great and are a real deal when you compare their price with a Michelin atlas.

GPS (Global Positioning System) Coordinates

You will note that for all of the campgrounds we have included a GPS coordinate. GPS is a new navigation tool that uses signals from satellites. For less than $150 you can now buy a hand-held receiver that will give you your latitude, longitude and altitude of your location anywhere in the world. You can also enter the coordinates we have given for the campgrounds in this book into the receiver and it will tell you exactly where the campground lies in relation to your position. If our maps and descriptions just don't lead you to the campground you can fall back onto the GPS information.

If you don't have a GPS receiver already you certainly don't need to go out and buy one to use this book. On the other hand, if you do have one bring it along. We expect that GPS will actually be installed in many vehicles during the next few years so we thought we'd get a jump on things. If you are finding that our readings are not entirely accurate you should check to see which map datum your machine is set to use. The coordinates in this book are based upon the World Geodetic System 1984 (WGS84). You should be able to reset your machine to use the same datum if it is using a different one, then the reading should be right on.

UNITS OF MEASUREMENT

One of the things that makes Europe really seem foreign is the fact that they use different units of measurement for almost everything: gas, distance, speed, money, temperature, food weight and volume, and even clothing sizes. If you are a Canadian you have already learned how to deal with most of this, you're lucky. For the rest of us it takes just a short time of working with all of these things, and there is no way to avoid it, to start to feel at home. Conversion tables and factors are available in most guidebooks but you will probably remember a few critical conversion numbers as we have.

For distance runners like ourselves, kilometers were easy. A kilometer is .62 miles. We can remember this because a 10 kilometer race is 6.2 miles long. For converting miles to kilometers, divide the number of miles by .62. For converting kilometers to miles, multiply the kilometers by .62. Since kilometers are shorter than miles the number of kilometers after the conversion will always be more than the number of miles, if they aren't you divided when you should have multiplied.

For liquid measurement it is usually enough to know that a liter is about the same as a quart. When you need more accuracy, like when you are trying to make some sense out of your miles per gallon calculations, there are 3.79 liters in a U.S. gallon.

Weight measurement is important when you're trying to decide how much cheese or hamburger you need to make a meal. Since a kilogram is about 2.2 pounds we just round to two pounds. This makes a half pound equal to about 250 grams and a pound equal to 500 grams. It's not exact, but it certainly works in the grocery store, and we get a little more than we expected for dinner.

Temperature is our biggest conversion problem. The easiest method is to just carry around a conversion chart of some kind. If you don't have it with you just remember a few key temperatures and interpolate. Freezing, of course, is 32 F and 0 C. Water boils at 212 F and 100 C. A nice 70 F day is 21 C. A cooler 50 F day is 10 C. An extremely hot 90 F day is 32 C. Since 50 - 90 F is our comfort zone we know that we're OK as long as the temperature in Europe is between 10 C and 32 C.

Here are a few useful conversion factors:

> 1 kilometer = .62 mile
> 1 mile = 1.61 kilometers
> 1 meter = 3.28 feet
> 1 foot = .30 meters
> 1 liter = .26 U.S. gallon
> 1 U.S. gallon = 3.79 liters
> 1 kilogram = 2.21 pounds
> 1 pound = .45 kilograms
> convert from °F to °C by subtracting 32 and multiplying by 5/9
> convert from °C to °F by multiplying by 1.8 and adding 32

CARAVAN TOURS

Caravan tours offer an easy first-class introduction to European camping. While the term caravan is also used in Europe for a camping trailer, that's not what we're talking about here. A caravan tour is a guided tour in rented motorhomes. Generally caravan tours last about a month. The caravan tour company plans the trip, sets up the motorhome rental, makes reservations at the campgrounds, arranges recreational activities like tours and special meals, and then provides a couple to guide the tour and an assistant (also called a tailgunner) to help out. You're provided with a complete written guide to the route to be traveled as well as maps and other materials.

Two companies dominate this business, even if you sign up for a European tour with one of the companies that offer caravan tours in North America you'll probably really be traveling with one of them. They are:

- **European Motorhome Tours**, Dieter and Gabriela Weigelt, 23701 Gothendorf, Germany. Telephone in the U.S. is 520 205-0841.

- **Overseas Motorhome Tours, Inc.**, Dennis and Tina Jaffe, 222 K South Irena Street, Redondo Beach, CA 90277. Telephone in U.S. is 800 322-2127, from outside U.S. dial (1) 310 543-2590.

Both of these companies have excellent websites containing lots of details. You will find links to them from our site: www.rollinghomes.com.

CHILDREN

There can be no better way to travel in Europe with children than by camping.

EUROPEAN TRAVEL IS A FUN EDUCATIONAL EXPERIENCE FOR CHILDREN

Children generally love camping and the opportunities it provides to be outdoors, meet other youngsters, and live in a way that is different and exciting.

Most campgrounds provide facilities for kids. They range from playground equipment and playing fields to swimming pools, beaches, and water slides, to bike trails to video games.

For most of us camping is the only way we can afford to bring the children to Europe for an extended tour. It costs little more to bring four or six to a campground than to bring two, and cooking for your family is much less expensive than taking them to a restaurant.

It is entirely possible to travel with children during the school year. Home schooling is now quite popular and most school districts will allow it, especially if it is only for a year or so and the object is to travel in an educational place like Europe. Policies vary, you may find that the school district will provide a lesson plan, give you assistance with your own, or require the use of a correspondence school. Check with your school or state department of education about the legalities and procedures. Don't forget about the advantages of a laptop computer with CD ROM drive. There is more and more reference and educational material available in a compact format on disk. Home schooling requires discipline but can be very rewarding.

HEALTH MATTERS

Europe is a modern, healthy place with no significant health risks that you wouldn't run into in North America. No special immunizations are required for the countries covered in this book. Health services in all of these countries are quite good.

You should review your health insurance coverage before any extended foreign trip. Check to see if your health expenditures will be reimbursed by your carrier and what procedures should be followed. If there is no coverage you may wish to consider supplemental travel insurance.

COMMUNICATION

Telephones

In the last few years Europe has been taken by storm by prepaid phone cards. They can be purchased at post offices and shops and are a reasonably inexpensive way to make calls, including international ones back home. The cards are inserted into slots in public phones and have a programmable chip preloaded with varying values of money. The cost of the call you make is deducted from the total in the chip, you can insert a new card in the middle of your call if your card runs out. Instructions in your choice of languages (including English) show on a screen on the phone, as does a running balance of the funds or time remaining on your card. Almost all European countries now have these phones.

Also available in Europe are so-called PIN cards. These cards are sold by private companies and use a programmed pin number, the rates vary widely but can be very cheap. If you buy them make sure that they are current and that they will work in the countries you plan to visit.

An alternative is a phone card from home (AT&T, MCI, or Sprint). These companies now have special numbers that you can call in all western European countries to reach an English-speaking operator (or you can direct dial if you're at a touch-tone phone), the call will be charged to your card. You can also use them to call anywhere else in Europe. There are different access phone numbers for each country so you need a list, these are distributed by the companies wherever there are tourists in any numbers. Sometimes they are even on the front page of USA Today. You may have to prime the public phone with some small change but only until you get through to the operator. It is more expensive to use this system than it is to use prepaid phone cards.

We like to use prepaid phone cards that we purchase in the U.S. These work the same way as the AT&T, MCI and Sprint cards described above. The only difference is that rather than your call being charged to your home phone it is deducted from a prepaid account associated with your card. The rates associated with prepaid cards are usually lower than cards associated with home phone cards. They are available in North America from many sources, the AT&T and MCI cards sold by Costco and

COMMUNICATION IS EASY WITH TELEPHONE, INTERNET CAFES, AND POCKETMAIL

Sam's Club have some of the best rates. You can generally recharge these cards over the phone using your credit card number.

If you are at a campground and can not use your AT&T, MCI, or Sprint card it may be because the phone has been blocked. This is primarily a problem in the Netherlands, apparently they want to sell you their own cards available in the office. Try using your card on a street-side phone to see if this is the problem.

Cell phones are very common in Europe. Everyone uses them and you'll be tempted. Unfortunately, there's really no inexpensive way to do it. Europe is on the GSM standard and most companies in the US are not, so most North American cell phones won't work in Europe. Some U.S. companies offer GSM telephones with European roaming but you'll soon find that rates are prohibitively expensive. If you must have a cell phone the cheapest thing you can do is to buy a GSM phone that takes prepaid SIM cards. It's best to do this in Europe so you can be sure that it will work with the system there. Each country in Europe has it's own offerings and you'll want the national SIM card for the country you're in to get the reasonable rates. This is the problem. The phone will work throughout Europe but you could end up paying for SIM cards from every country to get decent rates, and the SIM cards cost money too. You'll have to work out the cost trade-offs yourself. Regardless, with this setup local calls would be reasonable but any calls outside the country that your SIM card is from will be more expensive. In our opinion it makes no sense to even get involved with European cell phones unless you plan to be in one country for a significant period of time.

The phone systems in different European countries vary quite a bit. In general, the phone numbers in all countries have a two or three digit country code; a two, three, or four digit area code; and then individual subscriber numbers that vary from four to eight digits in length. Sometimes the same country will have varying length subscriber numbers, even in the same city. The area code always starts with a zero or a 9. If you are calling from outside the country you dial the country code but not this initial digit of the area code, if you are calling from inside the country you don't dial the country code but you do dial the leading 0 or 9 of the area code.

Country codes for Europe are as follows: Austria 43, Belgium 32, Czech Republic 420, Denmark 45, Finland 358, France 33, Germany 49, Greece 30, Gibraltar 350, Hungary 36, Ireland 353, Italy 39, Liechtenstein 423, Luxembourg 352, The Netherlands 31, Norway 47, Poland 48, Portugal 351, Slovakia 421, Slovenia 386, Spain 34, Sweden 46, Switzerland 41, Turkey 90, the U.K. 44.

Internet

As the internet matures it is becoming a wonderful tool for research and communication. Rather than fill the text of our books with web site addresses we have set up our own web site. At **www.rollinghomes.com** you will find links to many of the subjects covered in this book.

It is possible to use the internet for communication while you are in Europe but with today's cheap long-distance rates e-mail may not be the most economical or convenient way to keep in touch with home. Internet cafes are becoming more difficult to find and the fees and time involved may make using the phone the preferable communication alternative.

There is an excellent alternative to internet cafes that is widely used by RVers in North America but that is almost unknown outside that circle. It is called Pocketmail. A Pocketmail machine is a small keyboard and screen with an acoustical (telephone) modem attached to the back. The whole thing is slightly larger than a checkbook. To use it you type up your messages at your leisure at your campsite. Then you locate a telephone, dial a dedicated phone number, hold the acoustical modem on the back of the gadget up to the mouthpiece, and push a button. All of your messages are sent and the ones waiting for you are downloaded. It takes a minute or maybe two. Then you hang up, take your Pocketmail machine back to your campsite, and read your messages when you wish. It's extremely convenient, we use it every day for a telephone connection cost of perhaps a half-euro per day and we're always in touch. The machine cannot be used to surf the web, it's only for e-mail. You can purchase the machine for about $100 U.S. and service costs $90 for six months. There are dedicated telephone numbers in Europe but telephone calls between Europe and the U.S. are so inexpensive that we just use the U.S. dedicated number. We use it in conjunction with an AT&T prepaid card from home, see the Telephone section about that. The easiest way to get set up with Pocketmail is over the internet, just go to www.pocketmail.com. You can use it anywhere you travel where there are telephones, not just Europe.

REFERENCE BOOKS

A small set of reference books can make your trip more enjoyable. If you travel in your own vehicle they're much easier to bring along.

We have another much larger Europe camping book. It's called **Traveler's Guide to European Camping** by Mike and Terri Church, Rolling Homes Press, 2004, ISBN 0-9652968-9-X. It lists over 350 campgrounds (including the ones in this book, of course), and sightseeing information in the countries covered in this book as well as Scandinavia, Greece, Turkey, Portugal, Poland, and Slovenia. If you're planning to extend one of the tours in this book you'll find our other book very useful. It also has information about shipping cars and RVs from North America and about buying in Europe.

Europe By Van And Motorhome by David Shore and Patty Campbell (Odyssey Press, 2001 ISBN 0938297120) will help you raise your enthusiasm level about camping in Europe. It also has very good information about purchasing a van and evaluation of a used vehicle. When we first decided to go camping in Europe this was the only directly applicable book we could find in the U.S.

Budget travel guides like those published by **Lonely Planet**, the **Rough Guides**, and the **Let's Go** series are very useful for information about inexpensive restaurants and brief guides to what to see. They also list quite a few campgrounds, especially ones near cities useful to backpackers. You can find these in most bookstores.

The **Michelin Green Guides** go into a great deal of detail about the sights you will see. If you use them for that purpose and not your primary guide you will love them. They do tend to be a little dry. These are also widely available. In Europe you can find them almost everywhere. One big advantage is that they're smaller and easier to carry than many other guidebooks.

Guidebooks produced by **Fodor's**, **Fielding**, **Access**, and others seem to be written for folks willing to spend a lot of money for food and lodging so their sections about hotels and restaurants may not be very useful. On the other hand they often have very informative sections about things worth seeing. The best ones have beautiful modern graphics and good maps and are a pleasure to use.

The best camping guides to Europe in English are published by The Caravan Club in the U.K. Their address and phone number are published in the Camping section of the British Isles chapter. We highly recommend both the organization and their two-volume **Continental Sites Guide & Handbook**. You should consider giving them a call to get a copy of this guide, even if you aren't planning to visit the U.K. at the start of your visit to Europe.

The only guide that actually has people who visit every campground that they list each year is the Dutch **ACSI** guide. They publish several but the most useful is a two-volume set called **Internationale Campinggids Europe I and Europe II** that covers all of Europe. The campground listings are very compact and use a proprietary key system to convey a ton of information, you'll need a Dutch-English dictionary to work out the key before they can become really useful to you. They're available at travel bookstores throughout Europe but especially in the Netherlands.

If you find that you are short in background knowledge about European history and art you might enjoy two books by budget travel writer, television personality, and tour operator Rick Steves. These are **Europe 101** by Rick Steves and Gene Openshaw (Avalon Travel Publishing, 2001, ISBN 1562615351) about European history and art in general and **Mona Winks: Self-Guided Tours of Europe's Top Museums** by Rick Steves and Gene Openshaw (Avalon Travel Publishing, 2001, ISBN 1566913454) which has easy-to-follow guides to the some of the most important museums all over Europe. Rick also writes excellent individual guides to many European countries.

We like to have a dictionary covering the language of each country we visit. Language can be one of the most enjoyable parts of your trip if you are approaching it with a learning attitude.

Camping means that you will cook a great deal of your own food. Since you will be traveling in foreign countries you will probably enjoy knowing about their food and wine. There's nothing like a visit to a supermarket to pique your curiosity. We enjoy cookbooks and wine guides, but I have not found any that I would really recommend as both compact and outstanding. We're still looking, and carrying more of them than we probably should.

SECURITY

Europeans think that the U.S. is a very dangerous place. Statistics show that there is a lot more violent crime at home than there is in Europe. Don't let that make you overconfident during your trip. It is true that you are less likely to be murdered with a handgun in Europe but living in an RV leaves you relatively exposed to criminals.

Personal safety shouldn't be a problem if you make sure that you spend the nights in secure areas and avoid high crime areas in large cities. Europe really is safer than the U.S. in this way.

The security of your belongings, however, is another matter. It takes a thief almost no time to enter a locked vehicle. You yourself have probably seen the tool that tow truck drivers use to enter locked cars. Those tools are easy to get. Police always advise not leaving anything in a car that would attract a thief, but it is difficult to take this advice when traveling, you can't carry all your possessions with you everywhere you go. You should, however, consider strictly limiting the valuable items you bring to Europe to what you can comfortably carry along with you when you leave your rig.

The best way to protect yourself and your belongings is to always park in safe places. Campgrounds are great places to leave your rig. Public transportation is almost everywhere in Europe. Most campgrounds in this book have service. Use it to get in to the center of town while your RV or car sits safely in the campground. If you must park on the street do it where there are a lot of people or where there is security of some kind, like a parking attendant.

Another aspect of security is the security of the things that you carry with you. Pickpockets and purse snatchers are common in the places that tourists visit. We recommend that before you leave for Europe you make a Xerox copy of all of your documents including passports and both sides of the credit cards you will take with you. Keep the copies hidden somewhere safe in your RV or car so that if you do have your things stolen you will be able to accurately report the loss. You might also leave a copy with someone at home so that you can call and get the information if necessary. Most cards have a phone number to report losses on the back, you will have a copy of this.

Buy and use a money belt or purse that you carry inside your clothing. You can carry most of your cards, money and documents in it so that if your purse or wallet are stolen you won't lose everything.

TOURIST OFFICES

Almost every city, town, or village in Europe with any tourist potential at all has a tourist office. You will find them very useful. They are often the best place to get assistance in finding a room if you wish to spend the night indoors. They also usually have information about local campgrounds, sometimes with great maps, and also information about interesting local attractions.

Chapter 3

How To Use The Destination Chapters

The portion of this book that follows contains 10 tours in Europe. Each tour begins in a gateway city that offers places to rent automobiles and at least one place to rent RVs. Each tour then has either six or seven driving routes with a place to stay at the end of each day. The overnight stops are locations of special interest to visitors from North America. Each has at least one convenient campground.

Introductory Chapter Maps

We begin each tour chapter with a map that shows the tour route. The map is intended to give you an overview of the cities and places you will visit and the route you will take.

Top Attractions

The next portion of each tour chapter begins with a listing of the attractions we think that you'll probably want to see during your travels. These are the bare minimum, there are many more sights and attractions described in the text in each chapter.

General Description

The general description is just that. It's an overview of the tour to help you choose the tour you would like to take and to assist you in preparation.

Roads and Driving

This section talks in general about the characteristics of the roads and driving in each country visited by the tour. It generally talks about the quality of the roads, the numbering system, and the tolls.

Camping and Campgrounds

The campgrounds in each country are just a little different. Here is where we describe them.

Practical Tips

This is a section to bring you up to speed on the countries visited during the tour. It discusses money and shopping and other issues.

The Tour Sections

These sections are arranged in a day-by-day format. First there is a city and campground description of the gateway city. Then for each driving day there are three divisions: driving instructions, description of the destination, and campground descriptions.

Along the Way

Here we give a general description of the route as well as information about interesting stops along the way. We also include a map of the day's route in this section. At the beginning of the section we also give the day's driving distance in miles and kilometers along with an estimate of time it takes to drive the route at a relaxed pace.

City or Area Description

Each city or other selected destination has a few paragraphs describing the local attractions. In some cases there is also information about interesting side trips that you may wish to take while continuing to use this particular town and its campground as a base. Some of the destinations are famous and well known, others less familiar but still well worth a visit. We've made a big effort to select those places most interesting to visitors from outside Europe.

Our descriptions of the destinations in this book are intended to give you an idea of what the city or region has to offer. They are by no means complete, you will undoubtedly need additional guides during your visit. Exploring travel guides is almost as much fun as exploring the destinations themselves, you will no doubt acquire a small library before you finish your travels.

Campground Descriptions

Each campground section begins with address and telephone number. While it is not generally necessary to obtain reservations in Europe it is sometimes desirable to check ahead. This is particularly true during the busy July and August school holidays. You'll quickly become attuned to whether reservations are desirable in your locality at your time of year.

The internet has become as popular in Europe as it is here. Many campgrounds have websites and even more have e-mail address. We've included this information following the addresses and phone numbers. They're fun to look at before going to Europe to get an idea what to expect. They also sometimes list prices and a few allow you to book reservations.

One thing you will not find in our campground descriptions is a rating with some kind of system of stars, checks, or tree icons. Hopefully we've included enough information in our campground description to let you make your own analysis. We have found that the rating systems used by different organizations don't tell us much about what to expect in a campground. The things important to you may be different than the things important to us so we'll let you rely on the written information. While there are thousands of campgrounds in Europe, often there are few exactly where the traveler needs them to be. Location is the most important factor in selecting a campground, amenities are secondary as long as they are adequate for a comfortable and safe stay.

We have included a GPS location coordinate for every campground. This can be extremely useful in the unlikely (we hope) event that you just can't make sense of our maps and descriptions. See the discussion titled GPS (Global Positioning System) Coordinates in Chapter 2.

Campground prices vary considerably and are based upon different things in different countries. The price you pay depends upon the type of rig you drive, the number in your party, your use of electricity and the time of year.

Generally you can expect that tents are least expensive, followed by either caravans (camping trailers) or four-wheeled RVs (including campervans). The different prices paid by caravans and motorhomes is a contentious issue, particularly in England. Motorhomes are sometimes charged more because they must have a flatter parking pad, European rigs seldom have hydraulic levelers. Caravans, on the other hand, can park on a slope but need space for both the trailer and a car.

You'll almost always pay two or three euros for electricity. Sometimes electricity is metered, sometimes there is a flat fee. Sometimes, it is included without additional payment, but this is rare except in the U.K. Showers, too, are often extra. We've noted information about showers and electricity in the write-ups.

We have based our price categories on the euro rather than the dollar. We've done this for two reasons. First, now that the euro has been introduced it is used by the majority of the campgrounds covered in this guide. Second, in the six months prior to the publication of this book the dollar-euro exchange rate has changed about 35%. With such a large variation in such a short time we fear that our guide would be out of date within a very short time if we used dollars as our valuation yardstick. We don't know if the exchange rate will rise or fall, and neither does anyone else.

We've grouped campground fees into the following categories:

€	Inexpensive	Less than 15 euros
€€	Moderate	15 euros to 25 euros
€€€	Expensive	More than 25 euros

All of these prices are prices for a van conversion or small RV with two people using electricity and taking a shower. While methods of determining charges and prices vary you can come reasonably close to what would be right for your party by adding 3 euros per person for each person over two people, deducting 2 euros if you don't use electricity, and deducting 3 euros if you are using a tent.

If there is a difference between high and low season that moves the campground being covered into a different category we show both categories. In other words, if there are two different price icons that means that the campground is in a popular resort or recreation area and is in one category during the low season (usually winter but in winter sports areas sometimes summer) and another during high season.

Campground icons can be useful for a quick overview of campground facilities or if you are quickly looking for a particular feature. Keep in mind that even if a campground has an icon it may not have the service available during slow seasons. This is particularly true of restaurants, grocery shops, swimming pools, and sometimes special bus transportation.

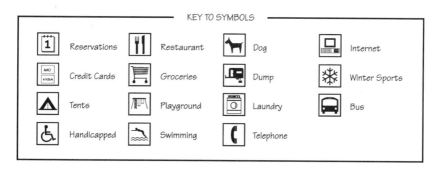

Reservations – While we do not generally make reservations it is sometimes possible. We show this icon if the campground accepts reservations.

Credit Cards – More and more campgrounds are accepting credit cards. Generally they accept Visa or MasterCard, sometimes American Express or Diners Club.

Tents – All of the campgrounds in this book accept RVs but not all accept tent campers. Each destination listed, however, does have at least one campground that accepts tent campers. We've included the tent symbol for all campgrounds that do accept tents.

Handicapped – Europe is becoming more friendly to those with disabilities. It has quite a distance to go to catch up with the U.S. and Canada but more and more campgrounds have handicap-accessible facilities. Unfortunately they are often limited and standards vary.

Restaurant – An on-site or nearby restaurant can provide a welcome change and a good way to meet people. In Europe most restaurants also include some kind of a bar provision. Campgrounds sporting this symbol have food service, they range from temporary kiosks with take-away items to full-service, white-tablecloth restaurants.

Groceries – If we've given the campground a shopping cart icon then it has some groceries. This could be a few items in the reception area or a large store with grocery carts. Check the write-up for more information. The write-up will often mention a larger store located conveniently near the campground.

Playground – Campgrounds with the playground icon have a playground facility of some kind, most have playground equipment or play fields.

Swimming – A swimming icon means that the campground has swimming either on-site or nearby. This may be a pool or the beach at an ocean or lake.

Dog – Many campgrounds accept pets. Generally this means one dog or cat and leashes are almost always required. Some campground limit pets during their busiest season so you might want to call ahead.

Dump – The dump station icon means that the campground has a dump station designed for motorhomes. Many of these stations are meant for only gray water because while many European RVs have gray-water systems for showers and sinks, few have black-water toilet systems. This should not be a problem for rental RVs since they are designed for the European standard and will usually not have a black-water dump requirement other than for the cassette toilet.

Laundry – Indicates that laundry machines are available at the campground. These are invariably coin-operated.

Telephone – Indicates that a public telephone is at or very near the campground.

Internet – Indicates that the campground offers internet service. In Europe this is generally a computer, not a place to connect your own. There is almost always a fee.

Winter Sports – Campgrounds with the winter sports snowflake icon are near a winter sports area (generally skiing) and are open during the winter. These places are popular during the winter, reservations are recommended, and this is often their high season.

Bus – Public transportation is convenient to the campground. It could be a bus, metro, or even a boat.

In the body of the text you'll usually find (in parenthesis) the outlet type (Euro, German, French, or Swiss) and amperage of the electrical hookups. At times we are unable to determine the exact electrical amperage of the hookups or one breaker protects many outlets, then we estimate either high (10-16 amps), medium (4 to 9 amps) or low (three or fewer amps).

You'll find that this book has a much larger campground description than most guidebooks. We've tried to include detailed information about the campground itself so you know what to expect when you arrive as well as information about the avail-ability and use of public transportation for traveling into town. While all campgrounds have a map we've also included a paragraph giving even more instructions about finding the campground.

Campground Maps

All of the campground descriptions include a small map to assist you in finding the campground. They show freeways and other identifying features to allow you to tie them into the country and city maps you will be using for primary navigation. You can use these maps to assist you in your search for campgrounds, they are meant to be used in conjunction with the written directions that we have included in the camp-ground descriptions. A picture often **IS** worth a thousand words, even if it only serves to give you a general idea of the campground location. We hope these maps will do more than that, we've spent many hours searching for campgrounds with only a brief description from other campers or campground guides to guide us. May you never have to do the same.

While the maps are for the most part self explanatory here is a key.

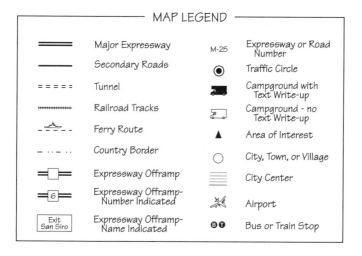

MAP LEGEND

Major Expressway	M-25	Expressway or Road Number
Secondary Roads		Traffic Circle
Tunnel		Campground with Text Write-up
Railroad Tracks		Campground - no Text Write-up
Ferry Route	▲	Area of Interest
Country Border	○	City, Town, or Village
Expressway Offramp		City Center
Expressway Offramp- Number Indicated		Airport
Expressway Offramp- Name Indicated		Bus or Train Stop

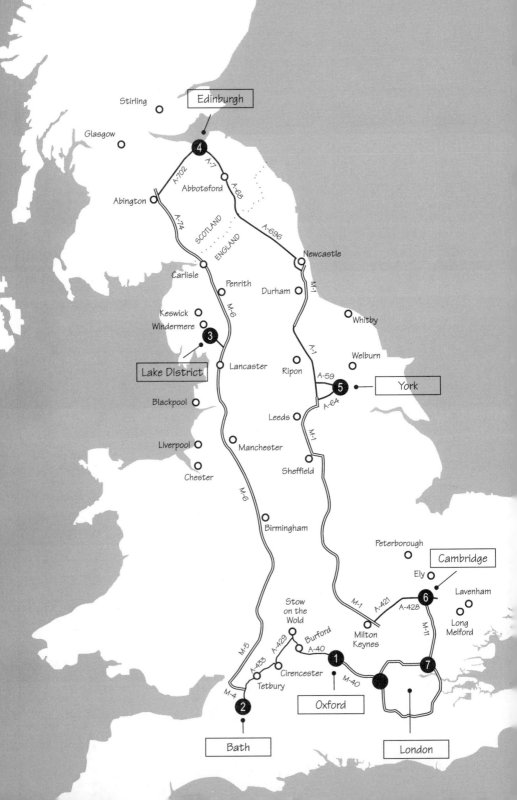

Stirling

Glasgow

Edinburgh

④

A-702 A-7 Abbotsford A-68

Abington

A-74 SCOTLAND ENGLAND A-696 Newcastle

Carlisle Penrith Durham M-1

Keswick M-6 Whitby

Windermere

③ Welburn

Lake District Lancaster Ripon A-1

A-59 ⑤ York

Blackpool A-64

Leeds

Liverpool Manchester M-1

Chester Sheffield

M-6

Birmingham

Peterborough

Cambridge

Ely

Lavenham

M-1 A-421 ⑥

Stow A-428

on the Long

Wold Burford Melford

A-40 Milton

M-5 A-429 Keynes M-11

A-433 Cirencester ① ⑦

Tetbury M-40

M-4 Oxford

②

Bath London

Chapter 4
Tour 1

England and Scotland

Top Attractions

- London
- Windsor Castle
- Oxford
- Blenheim Palace
- Uffington Horse
- Cotswolds
- Bath's Georgian Architecture
- Lake District

- Edinburgh
- Stirling Castle
- Melrose Abbey
- Durham Cathedral
- York
- Cambridge
- Ely Cathedral
- Duxford Airfield

General Description

This tour covers a total of 1,619 kilometers or 1,002 miles. That's a lot of driving but the long days are on motorways so the distances are manageable.

This is definitely a summer tour. Some of these campgrounds are closed during the winter months. Opening dates would allow you to make the tour any time from the beginning of April to about the middle of October but for comfort's sake it would be best to travel during the period from April 15 through the end of September.

The tour begins and ends in London. London is the easiest destination city for flying in and out of Britain, it's also a good place to find a rental automobile or RV. There's also lots to do and see before and after the road trip. You could easily spend a few days visiting London's attractions, pick up your rental car or RV and do the tour outlined here, and then spend another day or two in London.

From London the first drive is a short one to Oxford. The campground is within walking distance of the center, if a walk doesn't sound good there's a bus. It can be fun to drive out to Blenheim Palace, they do a great tour.

The second drive is a longer one. This time no motorways. The route takes you through some of England's loveliest countryside, the Cotswolds, to the Georgian resort town of Bath. The campground is in a very nice country setting. Again, you can walk in to town or take the bus. In town there's lots to see, this is one of England's top tourist towns, and rightly so.

The third drive is another long one, a full 400 kilometers (248 miles) on the motorways. An early start would be a good idea. You'll drive fully half way up the island to Cumbria, the Lake District. This is a favorite British holiday area with beautiful unspoiled countryside and lots of hiking opportunities, also boat cruises on the lakes.

The fourth drive will take you across the border into Scotland and Edinburgh. There are two good campgrounds here, one north and one south of town. Edinburgh is one of Europe's great cities, there's lots to see and do.

On the fifth driving day it's time to start south again. The route takes you through the Scottish border area with a possible stop at Sir Walter Scott's home at Abbotsford and the nearby Melrose Abbey. After crossing the border the route skirts Newcastle and there is another stop a few kilometers south to see Durham Cathedral. Continuing south the drive ends in York. The campground here is right in town and within easy walking distance of the center of this fascinating city.

The sixth drive is largely on motorways again, this time to England's other university town, Cambridge. If it's a nice day you might want to drive out to Ely and see the cathedral too, or even rent a punt to cruise the Backs.

The final drive is a short one and brings you back to London.

This tour can easily be altered, England has lots of campgrounds. You could also combine it with the Ireland tour in the following chapter by traveling to Ireland by ferry. There are many additional British and Irish destinations and campgrounds listed in our second Europe book – *Traveler's Guide to European Camping*.

Roads and Driving

The biggest concern most people have about driving in Britain is learning to drive on the left side of the road. You'll find that you adapt quickly. If you are driving a vehicle with the steering wheel on the left just remember to keep your side of the car next to the curb. The most persistent problem for many people is left or right turns onto intersecting streets, be alert when you make turns and you'll be fine. First thing in the morning as we pull out of the campground we often find ourselves on the wrong side of the road, so do other foreign travelers. Old habits are hard to break.

The United Kingdom is the only place in Western Europe that has not adopted the met-

REMINDER SIGN AT THE EXIT OF THE LEE VALLEY CAMPGROUND IN LONDON

ric system for its road signs. Maybe the familiar measurement system will offset some of the anxiety that folks from the North America will feel when driving on the left side of the road.

Speed limits in England are generally 70 mph (112 kph) on motorways or dual carriageways (divided highways), and 60 mph (96 kph) on other highways. In built-up areas the limit is usually 30 mph (48 kph). Motorhomes and cars with trailers sometimes have lower limits.

English freeways or expressways, called motorways, are plentiful and most are free. There is a movement afoot to start charging tolls but so far not many roads fall under the new scheme. The island is small by our standards and it is easy to cover ground quickly on the motorways. Avoid motorways near large cities during the morning and evening commute just as you would in North America.

Motorways are designated on maps with the letter "M". Secondary roads are designated with an "A" and a number, fewer digits indicate a more heavily-used and direct route. There are also "B" roads, these are small local roads.

The all-in-one police/ambulance/road help number in the British Isles is 999.

Camping and Campgrounds

The campground scene in England is dominated by two camping clubs: **The Caravan Club** and **The Camping and Caravanning Club**. Both have excellent campgrounds in useful locations. While you can use some of their campgrounds without joining you will find that there are advantages to being a member. You can join these clubs at any of their campgrounds or contact them before you head for Europe.

The Caravan Club has about 140 campgrounds located throughout the British Isles. It has over 800,000 members. The campgrounds are extremely well run. You seldom find extras like stores, restaurants, or swimming pools at these sites but they're generally immaculate and have some of the best restroom facilities anywhere. Some sites are closed to non-members, some do not accept tents, and those that are open to non-members charge an extra £5 (£6 at Abby Wood) fee if you're not a member. Rates at the Caravan Club sites almost always include electricity unless you are in a tent camping site or one of their few sites that have limited electricity available. There is a charge for the site (called a pitch), and a charge for each person. If you're not a member there's also the non-member fee. Rates vary quite a bit over the season going up during the middle of the summer and during bank holidays. There are also over a thousand Certified Locations. These are small locations accepting no more than five camping rigs. Most are on farms, in orchards, or on private country properties. They're relatively inexpensive and usually have minimal facilities and no hookups, but some do. It costs £36 to join the club for a year. They have a nice magazine and a website with quite a bit of information. You can also get an International Camping Card from them but must order it ahead, it takes some time to arrive. Don't expect to just pick it up at a campground. If you have an International Camping Card already and you are from overseas there is a £.50 reduction for each day's stay even if you aren't a member. If you join you get their book-length Sites Directory and Handbook with complete site descriptions and maps, Certified Site listings, and even listings for a few unrelated commercial campgrounds. The club sites can be reserved and accept credit

LONDON'S CHRYSTAL PALACE CARAVAN CLUB CAMPGROUND

cards as payment. You can join at the first Caravan Club campground you visit or by mail at the following address: East Grinstead House, East Grinstead, West Sussex RH19 1UA (phone 01342 326944) . There is also a link to the Caravan Club website on our site, www.rollinghomes.com. You can join on the website using a credit card.

The similarly named rival **Camping and Caravanning Club** has slightly different sites, rules and charges. They have some 90 sites throughout the United Kingdom. We find that their sites vary in quality more than the Caravan Club sites, they are more international-visitor friendly (see below), and they also seem to be slightly more tent-friendly. In general the sites are well-run, clean, and of superior quality. There is a nightly charge for the site (the pitch) and for each person. There is also a charge if you want electricity. If you are not a member there is an additional charge of from £4-£5 per night. This club also has the farm sites, here they're called Certificated Sites rather than Certified Sites, there are about 1,200 of them. It costs £32.50 to join but there's a special deal for visitors from overseas - £10 for three months. If you are a Camping Card International holder you are automatically considered a member and can stay in member-only campgrounds and do not have to pay the non-member fee. The club has it's own complete site guide called *Your Place in the Country* and also its own magazine. They too allow reservations and accept credit cards. Contact the Camping and Caravanning Club at Greenfields House, Westwood Way, Coventry CV4 8JH (phone 024 7685 6799) to join. There is also a link to the Camping and Caravanning website on our site, www.rollinghomes.com. You can join on the website using a credit card.

In this tour there is one destination requiring a stay at a Camping and Caravan Club site and a second requiring a stay at a Caravan Club site. Both sites accept non-members and tent campers.

Great Britain also has a lot of campgrounds that are not run by the camping clubs. These campgrounds vary considerably, many have a lot more amenities than club sites.

You can usually make reservations in England over the telephone directly with the campground office using your credit card. Being able to speak the language is a big help. While we don't normally make reservations while traveling in Europe we sometimes do when in England. Reservations are easier to make and the campgrounds in England do tend to fill up when the country is celebrating a holiday. Once you begin traveling in England you'll become aware of those bank holidays and you'll be able to decide whether you need to make reservations during your stay.

Electricity in British campgrounds is generally better than that available on the Continent. Sixteen amps are usually available and modern Euro (CEE17) outlets are the standard. Current is 230 volt, 50 cycles.

Practical Tips

We consider Britain to be one of the top camping regions in Europe. England and Scotland are full of destinations you've heard about and probably want to see. Many of us from North America have roots somewhere on the island.

The campgrounds are another attraction. We think British campgrounds are the best in Europe. Standards of cleanliness, quality of the facilities, and the friendly management are all outstanding.

Finally, as you might expect, virtually everyone speaks English. This will go a long way toward making you feel more comfortable and is a good reason to take your first European camping vacation in Great Britain.

It can be a little confusing talking about this country. The United Kingdom (UK) is made up of England, Scotland, Wales, and Northern Ireland. Great Britain is the largest island in the British Isles. The British Isles also contain the Republic of Ireland, a separate country and not part of the UK.

Despite what you may have heard about British cooking the British Isles offer the best selection of familiar foods in Europe. Modern hypermarket-type supermarkets like Sainsbury's, Tesco, ASDA (Wal-Mart) and Safeway are easy to find and offer good prices.

British pubs provide more than a place to drink a pint of beer. They're one of the best places to find an economical meal. They also provide an opportunity to meet some of the local people and often provide entertainment.

The U.K. still uses the pound. Credit cards are easy to use in the British Isles and cash machines are generally located at banks. You'll find them throughout Great Britain.

The best place to buy gasoline is the hypermarkets, many have gas stations in their parking lots and offer gasoline as a loss leader to attract shoppers. You can use credit cards to buy gas at most stations.

THE TOUR – ENGLAND AND SCOTLAND

TOUR 1 GATEWAY CITY – LONDON, ENGLAND
Population 12,000,000

Like Paris and Rome, London is circled by a freeway ring road, the M25 London Orbital Motorway. This one, however, is huge, you will cover 200 kilometers (124 miles) if you drive around it. For this reason we've included four campgrounds to use when visiting the city. When you arrive you can pick the closest because they're all good.

Transportation in London means subways (the tube), busses (many double-deckers), and suburban railways. Don't bring your vehicle in to the central city, the combined difficulties of overcrowded streets, a new toll system, and driving on the left are no fun. Avoid arriving in London during rush hours. All campgrounds listed in this book are outside the central city toll area.

London is arguably the most entertaining city in the world. The possibilities are endless, they include a **theater district** second to none. Museums are plentiful and include the **British Museum**, **National Gallery**, **National Portrait Gallery** and the **Tate Gallery**. There are monuments and sights to keep you busy for weeks: **Big Ben's clock tower**, the **Parliament Buildings**, **Buckingham Palace**, **The Tower of London**, **The Monument, St. Paul's Cathedral, The Tower Bridge, Kew Gardens** and much more.

LONDON'S TOWER BRIDGE

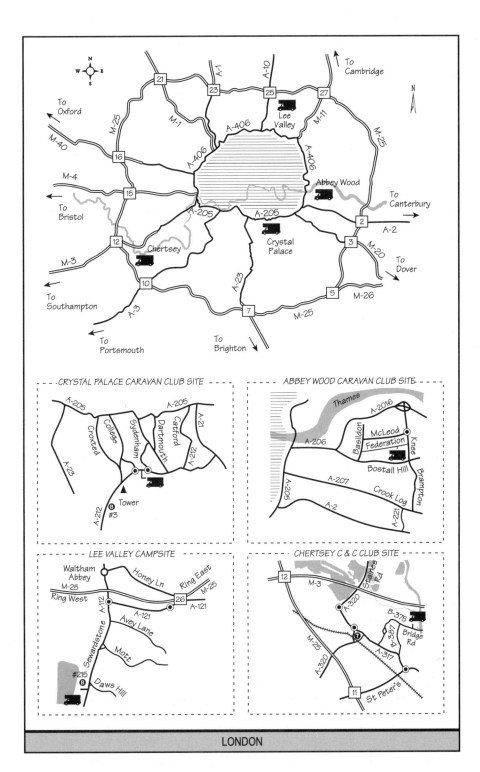

LONDON

There's no point in covering London in much detail here. There are information sources everywhere, start by checking with the campground reception office. You'll use public transportation quite a bit so buy daily pass tickets allowing unlimited use of subways and busses. The various sightseeing tours on double-decker busses are a good introduction to the city but you'll probably soon start thinking of locations in terms of tube stations because subways are so easy and convenient. Best of all, almost everyone in London speaks English

Windsor Castle is one of the queen's residences, in fact her family is named for it. Windsor is located west of London just outside the London ring road. You can most easily visit by using the suburban rail lines. From the Chertsey campground it doesn't take long at all to get there, from central London about forty minutes. At the castle you can tour the **State Apartments** if the family isn't in residence and also take a look at the Perpendicular Gothic **St. George's Chapel**.

London Campgrounds

▲ CRYSTAL PALACE CARAVAN CLUB SITE

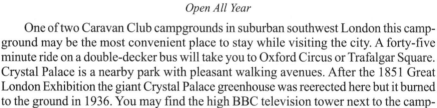

Address:	Crystal Palace Parade, London SE19 1UF
Telephone:	020 8778 7155
Fax:	020 8676 0980
GPS:	N 51° 25' 33.2", W 000° 04' 25.0"

Open All Year

One of two Caravan Club campgrounds in suburban southwest London this campground may be the most convenient place to stay while visiting the city. A forty-five minute ride on a double-decker bus will take you to Oxford Circus or Trafalgar Square. Crystal Palace is a nearby park with pleasant walking avenues. After the 1851 Great London Exhibition the giant Crystal Palace greenhouse was reerected here but it burned to the ground in 1936. You may find the high BBC television tower next to the campground helpful in locating it. You do not need to be a member of the Caravan Club to camp here and tents are allowed. In the summer this campground is very busy, arrive early or make reservations using phone and credit card. Try the Abbey Wood campground if you don't get lucky here.

The medium-sized campground is spread across a hillside but has flat, mostly gravel sites with convenient electrical outlets (Euro, 16 amp). It is nicely landscaped with some shade. The one shower/toilet building is immaculate and has lots of hot water for showers (adjustable), bathroom basins, and washing dishes. While there is no store at the campground you will find a Safeway about 2 kilometers (1.2 miles) away. Ask at the reception desk for directions. Many other shops and restaurants are much closer.

You can get downtown by taking the bus (the #3), it stops about 100 meters from the campground entrance. The campground reception desk sells daily tickets good for all London public transportation.

Directions for this campground will seem complicated but it is well signed once you are on the A205. Start on the London ring road east of the city. Exit the M25 ring road at Exit 2 and join A2. After 14 kilometers (8.7 miles) take the exit for and turn left onto A205. You'll be going west toward Catford. Continue for 5.6 kilometers (3.5

miles), then take the left onto A212. The campground is on the left in 4.4 kilometers (2.7 miles).

▲ ABBEY WOOD CARAVAN CLUB SITE

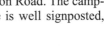

Address:	Federation Road,
	Abbey Wood, London SE2 OLS
Telephone:	020 8311 7708
Fax:	020 8311 1465
GPS:	N 51° 29' 12.5", E 000° 07' 11.1"

Open All Year

Another Caravan Club campground that is close to London, this site was recently completely redone. The place was leveled and rebuilt from scratch making it one of the newest and nicest of the Caravan Club sites. Note that non-members pay an additional 6 pounds here, that's not taken into account in the rate quoted above.

Abbey Wood is now a typical modern Caravan Club campground with 220 sites neatly laid out, convenient electricity (Euro, 16 amp), and great restroom facilities with lots of hot water and heated buildings.

Access to London is by suburban railroad. The Abbey Wood station is about one kilometer down the hill. The normal London Travel Card will work from this station, trains are frequent and it takes a half-hour to reach the Charing Cross station in the center of the theater district. As you can see by the longitude number in the GPS location reading above at Abbey Wood you're very near Greenwich with it's many interesting attractions. The train stops at the Greenwich station on the way in to London.

To reach the campground start on the M25 ring road east of London and then take Exit 2 onto A2 toward London. Take the A221 exit for Bexleyheath and proceed north on Danson Road. When you reach Crook Log Road you have to jog right and then left onto Brampton Road. Follow Brampton for 2.4 kilometers (1.5 miles) and turn left onto Bostall Hill Road at a stoplight. You're now very near the campground but have to take a circular route to make the easiest entrance. Drive 1.2 kilometers (.7 miles) down the hill and turn right at the light onto Basildon Road. In 0.3 kilometer turn right again on McLeod road. Proceed 0.8 kilometer to a roundabout, turn right onto Knee Hill Road, then after 0.1 kilometer turn right into Federation Road. The campground is on the left after about 100 meters. This entire route is well signposted, fortunately.

▲ LEE VALLEY CAMPSITE

Address:	Sewardstone Road, Chingford,
	Greater London E4 7RA
Telephone:	020 8529 5689
Fax:	020 8559 4070
Website:	www.leevalleypark.org.uk
E-mail:	scs@leevalleypark.org.uk
GPS:	N 51° 39' 17.9", W 000° 00' 22.1"

March 23 - Oct 26 (Varies)

This large campground is on the north side of London near the ring road. It is one of four sites in the area run by Lee Valley Park. Access to London takes about an hour and fifteen minutes via bus and then subway. You're really outside London and in the countryside at this campground.

The campground is a large flat field with trees separating it into several areas. Individual sites are not separated from each other. Electricity (Euro, high amp) is available to about half the sites. The shower/toilet buildings are modern and clean, hot showers are available.

To get to London you walk about 1 kilometer south and catch the number 215 double-decker to Walthamstow Underground Station. This is on the Victoria line and is a long way north, it's a long tube ride to central London. During the middle of the summer some of the number 215 busses actually stop at the campground so you don't have to walk that first kilometer.

From the M25 ring road take the exit at Junction 26, then from the roundabout on the south side of the freeway go west following signs for A121, you will proceed west just south of the ring road for 2 km (1.2 miles) to another roundabout. From here go south toward Chingford on A112 for 2.7 km (1.7 miles), the campground entrance is on the right.

▲ Chertsey Camping and Caravanning Club Site

Address:	Bridge Road, Chertsey, Surrey KT16 8JX
Telephone:	01932 56240
GPS:	N 51° 23' 22.6", W 000° 29' 22.3"

March 25 - Dec 31 (Varies)

A good choice for camping on the west side of London, Chertsey is a Camping and Caravanning Club Site, which means it's nice. Situated on the bank of the Thames, Chertsey is closer to Windsor Castle than it is to London, so it makes a good base for visiting the castle as well as being a convenient London campground.

The campground is a large grassy field running back from the banks of the river with the shower/toilet building in the center. Campsites are carefully assigned by the warden in person, fire regulations require good separation. Electricity (Euro, high amp) is available to most sites. The shower/toilet building is very good, it is heated and has hot water for showers, bathroom basins, dishwashing and laundry. There's a large supermarket in Chertsey about a kilometer from the campground, unfortunately it has barrier bars to prevent campers from entering its parking lot so you'll have to walk, ride your bike, or find a parking space somewhere else if you have a high-topped rig.

To reach central London from Chertsey you use the suburban rail lines. The Chertsey station has pretty good service but if you have the time walk up the left bank of the Thames about 6 km (4 miles) to the better-served Staines station at least once. The walk along the river is extremely pleasant and Staines has more frequent train service. Make sure to check schedules back to Chertsey if you plan to come back late in the evening, service to Chertsey at night stops about midnight, we almost had to walk from Staines one night.

To find the campground take the Junction 11 exit from the M25 London ring road. From the roundabout 1.2 km (.7 miles) east of the junction head northwest toward Chertsey on A317. Pass through Chertsey and at the T (B375) in 1.1 km (.7 mile) turn right. You'll see the campground entrance on the left in 0.3 km (.2 mile), just before the road crosses the Thames.

DRIVE 1 – LONDON TO OXFORD
90 Kilometers (56 Miles), 1 Hour

A long the Way – The drive from your London campground to Oxford could be as short as 90 km (56 miles) or as long as 170 km (105 miles) depending upon which campground you used in London. The day's mileage given in the heading is from the Chertsey campground, closest London campground to Oxford. London and its orbital (ring road) are huge so if you happen to be camped on the south or east side you'll have much farther to drive. There's a large population in the countryside around London so it's probably best to use the motorways as much as possible. If you are located on the east or south side you can drive to the ring road by the shortest route and then follow it around, don't try to drive through the city on surface streets.

From the orbital (ring road M25) take Exit 16 to head northwest on M40. After 45 kilometers (28 miles) you'll arrive at Exit 8 and from there you can follow A40 west to the Oxford ring road. Since the campground is on the southern edge of town follow the Eastern Bypass Road (A4142) to the left around the city to reach it. See the campground write-up and map for final approach instructions.

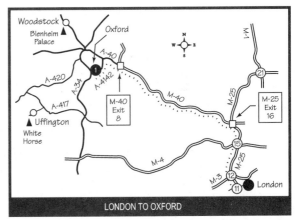

LONDON TO OXFORD

OXFORD, ENGLAND
Population 115,000

Oxford has been a university town longer than most, since at least the 11th century. Today almost a tenth of the city's population are students. On the other hand, Oxford is also home of the Rover automobile factory.

The central part of town is a virtual architectural museum. It is quite compact and easy to get around on foot. You'll want to tour several of the colleges, check with the Tourist Information Center in the middle of town, they actually conduct a walking tour although it is possible to visit on your own during scheduled visiting hours. Many colleges are arranged around quadrangles, famous names you'll probably recognize are **All Souls College**, **Christ Church College**, **Magdalen College**, **Merton College** and **Trinity College**. Book fans will want to join a tour of the three-million-volume **Bodleian Library** and visit **Blackwells's**, one of the world's largest bookstores.

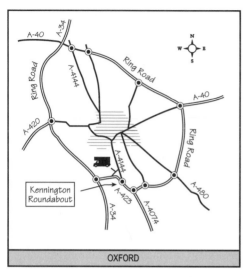

OXFORD

Blenheim Palace is located in the village of Woodstock, about 13 kilometers (8 miles) north of Oxford. Blenheim was the birthplace of Winston Churchill but not his home. It is the home of the Dukes of Marlborough and was given to the original Duke of Marlborough by Queen Anne in 1705 as a reward for winning the battle of Blenheim. Winston Churchill's father was a later duke's younger brother. Blenheim is one of Britain's largest palaces, the grounds cover over 200 acres, tours are quite entertaining. Winston himself is buried three kilometers (1.8 miles) south in Bladon.

Thirty kilometers (19 miles) south of Oxford near the village of **Uffington** the giant outline of a **white horse** is cut into a hillside. It was apparently created about 3000 BC. The chalk hills in England made this art-form popular with the early inhabitants of the island, but this figure has been unusually well maintained over the years.

Oxford Campground

 OXFORD CAMPING AND CARAVANNING CLUB SITE

Address: 426 Abindon Rd. Oxford OX1 4XN
Telephone: 01865 244088
GPS: N 51° 43' 54.9", W 001° 15' 03.6"

Open All Year

The Oxford is a medium-sized campground on the southern outskirts of town. It is a grassy field with campsites marked by small signs, many have electricity (Euro, high amp) conveniently located nearby. The shower/toilet building has coin-operated hot showers but free hot water for bathroom basins and washing dishes. You'll find a large Sainsbury's supermarket about one kilometer east on the ring road, there's a good bike path right to it. There's also a large camping supply store in front of this campground, very convenient if you've been looking for camping supplies. To get into town you can take a bus that stops near the campground, walk the streets, or follow a well-marked bike route that runs through a quiet residential neighborhood and several small parks. The distance is about 2 kilometers (1.2 miles) to the center.

To find the campground follow the signs from the ring road on the south side of town at the Kennington Roundabout. Head toward the center, the campground is just inside the ring road (A423 at this point). Immediately after leaving the roundabout you'll take the first left, then in a short distance at the camping store turn right to enter.

DRIVE 2 – OXFORD TO BATH
164 Kilometers (102 Miles), 3 Hours

A long The Way – Rather than driving directly to Bath, today you'll have a chance to spend the entire day driving on scenic country roads. The Cotswolds are one of the most famous and traditional regions of England. You'll find that the many direction signs pointing to upcoming towns will be very helpful on this tour.

Circle around the west side of Oxford until you reach the A40 and follow it about 13 km (8 miles) west to the town of Witney. This town is known as the eastern gateway to the Cotswolds, it specializes in the manufacture of wool blankets.

From Witney continue west on the Burford Road, also known as A4047, about 4 km (2 miles) and take a quick look at the beautiful little village of Minster Lovell. Then continue west on A3037 to the junction with the A40 and on to another perfect village – Burford.

From Burford drive north on A424 to Stow on the Wold. Then head southwest passing through a string of cute as a button towns including Upper and Lower Slaughter, Bourton on the Water, and Northleach. At Northleach jog south from A429 following signs to Bibury, another beautiful town. Pick up A4425 and follow it another 10 kilometers (6 miles) or so southwest to the capital of the Cotswolds, Cirencester.

Cirencester is a good place to stop, stretch your legs, and perhaps have a bite to eat. You can explore the Church of St. John Baptist, one of the largest parish churches in England. Cirencester Park and Cecily Hill show off the architecture produced by the wealth of the wool trade in this area during the 17th and 18th century. Cirencester was a Roman town too, the Corinium Museum exhibits Roman artifacts excavated there.

From Cirencester you can follow A433 southwest through Tetbury to connect with the A46 and then on south to Bath. You'll be entering town from the east and the campground is on the west. Just follow signs for the A4 to Bristol to get to the far side. See the campground write-up and map for final approach directions.

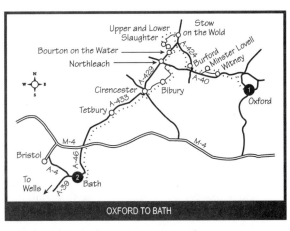

OXFORD TO BATH

BATH, ENGLAND
Population 88,000

Bath was England's 18th-century destination resort. Instead of golf courses or ski hills it was more fashionable in those days to visit baths and gardens. Much of the Georgian architecture remains, and Bath still draws many visitors. There are lots of expensive shops where you can spend your money.

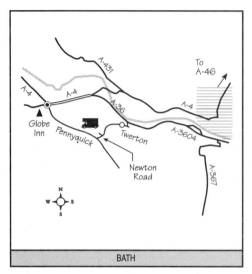

BATH

Even if you don't shop you'll admire Bath's handsome streets and gardens. Recommended reading before your visit are Jane Austen's novels *Persuasion* and *Northanger Abbey.* If you're a Jane Austen fan you'll want to visit the **Jane Austen Centre**.

Probably the best examples of Georgian architecture in town are **The Circus** and the nearby **Royal Crescent**, both situated northwest of the central area near **Royal Victoria Park**. East of the Circus on Alfred Street are the **Assembly Rooms** where the balls Austen wrote about were held, downstairs is a museum with examples of costumes including some from the days of Beau Nash, the fashion plate and social director of Bath's golden era in the 18th century. **Bath Abbey** marks the center of the city, nearby is the **Pump Room** and the well-preserved **Roman Baths,** they have a great tour. You'll also want to see **Pulteney Bridge**, built in 1771, it is similar to the Ponte Vecchio in Florence with shops on either side of the roadway. If you feel the need to soak you may want to visit the baths yourself, the newly restored **Hot and Cross Baths,** now known as the Themae Bath Spa, are the place to go.

Wells is England's smallest cathedral town with the country's oldest Gothic cathedral, the **Cathedral of St. Andrew**. The medieval town is well worth the 37-kilometer drive down Highway A39 from Bath.

Bath Campground

▲ Newton Mill Caravan and Camping Park

Address:	Newton Road, Bath, BA2 9JF
Telephone:	01225 333909
Website:	www.campinginbath.co.uk
E-mail:	newtonmill@hotmail.com
GPS:	N 51° 22' 42.3", W 002° 24' 37.2"

Open All Year

This is a beautiful medium-sized campground in a country location but convenient for visiting Bath. The RV sites are gravel back-ins, surrounded by grass and with convenient electrical outlets (Euro, 16 amp) and cable TV. Tent sites are separate and are on grass. Restrooms have hot showers (adjustable) and there is hot water for washing dishes. Access to town is by very frequent bus from just outside the campground. To reach the campground from town take the No. 5 First Badgerline bus from the central bus station opposite the train station. Get off at the Pennyquick View stop, walk across the road, down the path between the houses and playing field, through the

THE KING'S AND QUEEN'S BATHS

gate to the left, down the hill and turn right at the road to reach the reception office. The town is also accessible by a three-kilometer bicycle path.

To find the campground in a vehicle start at the roundabout 3 km (1.8 miles) west of Bath on the A4 Bath to Bristol road. The intersection is marked by the Globe Inn, a pub. Follow the road south for Newton St. Loe and Twerton, the campground is on the left in 1.5 km (.9 miles).

DRIVE 3 – BATH TO THE LAKE DISTRICT
400 Kilometers (248 Miles), 4.5 Hours

Along The Way – By English standards this day's drive is a long one although for those of us from North America it doesn't really seem bad. Rather than taking the most direct route through busy Bristol retrace your steps through Bath and head north on A46 to the M4 motorway. Once you reach the M4 head westward for about 17 km (11 miles) to the intersection with the M5, Exit 20. The M5 and then the M6 will take you north effortlessly for 360 km (223 miles) past much of central England.

North of Lancaster, at Exit 36, leave the M6 and follow A590 northwest into the Lake District. Twenty-four kilometers (15 miles) on A591 will put you in Windermere.

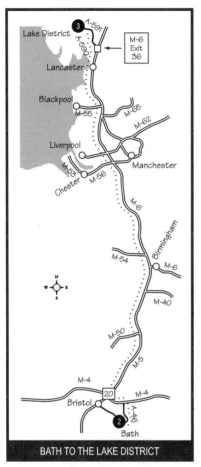

BATH TO THE LAKE DISTRICT

See the map and campground descriptions for detailed information which will allow you to select and drive to a campground.

LAKE DISTRICT, ENGLAND

The English Lake District is a region of long lakes and small but often rugged mountains. The whole area covers about 1,200 square miles (35 miles to a side), the longest lake is 11 miles long, and the highest peak in the Lake District is also the highest in England at 3,210 feet. It is a region with many literary associations, the best known are William Wordsworth and the Romantic Poets and the children's writer Beatrix Potter, creator of stories about Peter Rabbit, Benjamin Bunny, and Jemima Puddle-Duck. The region can be easily explored from two bases, Windermere and Keswick. Both have campgrounds.

Located on the east side of Lake Windermere, the region's largest lake, **Windermere** (population 9,000) can be considered the center of the district's tourist trade. This is actually a double town, Bowness-on-Windermere was originally a lakeside town separate from Windermere but the two have grown together.

The lake shore and docks are quite attractive, you can ride one of the lake cruise boats or catch a cable-propelled car and pedestrian ferry to the far side of the lake where things are much quieter and the walking is good on the small quiet lanes around Near Sawrey. The **Windermere Steamboat Museum** has a collection of lake boats and, as you would expect, the town is full of restaurants and shops oriented toward the tourist trade.

The Braithwaite Fold campground, identified below as **Lake District Campground No. 1 - Windermere** is popular and often full. A good alternative is Limefitt Park, 5 km (3 miles) north of Windermere in a mountain setting and identified below as **Lake District Campground No. 2 - Windermere**.

For your Wordsworth tour drive north along the east side of Lake Windermere for about 5 kilometers (3 miles) to the **Lake District National Park Visitor Center**. You'll find information about the region and also about its literary legacy. Continue north through Ambleside to two lakes that are in the heart of Wordsworth country: Rydal Water and Grasmere. Two of Wordsworth's former residences are in the area, Rydal Mount and Dove Cottage. Dove Cottage is the headquarters of the Centre for British Romanticism and is full of information for those with an interest.

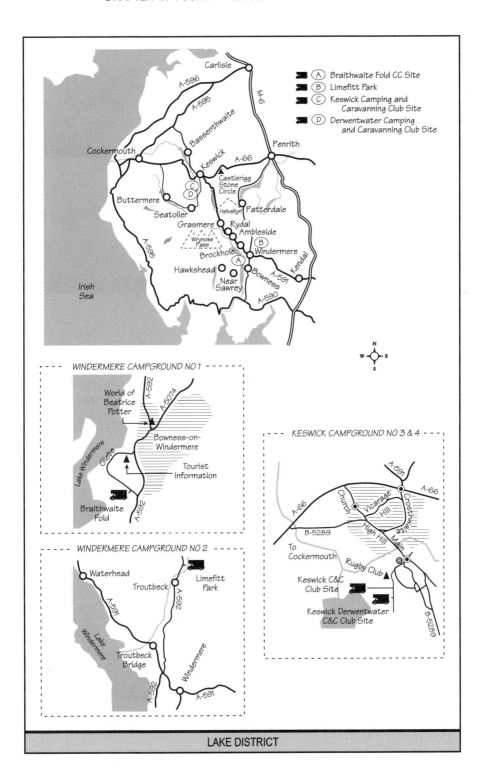

LAKE DISTRICT

For your Beatrix Potter tour either drive around the south end of Lake Windermere or take the ferry across the lake. Near Sawrey and Hawkshead on Esthwaite Water, you'll find the **Hill House**, which was her home, and also the **Beatrix Potter Gallery**. You may also wish to visit the **World of Beatrix Potter Exhibition** in Bowness.

If you want to get out and see the high country try hiking to the top of 3,118 foot **Helvellyn**. The trail starts at Patterdale which is north of Windermere on A592. A much shorter walk will take you in to the waterfalls at **Aira Force**, 5 miles farther north. To see the high country from the comfort of your vehicle try crossing **Wrynose Pass**, located just west of Ambleside. You'll climb to 1,280 feet on a very tiny paved road with very steep grades. Don't try this in wet weather or with a motorhome or trailer, it is sometimes possible in a lightly loaded VW van (a short section of slope exceeds one in three). In fact, we've seen front-wheeled vehicles backing over the pass in order to get enough traction.

Keswick (population 6,000) is a small town on the north shore of Derwent Water, one of the region's most scenic lakes. Think of the town as a base for hiking, there are few attractions within the village. An exception is the **Cumberland Pencil Museum**, this is the first place in the world where they were manufactured.

Check at the Tourist Information Center for information about hiking routes in the area. A nice local stroll is the **Friar's Crag path** to a viewpoint over the lake. It is also possible to walk entirely around Derwent Water, a distance of about 13 km (8 miles).

The two campgrounds listed below in Keswick are very near each other and give you a choice of amenities. They are identified as **Lake District Campground No. 3 - Keswick** and **Lake District Campground No. 4 - Keswick**.

Just east of Keswick is the **Castlerigg Stone Circle**. Follow signposts to this circle of stones dating from before Stonehenge.

For a nice driving tour head south from Keswick along the east side of Derwent Water on Highway B5289. Take a look at the **Ladore Waterfall** near the south end of the lake and then drive on to **Seatoller**. There's another information center here, Seatoller is the starting point for several hiking routes. From here you can drive on through **Honister Pass** to **Buttermere** and then return to Keswick over **Newlands Pass**.

Lake District Campgrounds

Campground No. 1 - Windermere

▲ BRAITHWAITE FOLD CARAVAN CLUB SITE   €€ 1 [MC VISA] 🐕 ⊡

Address:	Glebe Road, Bowness-on-Windermere, Windermere LA23 3GZ
Telephone:	01539 442177
GPS:	N 54° 21' 29.9", W 002° 55' 25.7"

March 28 - Nov 3 (Varies)

This Caravan Club site is located just about as close to the action on Windermere as you can get. It's just south of Windermere's lakeside companion town, Bowness.

The campground is an open, grassy field, separated into three smaller sections by hedge, with cement strips to park your rig on. The campground is so popular that the warden says it is full every evening from June through August. You would be well-advised to make reservations if you wish to spend some time here. The shower/toilet building is not standard Caravan Club issue (unfortunately) but does offer hot water for showers, bathroom basins, and laundry tub. There are no dishwashing stations but there is a coin-operated washer and dryer. Tenters are not accepted here but membership in the Caravan Club is not required.

The campground is located at the south end of Bowness. It is well signed from the pier and tourist information office area. Follow Glebe Road which makes a counter-clockwise circle (one way) from near the tourist office on the waterfront, you will see the campground entrance on the right 0.8 km (.5 miles) from the tourist-office turn.

Campground No. 2 - Windermere

▲ LIMEFITT PARK

Address:	Windermere, The Lake District, Cumbria, LA23 1PA
Telephone:	015494 32300
Fax:	015394 32848
Website:	www.limefitt.co.uk
GPS:	N 54° 25' 07.8", W 002° 54' 14.6"

April 1 - Oct 31 (Varies)

This is a large campground located high in a mountain valley just 5 kilometers (3 miles) north of Windermere. There are lots of amenities but the price is reasonable and it's one of the easier places to get into in the Lake District. Even so, you might consider making a reservation by phone using a credit card to make sure you have a place to stay in this popular area.

Sites for RVs are back-in and gravel, electricity is easily accessed (Euro, high amp), and there are also large areas for tenters. Restrooms are modern and clean and have hot water for showers, sinks, and dishwashing. There is a kitchen area with gas stoves for tenters to cook indoors as well as a well-stocked Spar grocery store on-site and a pub that serves food.

To find the campground drive north from Bowness on A592 or from Windermere on A591. These roads intersect about a kilometer north of Bowness. From the intersection drive north on A592 following signs for Ullswater for 4 km (2.5 miles), the campground entrance is on the right.

Campground No. 3 - Keswick

▲ KESWICK CAMPING AND CARAVANNING CLUB SITE

Address:	Derwentwater, Keswick, Cumbria CA12 5EP
Telephone:	01768 772392
GPS:	N 54° 36' 03.1", W 003° 08' 57.9"

Feb 5 - Nov 29 (Varies)

This Camping and Caravanning Club Site is handily located on the shore of Derwent Water in the town of Keswick. It has its own beach so it is convenient for kayakers and sailboarders and the walk into town for shopping, a meal, or a movie takes only five minutes.

The campground is a large one, it is two large grassy meadows on the shore of the lake. Electrical hook-ups are available and conveniently located. There are two shower/toilet buildings with hot water for showers, bathroom basins, and dishwashing. There is a nice supermarket not far from the campground entrance. There is also a boat launch facility.

To reach the campground start on A66 north of town. At the roundabout where A66 and A591 meet turn south toward Keswick on A591 (Crosthwaite Road) and proceed for 0.6 kilometers (.4 miles) to the intersection with High Hill Road. Turn left on High Hill, it quickly becomes Main Street. Proceed for 0.5 kilometers (.3 miles), turn right on B5289 at a roundabout (Tithenebarne St. or The Headlands). Stay to the right as you pass a Methodist Church on a corner on your left, and again keep right at the next split in the road. You'll see the campground entrance on the right about 0.3 km (.2 miles) after the point where you turned off Main Street.

Campground No. 4 - Keswick

▲ **Derwentwater Camping and Caravanning Club Site**

Address:	Crow Park Road, Keswick,
	Cumbria CA12 5EN
Telephone:	01768 772579
GPS:	N 54° 35' 59.8", W 003° 08' 36.0"

March 1 - Nov 14 (Varies)

This is a very nice campground with new facilities. Parking is on gravel surrounded by clipped grass, electricity (Euro, high amp) is available to all sites and a few also have water and drains. Restrooms have hot water for showers, sinks, and dishwashing. There are two other camping areas that are part of this campground. They are a little farther down the road and known as Walker Park and The Oval. One of these has back-in sites with gravel surfaces off an oval paved road (The Oval), the other is a grassy playfield with parking around the edges. Both are serviced by a portable toilet building and electricity is available.

To reach the campground start on A66 north of town. At the roundabout where A66 and A591 meet turn south toward Keswick on A591 (Crosthwaite Road) and proceed for 0.6 kilometers (.4 miles) to the intersection with High Hill Road. Turn left on High Hill, it quickly becomes Main Street. Proceed for 0.5 kilometers (.3 miles), turn right on B5289 at a roundabout (Tithenebarne Steet or The Headlands). Stay to the right as you pass a Methodist Church on a corner on your left, and again keep right at the next split in the road. You'll see the campground entrance on the right about 0.5 km (.3 miles) after the point where you turned off Main Street and just after you pass the entrance for Keswick Camping and Caravanning Club Site.

DRIVE 4 – LAKE DISTRICT TO EDINBURGH
250 Kilometers (155 Miles), 3 Hours

Along **The Way** – From the Lake District work your way east on secondary roads to the M6 motorway and head north. Somewhere just past Carlisle the name of the motorway changes to A74 and you're in Scotland. After a total of about 165 km (102 miles) on the motorway take Exit 13 near Abington and drive northeastward on A702 toward Edinburgh. In about 57 km (35 miles) you'll reach the Edinburgh bypass, also called the A720.

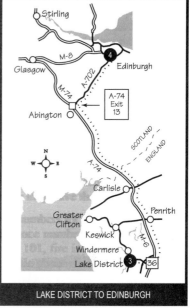

LAKE DISTRICT TO EDINBURGH

There are two good campgrounds in Edinburgh. To reach the Caravan Club's Edinburgh Caravan Club Site you'll have to circle around Edinburgh to the left since the campground is on the north side of town. Mortonhall Park Caravan Park is closer, circle to the right on A720 to get there. See the campground write-ups and maps for detailed driving instructions for finding the campgrounds.

EDINBURGH, SCOTLAND
Population 450,000

Edinburgh is a great town to visit. This is no secret, you will probably see more foreign tourists here than any other city you visit in the British Isles, excepting maybe London. Don't let that put you off, however. The campgrounds here are very convenient to the city and there's lots to see.

As a visitor you'll find that Edinburgh's attractions are in two areas: the **Royal Mile** which stretches from the Edinburgh Castle to Holyroodhouse Palace, and the **New Town** to the north. These are separated by a deep chasm, now the **Prince Street Gardens**, which is spanned by several bridges and paths. Busses from the campground will drop you in either place, but the whole central city area is quite compact. Both **Edinburgh Castle** and **Holyroodhouse Palace** can be toured and the **Royal Mile** between them is full of worthwhile stops like the **Scotch Whiskey Heritage Center** where you can plan your tour of highland distilleries. Between the old and new town you'll find the **National Gallery of Scotland**, filled with a wide selection of European paintings from the 15th to the 19th century.

Edinburgh is most crowded with tourists during the **Edinburgh Festival** during the last half of August. This is the best time to visit the town but reservations are recommended. It's an exciting place to be with cultural events of all kinds going full blast all the time.

Stirling is located about 50 km (31 miles) east of Edinburgh. **Stirling Castle** played an important part in Scottish history and remains an impressive and interesting destination. Many important battles were fought nearby, including the long-remembered defeat of the English by Robert the Bruce at the Battle of Bannockburn in 1314. The **Bannockburn Heritage Centre** stands on the field of battle some 3 kilometers (2 miles) south of Stirling Castle. North of Stirling is the **Wallace Monument**, Scottish hero William Wallace was played by the actor Mel Gibson in the movie *Braveheart.*

The area around Edinburgh is **Sir Walter Scott country**. The famous novelist immortalized many sights in the region including **Glamis Castle** (also associated with Shakespeare's *Macbeth*), **Inveraray Castle**, and **Melrose Abbey**. Scott's home, **Abbotsford**, is situated south of Edinburgh.

Edinburgh Campgrounds

▲ EDINBURGH CARAVAN CLUB SITE

    Address: Marine Drive, Edinburgh EH4 5EN
    Telephone: 01313 126874
    GPS: N 55° 58' 39.7", W 003° 15' 54.6"

Open All Year

This large Caravan Club campground with 200 sites is located in the northern suburbs of Edinburgh. Good bus service makes visiting central Edinburgh very easy and it's a very comfortable place to stay.

Parking is on gravel separated by well-clipped grass and hedges. Electricity is close to each site (Euro, high amp) and heated restrooms have hot water for showers, bathroom basins, and for dishwashing. The bus stop is just outside the campground and takes about 40 minutes to reach Princes Street. From the intersection of Silverknowes Road and Marine Drive west of the campground there's a very nice walk westward on a walkway along the Firth to Cramond.

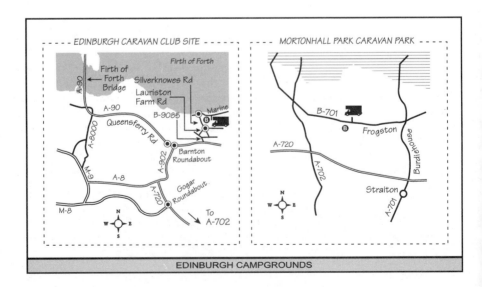

EDINBURGH CAMPGROUNDS

THE ROYAL MILE PUB IN EDINBURGH

The easiest access route to the campground is the A90 which comes from the north across the Firth of Forth Bridge. From the southwest on A702 you can follow the Edinburgh bypass (A720) around the west side of town for 10 kilometers (6 miles) and then the A902 (signed Forth Road Bridge), which form a sort of ring road around western Edinburgh. You will meet the A90 at Barnton roundabout. Once you are heading inbound toward the city from the Barnton roundabout on the A90 (which is called Queensferry Road) drive 2 km (1.2 miles) and turn left onto B9085 which is signposted for Davidsons Mains. On B9085 proceed north for 0.6 km (.4 miles) past a Safeway on the right to Lauriston Farm Road and turn right, proceed 0.5 km (.3 miles) to a roundabout and turn left onto Silverknowes Road, drive 0.9 km (.6 miles) to a T, turn right into Marine Drive, and you'll see the campground on the right in another 0.9 km (.6 miles).

▲ MORTONHALL PARK CARAVAN PARK

Address:	38 Frogston Road East, Edinburgh, Lothian EH16 6TJ
Telephone:	01316 641533
Fax:	01316 645387
Website:	www.meadowhead.co.uk/mortonhall
E-mail:	enquiries@mortonhallcp.demon.co.uk
GPS:	N 55° 54' 10.7", W 003° 10' 48.3"

March 15 - Nov 1

This is a very large private campground located south of the city. It has convenient bus service and lots of amenities. Sites are grass or paved and electricity (Euro, high amp) is available. Several restroom buildings provide hot showers. There is also a restaurant and a shop for supplies.

To reach the campground start from the A720 which forms a bypass around southern Edinburgh. Turn north near Straiton on A701 (Burdiehouse Rd.) and proceed 1.1 km (.7 miles). Turn left on B701 which is Frogston Road, the campground entrance is on the right after 0.9 km (.6 miles).

DRIVE 5 – EDINBURGH TO YORK
336 Kilometers (208 Miles), 4.5 Hours

A long The Way – Rather than travel by motorway drive south via the A7, the A68 highway and the A696 to Newcastle, a distance of about 160 km (99 miles). About 50 km (31 miles) south of Edinburgh you will pass through Abbotsford, which has two interesting places that you may want stop and visit. One is Abbotsford, the manor of Sir Walter Scott, author of Ivanhoe and the Waverly novels. The other is the ruins of Melrose Abbey.

At the western edge of Newcastle pick up the M1 motorway which will take you 125 kilometers (77 miles) south to a point just 25 kilometers (15 miles) west of York.

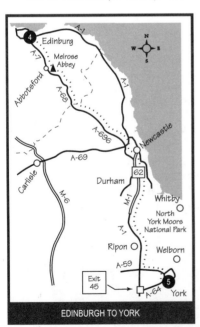

EDINBURGH TO YORK

As you drive south there's another interesting treat. Thirteen kilometers (8 miles) south of Newcastle at Exit 62 you can drive a few kilometers west to Durham, home of one of England's most impressive cathedrals.

After Durham, continue south and then leave the motorway at Exit 45. Follow A64 east to pass south of York, see the campground write-up for final approach instructions.

YORK, ENGLAND
Population 120,000

While Newcastle is the major city of northeast England the city of York must certainly be the tourist capital. A smaller city, bisected by the tranquil River Ouse, and partially surrounded by medieval walls, York's streets teem with tourists shopping at dozens of large and small shops and restaurants. When you've had your fill of shopping and crowd watching you might want to visit **York Minster**, the largest Gothic cathedral in northern Europe or take a stroll along the top of the **old city walls**.

York was also a Roman and Viking city as you'll see if you visit some of the city's many museums including the **Undercroft Museum and Treasury** in the Minster and the newly revamped **Jorvik Viking Centre** which shows off the old Viking town which underlies modern York and includes animated characters. York also has the **National Railway Museum**, the world's largest train museum.

Fortunately York is one of the easiest towns in Europe for the camper to visit. The Rowntree Park Caravan Club Site is almost inside the city walls, it sits next to the river and is no more than five minutes walk from the action.

Studley Royal and the ruins of **Fountains Abbey** are run by the National Trust are known for their impressive gardens. The complex is located 40 kilometers (25 miles) northwest of York near Ripon.

Castle Howard, setting for the TV series *Brideshead Revisited*, is about 25 kilometers (15 miles) northeast of York via A64 near Welburn. The house and gardens are the most impressive in the region. The architect was Sir John Vanbrugh, he also did Blenheim Palace.

The **North York Moors National Park** is easily visited. It is 70 kilometers (43 miles) north of York and west of Whitby.

York Campground

▲ ROWNTREE PARK CARAVAN CLUB SITE

Address:	Terry Avenue, York YO2 IJ	
Telephone:	01904 658997	
GPS:	N 53° 57' 02.7", E 001° 04' 46.0"	

Open All Year

This medium to large campground is a classic Caravan Club Site. It has hard-surfaced gravel sites in small groups surrounded by well-clipped grass and separated by tall hedges. Each site has a convenient electrical outlet (Euro, 16 amp). The shower/toilet building is heated and has lots of hot water for showers, bathroom basins, and dish and clothes washing. Unlike some Caravan Club sites this one accepts tent campers. Since this is a very popular campground you'll want to make reservations. You do not need to be a member of the Caravan Club to camp here. The campground's location is extremely handy. You can walk in to town by heading out the gate, turning left to walk along the river for a short distance, and then crossing a bridge into the central area.

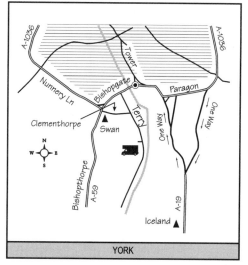

Driving around inner York is difficult because traffic is heavy and roads are cramped. Here's the route recommended by the Caravan Club to get to the site. From the A64 south of the city take the A19 exit following signs for York. Zero your odometer as you exit. At the roundabout at the bottom of the ramp take the first exit. Proceed north toward the city, you'll see an Iceland supermarket on your left at 2.4 km (1.5 miles) on your odometer. Continue straight, the road goes left at a Y at 3.4 km (2.1 miles) on your odometer and becomes one way. You'll come to a traffic circle at 3.8 on your odometer, turn left and cross the river. At 4.1 km (2.5 miles) on your odometer you'll spot the Swan Tavern on the left, turn left immediately before the tavern, there is a camping sign at this corner. Proceed straight ahead to the river, then turn right to drive along the bank, you'll see the campground on the right in about 250 meters.

Drive 6 – York to Cambridge
340 Kilometers (211 Miles), 3.5 Hours

Along **The Way** – Drive southeast on A64 for 21 kilometers (13 miles) to pick up the M1. The motorway will carry you south 252 km (156 miles) to Exit 13 south of Milton Keynes. From the exit follow A421 and A428 for 76 km (47 miles) east-

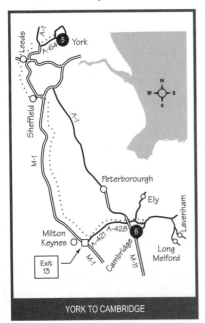

ward to Cambridge. For the Caravan Club's Cherry Hinton campground head north to circle the city on the A14 and then follow the instructions in the campground write-up. For the Camping and Caravanning Club's Cambridge site head south on M11 and then follow the instructions in the campground write-up.

YORK TO CAMBRIDGE

Cambridge, England
Population 90,000

The first or second university town in England, depending upon your information source's bias, Cambridge is not quite as old as Oxford. The university originated in the 12th century with Benedictine monk teachers from the nearby cathedral town of Ely. Residential colleges eventually opened and gradually became today's university town. Your visit to the British Isles won't be complete if you don't visit **King's College Chapel,** a Perpendicular Gothic style church inspired by St-Chapelle in Paris. You can also rent a punt and tour the **"The Backs"**, the lawns and waterways behind the colleges. Touring the colleges usually requires payment of a fee and may require joining a tour. The last half of April, May, and June are exam time and the colleges are not open for visitors at that time. Cambridge is fun and easily visited from the campground. Don't miss the **Fitzwilliam Museum** with a fine collection including French Impressionists and English paintings by Hogarth, Gainsborough, Constable and Turner.

North of Cambridge lie the **Fenlands**, a large swampy area, much of which has been drained for farming. The most important city of the Fenlands is **Ely**. Building of

PUNTERS IN CAMBRIDGE

the **Ely Cathedral** or "Ship of the Fens" began in 1083. Ely is known for the way the cathedral towers above the little town, visible for miles across the low-lying surroundings. Ely is where Oliver Cromwell headquartered during the civil wars against King Charles I, his house is now the tourist office. To reach Ely drive 20 kilometers (12 miles) north from Cambridge on A10.

Fifteen kilometers (9 miles) south of Cambridge just off the M11 at Exit 10 is **Duxford Airfield**, now the location of the aviation exhibits of the Imperial War Museum. This was a World War II air base and many of the exhibits reflect this, although there is also a Concorde, a Harrier, and a U-2. This may be the best aviation museum in Europe, aviation buffs shouldn't miss it!

The wool trade made East Anglia a very rich area during the 15th and 16th centuries. Towns built showpiece churches and the merchants and weavers had impressive homes. Two of the best towns to visit are **Lavenham** and **Long Melford**. They are located about 70 kilometers (43 miles) east of Cambridge.

Cambridge Campgrounds

▲ CHERRY HINTON CARAVAN CLUB SITE

Address:	Lime Kiln Rovad, Cherry Hinton, Cambridge CB1 8NQ
Telephone:	01223 244088
GPS:	N 52° 10' 53.6", E 000° 10' 08.6"

March 28 - Jan 5 (Varies)

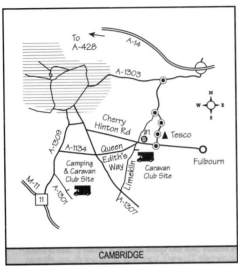

CAMBRIDGE

This medium-sized Caravan Club site is unusual because it is located in an old limestone quarry. Now covered with grass and plants the sites are arranged in groups beneath the quarry walls. Parking is on grass or gravel in marked sites off paved access roads. Electricity (Euro, high amp) is available at all sites except in the area set aside for tents. The shower/toilet building is a typical heated Caravan Club type with plentiful hot water for showers, bathroom basins, dishwashing and laundry. Transportation to Cambridge is quite good. A bus stop is located about 500 meters from the site with the trip to town taking about 10 minutes. Bus #1 stops across the road from the Robin Hood Pub just down the hill from the site. If you elect to walk you can do so in about 45 minutes, the distance is about 5 kilometers (3 miles) to the center of town.

This campground is not easy to find without good instructions as there are few signs. The best route is from the A14 running east/west north of town. Take the exit for A1303 and at the roundabout located at the exit follow the signs for Cambridge and A1303. In 1.8 kilometers (1.1 miles) turn left following the sign for Cherry Hinton. In 1.8 kilometers (1.1 miles) you will come to a roundabout, turn left into Gazelle Way following signs to Fulbourn. Pass through two roundabouts continuing straight and at the third (after 1.5 kilometers) turn right. At the traffic light in 0.9 kilometer turn left into Queen Edith's Way (opposite the Robin Hood and Little John Pub) and then in a short distance turn left into Lime Kiln Road. The campground is up this road about 200 meters on the right.

▲ Cambridge Camping and Caravanning Club Site

Address: 9 Cabbage Moor, Great Shelford,
                  Cambridgeshire CB2 5NB
Telephone: 01223 841185
GPS: N 52° 09' 53.5", E 000° 07' 25.6"

March 25 - Nov 1 (Varies)

The Camping and Caravanning site just outside Cambridge is one of their modern ones. Sites are on grass in a large open field with convenient electricity (Euro, high amp) and there is a modern restroom building with hot showers as well as dishwashing and laundry facilities. Bus service to central Cambridge is conveniently close to the site.

You'll find this campground about 5 km (3 miles) south of central Cambridge. Easiest access is from Exit 11 of the M11 motorway. Drive north toward Cambridge on the A1309 for 1.2 km (.7 miles), then turn right toward Great Shelford on Shelford Road. The campground entrance is on the left 1 km (.6 miles) from the turn.

Drive 7 – Cambridge to London
65 Kilometers (40 Miles), 1 Hour

Along The Way – Don't let today's the short mileage fool you. That only takes you to the London ring road. From there you might have as much as 100 km (62miles) more to reach your campground or return your vehicle. The route follows M11 south to the London ring road.

Information Resources

See our Internet site at www.rolling homes.com for many links to information sources.

British Tourist Authority, 551 Fifth Ave, Suite 701, New York, NY 10176 (800 462 2748). In Canada the address is 5915 Airport Rd, Suite 120, Mississauga, Ontario L4V 1T1.

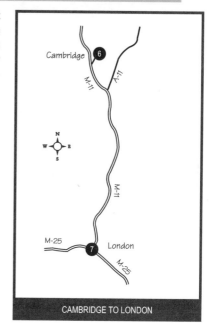

CAMBRIDGE TO LONDON

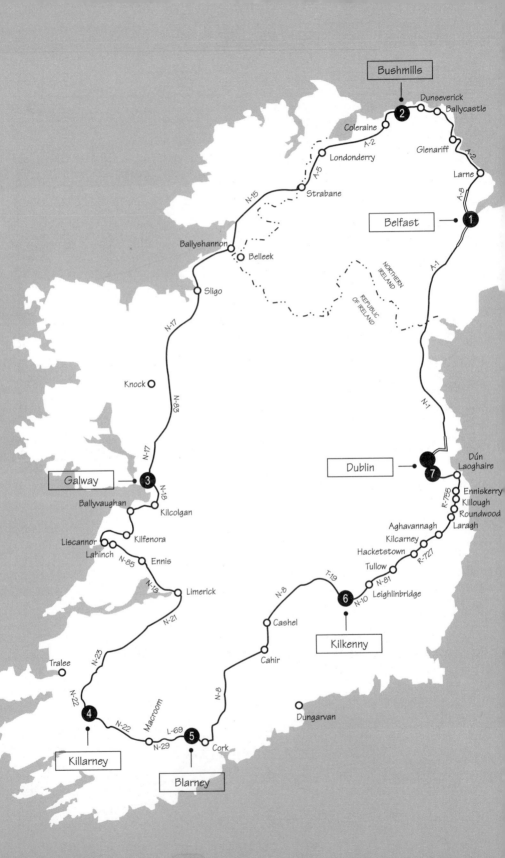

Chapter 5
Tour 2

Ireland

Top Attractions

- Dublin
- Belfast
- Ulster Folk Museum
- Antrim Coast
- Bushmills Irish Whiskey Distillery
- Giant's Causeway
- Belleek Pottery Works
- The Burren

- Cliffs of Moher
- Knock Catholic Shrine
- Lakes of Killarney
- Ring of Kerry
- Blarney Stone and Castle
- Rock of Cashel
- Glaendalough
- Powerscourt Waterfall and Gardens

General Description

This tour covers a total of 1,252 kilometers or 776 miles. It traverses a great deal of the island, starting in Dublin and driving counter-clockwise around the perimeter.

The opening dates for the campgrounds on this tour would allow travel from the middle of April to the middle of September. Travel anytime during this period will work, the middle of the summer is best, however, due to the weather.

The tour begins in Dublin. This is undoubtedly the most interesting city on the island and makes an excellent gateway city. Both rental automobiles and RVs are available in Dublin.

The first drive takes you north and out of the Republic of Ireland into Northern Ireland. The day's destination is Belfast, the north's largest and leading city. Belfast now offers two campgrounds, the most convenient is probably Larne, the nicest is the one in Killyleagh.

The second drive is very scenic. It follows Ireland's northern coast to the west. The distance is short, only about 80 kilometers (50 miles), but the roads aren't for high speed driving, you'd miss the scenery. Once in Bushmills you'll want to visit the Giant's Causeway and perhaps tour the Bushmills Distillery.

The third drive is another long one. You leave Northern Ireland and again enter the Republic. To break up this long day's drive there are two interesting stops. The first is actually a quick crossing back into Northern Ireland to the world famous Belleek Pottery Works. The second is the Catholic shrine at Knock. The day ends in Galway, or, if you prefer, at a campground that is actually in Knock.

Drive four is a chance to explore the back roads in one of Irelands most unusual places, the limestone plateau known as the Burren. Driving south from Galway you soon leave the main roads and cross the Burren, then visit the dramatic Cliffs of Moher. Then it's time to drive south again, crossing the Shannon at Limerick and finishing the day in Killarney, a holiday town in a national park.

Drive five is a short drive to Blarney. You can visit the castle and kiss the stone, then travel on in to Cork, the Republic's second largest city.

On drive six you drive across southern Ireland to Kilkenny. Along the way you can stop and see Cahir Castle and the Rock of Cashel.

Drive seven takes you back to Dublin, but the driving route is a highlight as it

THE IMPRESSIVE CLIFFS OF MOHER ON IRELAND'S WEST COAST

winds through the Wicklow Mountains with stops at the Glaendalough Valley and the Powerscourt Waterfall and Powerscourt Gardens.

This tour can easily be shortened, perhaps by leaving out Northern Ireland and traveling directly west from Dublin to Galway or Killarney. You could also combine it with the Great Britain tour in the preceding chapter by traveling from Dublin or Belfast to Wales. There are many additional destinations and campgrounds listed in our second Europe book – *Traveler's Guide to European Camping*.

Roads and Driving

Traffic in both Ireland and the Republic of Ireland drives on the left. There's some advice about driving on the left in the Roads and Driving section of the previous chapter.

The Republic of Ireland uses metric road signs although you may still see some marked in miles. Northern Ireland, on the other hand, has for the most part stuck with miles for speeds and distances.

Speed limits in both Northern Ireland and the Republic of Ireland are generally as follows unless otherwise marked: built-up areas – 50 kph (30 mph), outside built-up areas – 95 kph (60 mph), highways 110 kph (70 mph).

In the Republic of Ireland and Northern Ireland there are few four-lane roads and traffic is often held up by slow-moving farm tractors and trucks. In Northern Ireland, like in England and Scotland, motorways are designated on maps with the letter "M". Secondary roads are designated with an "A" and a number, fewer digits indicate a more heavily-used and direct route. There are also "B" roads, these are small local roads.

The Republic of Ireland uses a somewhat different system. Motorways are designated as "M" roads, but the next level is "N" or national roads with the smallest roads being "L", "R", and "T" roads.

Toll roads in Ireland are scarce, there is a toll on the M50 around Dublin and also on the M1 between Dublin and Belfast.

The all-in-one police/ambulance/road help number on the island is 999.

Camping and Campgrounds

Irish campgrounds tend to be pretty good although quality does vary. All of the campgrounds in this book have electrical hookups and decent restroom facilities.

You will find a very few examples of the two major British camping clubs in the campgrounds included in the tours in this chapter. These are the Caravan Club and the Camping and Caravanning Club. You'll find more information about these clubs in the Camping and Campgrounds section of the prior chapter. It is not necessary to join either of them in order to use the campgrounds listed in this chapter.

You can often make reservations in Ireland over the telephone directly with the campground office using your credit card. Being able to speak the language is a big help.

CAMPING AT THE BALLYNESS CARAVAN PARK NEAR BUSHMILLS

Electricity in Irish campgrounds is generally better than that available on the Continent. Sixteen amps are usually available and modern Euro (CEE17) outlets are the standard. Current is 230 volt, 50 cycles.

Irish local tourist offices can be a good place to get information about camping. Some can provide small guidebooks to camping sites, but there is usually a fee for these.

Practical Tips

Ireland is a great destination. Outside Dublin and Belfast the pace is slow and the countryside beautiful. Ireland is composed of two countries: the Republic of Ireland in the south and Northern Ireland (part of the UK) in the north. There are no border stations so you may not even know when you cross from one to the other.

The major difference between the two as a short-term visitor is the currency. The Republic of Ireland uses the euro while Northern Ireland still uses the pound. Both countries are well-supplied with bank machines in larger towns so obtaining the local currency is generally easy.

English is widely and beautifully spoken here although in some of the rural areas you will visit on these tours you may meet the occasional Gaelic speaker who has no English.

THE TOUR – IRELAND

TOUR 2 GATEWAY CITY – DUBLIN, REPUBLIC OF IRELAND
Population 950,000

This is the only really large urban center in the Republic of Ireland, Dublin's one million or so people comprise about a third of the Republic's inhabitants. Although a large city Dublin is easy for a camper to visit with a convenient campground and good public transportation to get you in to town.

Dublin is bisected by the west to east-flowing River Liffey. O'Connel Street, running north from the river, is the central thoroughfare and a good point of reference. The north half of Dublin was the posh area during the 18th century, but it is a little run-down today. It contains much that you'll want to see, **O'Connel Street** is probably the best known boulevard in Dublin. Near the street's north end you'll find **Parnell Square**, home to the **Hugh Lane Municipal Art Gallery**, the **Gate Theater** and the **Dublin Writer's Museum**. About halfway up O'Connel a major shopping street, **Henry Street**, runs westward.

South of the Liffey the streets are smaller and more crowded and the sights more concentrated. This is the home of **Trinity College** and its **Book of Kells**. You'll also find **Dublin Castle** and **St. Stephen's Green** here. **Merrion Square** is east of Stephen's Green and home of the excellent **National Gallery of Ireland**. Good shopping streets are **Nassau Street** which runs south of Trinity College and **Grafton Street**, a pedestrian street running from College Green in front of the Trinity College to St. Stephen's Green.

There are some attractions upstream of the town center to the west. Best known is probably the **Guinness Brewery** with its museum and recreated 19th-century pub. The giant **Phoenix Park** has flowers, a castle, and the **Dublin Zoo**.

Dublin is known for its pubs. The drink of choice is Guinness, of course. There's an organized Literary Pub Crawl tour or you can select your own pubs. Look for some of the best along Grafton Street or in the **Temple Bar Area** which is just south of the Liffey near the Ha'penny Bridge crossing.

The area around Dublin, known as "The Pale" during the years of English occupation, has many rewarding side trip destinations. One of the most prosperous English communities was at **Dún Laoghaire**, located on the coast south of Dublin. You can ride the Dart train to Dún Laoghaire in just a few minutes. Today the town is a pleasant ferry port for the run to Holyhead in north Wales but it also is home to the **James Joyce Martello Tower Museum**.

Fifteen kilometers (9 miles) north of Dublin is Malahide village and **Malahide Castle**. You can tour the castle which houses part of the **Portrait Collection of the National Gallery** and the **Fry Model Railroad Museum** and wander the surrounding gardens.

Dublin Campground

🔺 **Carmac Valley Tourist Caravan and Camping Park**

Address:	Road, Clondalkin, Co Dublin (Eire)
Telephone:	01 4640644
Fax:	01 4640643
Website:	www.irishcamping.com
E-mail:	camacvalley@eircom.net
GPS:	N 53° 18' 15.6", W 006° 24' 52.6"

Open All Year

This is a modern large campground in good condition. It is located west of Dublin along the N7, about 40 minutes by bus from the center of the city.

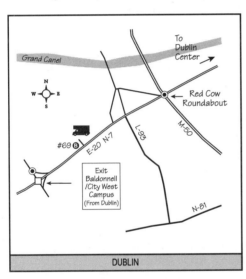

There are large areas of grass for tent camping as well as over 100 sites for vehicle campers. Sites are paved back-ins separated by hedges, they have electricity (Euro, 10 amp), water, and drains. The restroom buildings are excellent with hot showers (require a token) in individual rooms. Access to town is via Bus 69 which stops outside the gate going into town, coming from town tell the driver and he'll tell you where to get off for the shortest walk. There's also a special bus from the campground each morning.

Access to the campground is off the eastbound lanes of N7. Arriving from the west on N7 you can turn directly into the campground, it is easy to see on the left about 8 km (5 miles) outside of the city. From the Dublin direction watch for the campground on the right 3.5 km (2 miles) past the Red Cow roundabout over M50. After seeing the campground on the right go 1.4 km (.9 miles) to the Baldonnell exit and reverse direction to return to the campground.

Drive 1 – Dublin to Belfast
160 Kilometers (98 Miles), 2.5 Hours

Along The Way – Today's drive is a simple one. Just drive north on the N1 (also called the M1 and A1 in some sections) to Belfast. Once you arrive in Belfast you have a choice of campgrounds, the Curran Court in Larne is more convenient since the next day's drive heads off to the north through Larne and because it has direct rail connections to central Belfast. The Delamont Country Park in Killyleagh is less convenient but nicer since it's almost new and is in a country setting. It's your choice. See the campground write-ups below for driving directions.

BELFAST, NORTHERN IRELAND
Population 420,000

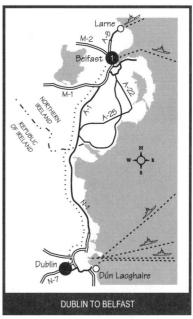

DUBLIN TO BELFAST

Belfast is a big industrial city with a bad reputation stemming from the "Troubles", the long-running struggle between the Protestant and Catholic citizens of the area. If you are there during a quiet period you may want to visit some of the more notorious trouble spots like the Protestant **Shankill Road** and the Catholic **Falls Road**. Both of these are west of the city center.

In the central city area **Donegall Square** marks the center with the **City Hall**, gardens, and the city bus station. **Donegall Place** is a pedestrian shopping street that runs north from the square. Most bars, restaurants, and nightlife are along the **Golden Mile** on Great Victoria Street which is southwest of Donegall Square. Here you'll find the **Crown Liquor Saloon**, a Victorian pub owned by the National Trust.

Both of the campgrounds listed below are outside Belfast. Larne is a ferry port to the north with good rail transportation to Belfast. Delamont is located to the southeast toward the coast, it's less convenient but still has public transportation to the center of the city and is a nicer campground. Take your pick.

The **Ulster Folk Museum** and **Ulster Transport Museum** are located 11 kilometers (7 miles) northeast of Belfast toward Bangor on the A2 motorway. The folk museum is a European-style open-air museum with typical buildings from around Northern Ireland.

Belfast Campgrounds

▲ CURRAN COURT CARAVAN AND CAMPING SITE

Address:	Curren Court Hotel, 84-86 Curren Rd, Larne, Co Antrim BT40 1BU
Telephone:	01574 275505
Fax:	01574 260096
E-mail:	curren.court-hotel@virgin.net
GPS:	N 54° 51' 02.4", W 005° 48' 15.3"

Easter - Sept (Varies)

This is a municipal campground. Ideally located near ferry docks, train station, and the center of the town of Larne, the price is right and the facilities are more than adequate. Larne is located about 35 kilometers (22 miles) north of Belfast. Larne is a ferry port and as such has outstanding train connections to Belfast. Trains leave at least every hour, the trip takes about an hour, and a round trip costs roughly four pounds.

This medium-sized campground is a grassy site sitting in a residential area near the ferry dock. There are about 30 hard-surfaced parking spots for caravans or motorhomes and a large grassy area for tents or even vans if the campground is crowded. Electricity (Euro, medium amp) is scarce, only a few sites have it. The shower/toilet building has free hot water in sinks, showers and laundry room, also a coin-operated washer and dryer. There is a playground next door for the kids and three small supermarkets are less than 10 minutes away on foot in the center of town.

Approaching from the south from Belfast on A8 just continue to where the highway terminates at a roundabout with a Kentucky Fried Chicken restaurant next to it, exit the roundabout to the north toward the ferry dock, in 0.4 km (.2 miles) you'll enter the Larne Harbor Roundabout, exit it to the north toward the ferry docks on Olderfleet Street. In 0.2 km (.1 mile) turn left onto Fleet Street, then in 0.2 km (.1 mile) turn right on Curren Rd. The campground is on the left in another 0.3 km (.2 mile). If you arrive by ferry turn right immediately after leaving the port gate onto Fleet Street, proceed 0.2 km (.1 mile), turn right onto Curren Road, proceed 0.3 km (.2 mile), the campground will be on your left.

▲ DELAMONT COUNTRY PARK

Address: Downpatrick Road, Killyleagh,
Northern Ireland, BT30 9TZ
Telephone: 028 4482 1833
GPS: N 54° 23' 08.3", W 005° 40' 25.3"

March 22 - Oct 30 (Varies)

The access to Belfast from this campground isn't as easy as from Larne, but this is a nice place and the extra difficulty may be worth the effort. The campground is located about 30 kilometers (19 miles) southeast of Belfast near the shores of the Strangford Lough and the town of Killyleagh.

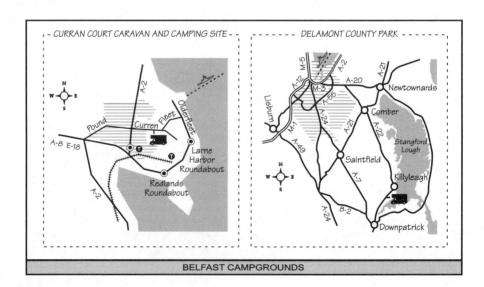

BELFAST CAMPGROUNDS

This Camping and Caravanning Club site is a new one and has excellent facilities. The sites themselves have a brick lattice to park on, they have electricity (Euro, high amp), water, and gray water drains. Tenters use the same sites as vehicle campers. Restrooms have hot showers and hot water for dishwashing. The Country park that this campground is a part of has excellent hiking trails with views of the Strangford Lough.

From Downpatrick drive north on the A22. In seven kilometers (4 miles) you'll see the campground entrance on your right.

Drive 2 – Belfast to Bushmills
110 Kilometers (68 Miles), 1.5 Hours

A long The Way – Today's drive is a beautiful one along the north coast of the island. From Larne follow A2 along to the westward some 80 kilometers (50 miles) to Bushmills. You'll pass the famous Antrim Glens, short steep valleys that open onto the coast.

Bushmills, Northern Ireland
Population 1,500

Bushmills is a small town that is well located for exploring one of the most interesting areas of Northern Ireland, the western Antrim Coast. Nearby you'll find the **Giant's Causeway** and long sandy beaches. In town is the **Bushmills Irish Whiskey Distillery** which offers a popular half-hour tour culminating in a tasting. This is probably the best known Irish Whiskey label to North Americans and the distillery tour is fun, lots of good smells.

The **Giant's Causeway**, a favorite Northern Ireland tourist attraction, is just 6 kilometers (4 miles) away by car. The

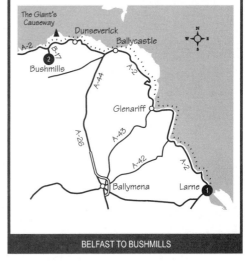

BELFAST TO BUSHMILLS

causeway is an unusual rock formation of octagonal-shaped basalt columns that almost appear to be the remains of a causeway leading into the sea toward Scotland. If you wish you can ride a bike from the campground to the causeway on a good bike trail, the distance this way is about 5 kilometers (3 miles) as the route is more direct than the road. Another option is a small tourist railway along the same route from Bushmills. Once you reach the Causeway Visitor's Center you have access to another 16 kilometers (10 miles) of trail running eastward along the coast as far as White Park Bay.

Farther east along the coast is **Carrick-a-Rede rope bridge**. This is a precarious rope bridge that crosses to a small island used for commercial salmon fishing during the summer. The seabird rookery is fascinating, particularly if you like puffins, and the rope bridge you have to use to get there is challenging if heights make you nervous. There's a nice paved 1 kilometer (.6 mile) path along the rocky shoreline from the parking lot to the bridge.

Bushmills Campground

▲ BALLYNESS CARAVAN PARK

Address:	40 Castlecatt Road, Bushmills, CO Antrim, BT57 8TN
Telephone:	(0)28 2073 2393
Fax:	(0)28 2073 2713
Website:	www.ballynesscaravanpark.com
E-mail:	info@ballynesscaravanpark.com
GPS:	N 55° 11' 40.4", W 006° 31' 02.5"

March - Oct (Varies)

This is an extremely nice campground. It's new, the facilities are excellent, and the location is terrific. With only 30 sites it can fill quickly, reservations are definitely recommended. There are also grass tent sites.

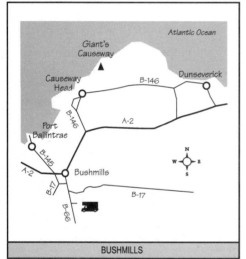

BUSHMILLS

Parking is on paved back-in sites. They have electricity (Euro, 16 amp) water, and gray water drains. Restrooms are new and clean with hot water for showers, bathroom basins, and for dishwashing. The Bushmills distillery is about a half-kilometer (.3 mile) distant and the small tourist train to the Giant's Causeway just on the far side of the village. Restaurants and shops in the village of Bushmills are easily reached with a short stroll.

To find the campground just head south from the center of Bushmills village on B66. You'll see the distillery on the left and then the campground.

DRIVE 3 – BUSHMILLS TO GALWAY
325 Kilometers (201 Miles), 4.5 Hours

A long The Way – Get an early start today because this is a long day's drive with a couple of interesting possible stops. Follow the A2 westward along the coast to Coleraine and then on to Londonderry, a distance of 69 km (43 miles). Then head south for 23 km (14 miles) along A5 to Strabane. From Strabane go west to cross the border into the Republic of Ireland and then follow N15 south to Sligo and then N17 on to Galway, a long run of 250 km (155 miles). For easiest access to the campground take N18 south from the junction about 7 km (4 miles) north of Galway near

Claregalway. It connects with N6 east of Galway and you can easily follow N6 and R338 in to the campground.

To break up this long day of driving you might want to stop in Belleek to tour the famous **Belleek Pottery Works**. To get there you detour just 8 km (5 km) east from Ballyshannon, that would be about half-way through the day's drive.

Another interesting place along the way is the famous **Catholic shrine at Knock**. It's well worth the stop and is located an hour or so north of Galway. It commemorates the miracle sighting of Mary, Joseph and St. John the Evangelist in 1879. It's similar to shrines in Lourdes and Fatima. The shrine grounds are huge, there you'll find **The Church of the Apparition** at the location where the sighting actually occurred, the **Basilica of Our Lady Queen of Ireland** which seats 12,000, and the **Knock Folk Museum** which explains the whole thing. There's even a campground there if you just don't feel like driving the remaining 70 km (43 miles) to Galway. A description of the campground is included in the Galway write-up below.

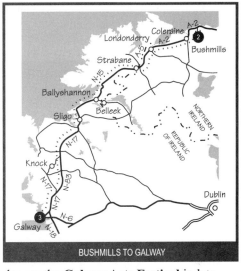

BUSHMILLS TO GALWAY

GALWAY, REPUBLIC OF IRELAND
Population 60,000

Galway is Ireland's fourth largest city. It's a dynamic business and college town. The interesting place to visit here is the center; walk the streets, visit the pubs, watch the people. There are many festivals and events in this town, the most popular are the **Galway Arts Festival** in late July and **Galway Race Week** (horse racing) at the end of July or beginning of August.

Galway Campground

▲ BALLYLOUGHANE CARAVAN AND CAMPING PARK

Address:	Ballyloughane Beach, Renmore, Galway City
Telephone:	091 755338
Fax:	091 752029
E-mail:	galwcamp@iol.ie
GPS:	N 53° 16' 08.0", E 009° 00' 57.0"

April 14 - Sept 15 (Varies)

This is a small private campground overlooking Galway Bay to the east of the city. Access to town is either a 3 kilometer (2 mile) walk or by frequent bus service from near the campground.

Most sites here are on grass in two large fields, there are about ten gravel spaces for vehicles at the top of one of the fields. Electricity (Euro, 6 amp) is available to the vehicle sites. Restrooms have hot showers (tokens required) and there is hot water in the dishwashing area. This campground gets a lot of tent campers and there are cooking facilities for them as well as a dining/lounge area. There's a grocery store just up the lane.

To find the campground approaching from the north you will come to a roundabout, follow signs for N18 and N6. In 0.5 km (.3 mile) at a second roundabout follow signs for Merlin Park. In another 1.1 km (.7 mile) you will reach a third roundabout, follow signs for City Center and in 0.3 km (.2 mile) make a left turn at Dawn Dairies. You'll reach the end of the road and the campground in another 0.9 kilometers (.6 miles). Approaching from the east on N6 at the first roundabout (7.2 km (5 miles) from Oranmore) follow signs for Galway City East Route and Merlin Park, In 1.1 km (.7 mile) at the roundabout follow signs for City Center and in 0.3 km (.2 mile) make a left turn at Dawn Dairies and in another 0.9 km (.6 mile) you'll reach the campground. Coming from the city center follow signs for Dublin/Limerick via Renmore and turn at Dawn Dairies after passing Flannery's Motor Hotel, you'll come to the campground in 0.9 km (.6 mile).

Knock Campground

▲ KNOCK CARAVAN AND CAMPING PARK   €€ 1 ▲ ♿ ▣

Address:	Claremorris Road, Knock, Co. Mayo
Telephone:	094 88100
Fax:	094 88295
Website:	www.knock-shrine.ie
E-mail:	info@knock-shrine.ie
GPS:	N 53° 47' 19.4", W 008° 55' 10.8"

March 1 - Oct 31

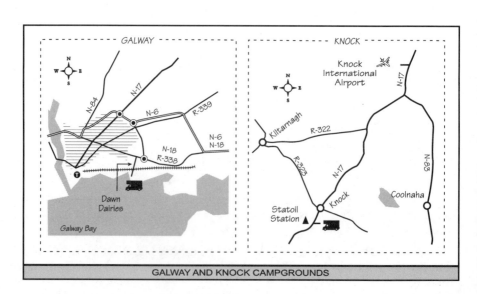

GALWAY AND KNOCK CAMPGROUNDS

The campground here is very convenient, just a short walk from the village and shrine. Camping sites are paved back-ins with electricity (Euro, high amp). Restrooms have hot showers and there is hot water for dishwashing. This campground also has a TV room.

The campground is easy to find, it's just on the southern edge of the village of Knock on the east side of the N17.

DRIVE 4 – GALWAY TO KILLARNEY
264 Kilometers (164 Miles), 4 Hours

Along The Way – Today's route is not the most direct route to Killarney, but a detour will take us through a scenic and unusual Burren region.

From Galway follow N6 east and then south N18 south to Kilcolgan, a distance of 16 km (10 miles). Now head west on N67 for 28 km (17 miles) to Ballyvaughan.

From Ballyvaughan drive south and take R480 across the top of the Burren, a barren limestone plateau covered with flowers in the spring. Watch for signs for the Portal Dolman on the left side of the road, you'll want to stop and take a look at this 4,000-year-old gravesite that looks a little like a large rock table.

After the dolman continue south following signs for Kilfenora which has a small museum about the Burren. It's 21 km (13 miles) from Ballyvaughan along the route across the Burren to Kilfenora.

Then on to coast to the west where the impressive Cliffs of Moher are well signed from all directions. Stop and take a look.

From the cliffs follow L54 through Liscannor to Lahinch and then N85 to Ennis and N18 to Limerick. From there it's a fairly straight shot of 108 km (67 miles) south on N21, N23 and N22 to Killarney.

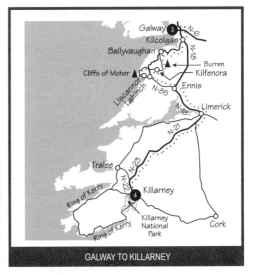

GALWAY TO KILLARNEY

KILLARNEY, REPUBLIC OF IRELAND
Population 9,000

Killarney has a deserved reputation as a tourist town and it is an excellent base for exploring this part of Ireland. Probably the best known side trip from Killarney is the **Ring of Kerry** around the Iveragh Peninsula. On days when a longer trip doesn't sound attractive you can visit closer attractions in the **Killarney National Park**. A good way to explore the nearby attractions is by bike, if you didn't bring one along you can always rent one at the campground.

Killarney is perfectly situated for a circular day trip around the **Ring of Kerry.** The circuit around the Iveragh Peninsula is about 175 kilometers (108 miles) when done from Killarney but many of the roads are slow and narrow. There are also many places to stop and explore. Most tour busses travel counter-clockwise around the circle and for safety's sake you probably should too.

The three **Lakes of Killarney** (Lough Leane, Muckross Lake, and Upper Lake) are famed for their scenery. They are within the **Killarney National Park** and located just southwest of Killarney. There are many attractions including **Muckross Abbey**, **Muckross House**, **Ross Castle and Torc Waterfall**. You can take a boat out to Innisfallen Island or hike or bike the **Gap of Dunloe.**

Killarney Campgrounds

▲ FLEMINGS WHITE BRIDGE CARAVAN AND CAMPING PARK

Address:	Ballycasheen Rd, Killarney, Co. Kerry
Telephone:	064 31590
Fax:	064 37474
Website:	www.killarneycamping.com
E-mail:	fwbcamping@eircom.net
GPS:	N 52° 03' 25.3", W 009° 28' 32.7"

March 14 - Oct 31 (Varies)

White Bridge is a large well kept campground about 1.5 kilometers (.9 miles) from the center of Killarney next to the River Flesk. It covers two large grassy fields.

A few pitches near the entrance have hard all-weather surfaces, the remainder of the campground sites are on the grass and not delineated in any way. Adequate electrical outlets (Euro, 10 amp) are provided. There are three shower/toilet buildings with hot water for showers, dishes and laundry. Showers require a token. There is a small grocery store on-site and bicycles for rent.

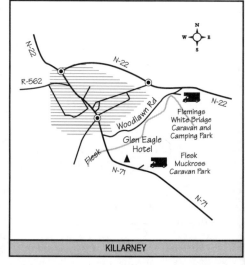

You'll find the campground on the southeast edge of town, just off Highway N22. A sign on the highway will show you where to turn. If you approach town from the southwest on N71 a sign just outside the central area of town at the Shell station will direct you to the right along Woodlawn Road, a convenient bypass route south of town.

▲ **FLESK MUCKROSS CARAVAN PARK**

Address:	Muckross Rd, Killarney, Co Kerry (Eire)
Telephone:	064 31704
Fax:	064 34681
Website:	www.homepage. tinet.ie/~jcourtney/Victoria.house/
E-mail:	killarneylakes@eircom.net
GPS:	N 52° 02' 34.8", W 009° 29' 59.5"

April 20 - Sept 30 (Varies)

This simple campground is located behind a gas station just south of Killarney. Sites for vehicles are gravel back-ins with electricity (Euro, high amp) and there are large grassy areas for tents. Restrooms have warm showers (tokens required).

The campground is on the east side of the N71 about 1.5 km (1 mile) south of central Killarney.

DRIVE 5 – KILLARNEY TO BLARNEY
80 Kilometers (50 Miles), 1.25 Hours

A long The Way – It's only a short drive from Killarney to Blarney which leaves lots of time for some touring in either Killarney or Blarney and Cork. From Killarney head east on N22. As you near Cork you'll find that signs will direct you toward Blarney along minor roads along the north shore of the River Lee from the vicinity of Macroom.

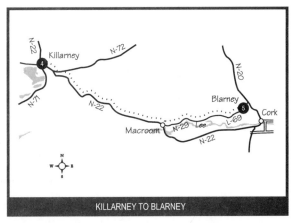

KILLARNEY TO BLARNEY

CORK AND BLARNEY, REPUBLIC OF IRELAND
Population 180,000

Cork is the second largest city in The Republic of Ireland. It is a fun city, there are good restaurants and pubs, excellent shopping, and even some decent architecture. The center of the city is on an island in the River Lee. There is a shortage of famous visitor attractions here, that should give you more time to enjoy the city's ambiance.

The village of Blarney, just seven kilometers (4 miles) to the north, does have a famous attraction and little else. The **Blarney Stone** is part of the walls of **Blarney Castle**, dating from 1446. If you want to kiss the stone yourself be prepared to climb old spiral staircases and then wait while one at a time a long line of folks ahead of you lay on their backs and stretch out over almost-empty space to kiss the stone. They have a lot of help, as you strain to kiss the stone assistants keep a good hold on you (and there's a safety grill), they told us they've not lost anyone in the last few years.

Cork and Blarney Campground

▲ Blarney Caravan and Camping Park

Address:	Stoneview, Blarney, Co Cork, Ireland
Telephone and Fax:	021 438 5167
Website:	www.blarneycaravan park.com
E-mail:	info@blarneycaravanpark.com
GPS:	N 51° 56' 50.9", W 008° 32' 50.0"

Feb 1 - Nov 15 (Varies)

Located about 2 kilometers (1.2 miles) from Blarney Castle, this campground gives you the opportunity to easily kiss the Blarney Stone and the bonus of being within easy visiting range of Cork.

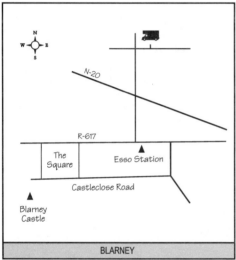

The clean and modern campground has back-in gravel surfaced sites with electricity (Euro, high amp) and good restrooms with hot showers. There is also a lot of grass for tent campers. There's a campers' kitchen and dining area as well as a nearby restaurant and pitch-and-putt golf course. Central Blarney is a two-kilometer (1.2 mile) walk, from there you can easily catch one of the frequent busses into Cork. The castle itself has quite a bit of parking so you can visit in your RV.

To reach the campground from Blarney follow signs north from the Esso service station over the N20. The campground is 2 kilometers (1.2 miles) from the service station.

Drive 6 – Blarney to Kilkenny
160 Kilometers (100 Miles), 2.25 Hours

Along The Way – From Blarney follow L69 toward Cork and join the N8. This highway will take you 80 kilometers (50 miles) to the northeast to Cahir. Here you can tour **Cahir Castle**, one of the largest in Ireland.

Another 20 kilometers (12 miles) north, still on N8, is Cashel and the **Rock of Cashel**. There has been a fortress here for over a thousand years, it's one of the most evocative sites in Ireland. Today there are a round tower, a roofless abbey, and a Romanesque chapel.

From Cashel continue northeast on N8 for another 32 kilometers (20 miles), then turn southward on T19 and you'll soon arrive in Kilkenny.

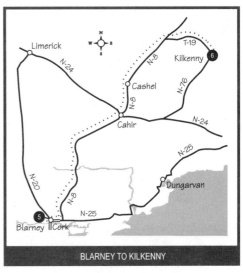

BLARNEY TO KILKENNY

KILKENNY, REPUBLIC OF IRELAND
Population 19,000

Kilkenny is a very old town, it dates from at least the fifth century. Many people consider Kilkenny to be the most beautiful city in Ireland. You'll want to see **St. Candice's Cathedral**, dating from about 1200. There's also **Kilkenny Castle** which traces it's roots to a wooden structure built by Strongbow in 1172. The city gained title to the castle in 1967 and it is being restored, it is open to the public.

Kilkenny has many festivals during the year, the best attended is the **Kilkenny Arts Festival** in late August.

Kilkenny Campground

▲ TREE GROVE CARAVAN & CAMPING PARK

Address:	Danville House, Kilkenny, Co Kilkenny (Eire)
Telephone:	056 70302
Fax:	056 21512
E-mail:	tree.cc@101.ie
GPS:	N 52° 38' 22.3", W 007° 13' 45.1"

Open All Year

Located just outside the Kilkenny ring road this little campground is a pleasant and convenient place to stay while visiting the town. The sites here are gravel back-ins with electricity (Euro, 10 amp). The restroom building has hot showers and the dishwashing room is large enough to make a convenient place for tent campers to gather out of the weather if necessary. The walk in to town is only a kilometer and a half.

Look for the campground on the right (heading out) just outside the ring road on the road south toward Thomastown and Wexford.

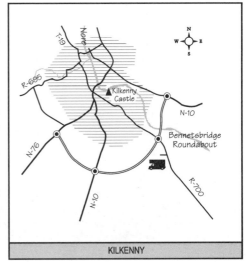

KILKENNY

DRIVE 7 – KILKENNY TO DUBLIN
153 Kilometers (95 Miles), 3 Hours

A long The Way – Today's route follows small roads across southeast Ireland and then crosses from south to north through the scenic Wicklow Mountains to Dublin. There are several very interesting stops along the way.

From Kilkenny follow N10 east to meet N9 and then north to Leighlinbridge. Cross the river and follow small roads eastward toward Tullow on N81. A few kilometers north of Tullow turn east again onto R727 and follow it through Hacketstown, Kilcarney, and Aghavannagh and then north into the Wicklow Mountains.

About 15 km (9 miles) north of Aghavannagh you'll reach Laragh. Glaendalough, the valley of two lakes, is just to the west. Sitting near the lakes and connected by

ROUND TOWER AND GRAVEYARD AT GLENDALOUGH

trails are two groups of very old buildings that were part of a monastery founded by St. Kevin in the 6th century.

From there follow R755 north through Roundwood (the highest village in Ireland) and Killough toward Enniskerry and Dublin. Near Killough you can take a short side trip to the west to see the 425-foot Powerscourt Waterfall and a few kilometers beyond stop to see the Powerscourt Gardens.

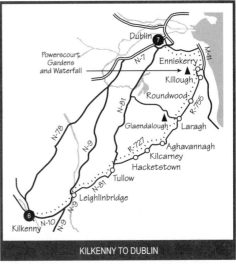

KILKENNY TO DUBLIN

When you leave the gardens head east to the M11 motorway and then north toward Dublin. If you are headed for Carmac Valley Tourist Campground (see write-up under Dublin above) follow signs around the M50 ring road to the N7. Heading southwest on the N7 you'll spot the campground on the right, go to the next off-ramp to reverse directions to reach it.

Information Resources

See our internet site at www.rollinghomes.com for many links to information sources.

Bord Fáilte (Republic of Ireland), 345 Park Ave, New York, NY 10154 (800 223-6470).

NITB (Northern Ireland), 551 5th Ave, Suite 701, New York, NY 10154 (212 922-0101).

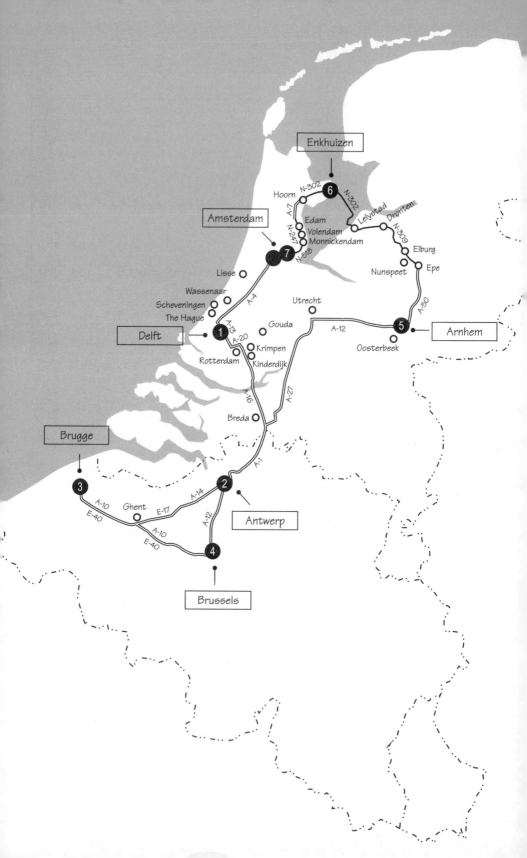

Chapter 6
Tour 3

Benelux

Top Attractions

- Amsterdam
- Delft
- Gouda
- Kinderdijk Windmills
- Ghent
- Rubens Huis
- Brugge
- Brussels

- Hoge Veluwe
- Kröller-Müller Museum
- Airborne Museum
- Nieuw Land Poldermuseum
- Zuiderzeemuseum
- Edam
- Volendam, Marken, and Monnickendam

General Description

This tour covers 805 kilometers (499 miles). While the distances are short the overnight stops are full of interesting sights and things to do. You'll definitely find your days full of activity. For this reason most of the routes follow the autobahns which let you move from place to place easily in these crowded countries.

The opening dates of the campgrounds in this section would allow you to complete the entire tour from April 1 to September 30. Be advised that the first part of April can be a little chilly for tent camping, we've seen temperatures below freezing during the first week of the month.

The tour starts in Amsterdam, without a doubt one of Europe's top tourist destinations as well as one of the world's favorite cities. Once you've spent a few days you can pick up your rental automobile or RV and start the tour.

On the first drive you'll travel to Delft, a short drive to a good campground and another place that tops most visitor's lists of their favorite towns in the Netherlands. It's a very short drive.

Drive two takes you into Belgium. The city of Antwerp is a great camping destination with a campground conveniently located just across the river from action in the central part of town.

Drive three is 100 kilometers (62 miles), it ends in Medieval Brugge. This must be Belgium's top visitor destination, the old canal-ringed city is filled with restaurants and shops, it's a great walking city.

On drive four the tour moves on to Brussels. This is a big city, the capital of Belgium. You have a choice of two campgrounds outside the center, both have good transportation options for traveling in to the center.

Drive five takes you back north into the Netherlands. Arnhem is a small city with a location just south of the Hoge Veluwe National Park. You can ride the extensive trails in the park on the free bicycles supplied to visitors. There's a great art museum in the center of the park. Arnhem is also known as the location of World War II's Operation Market Garden, there is a good museum covering that battle in the town.

The next drive, the sixth, takes you north across the polders to Enkhuizen. You should stop along the way to see how the Dutch have drained this area at the Nieuw Land Poldermuseum in Lelystad. Then, you'll cross what is left of the old Zuider Zee (now divided by the causeway you are driving across into the Markermeer and the Ijsselmeer) and overnight in a town along it's shore. Enkhuizen is the site of an open-air museum dedicated to the fishing lifestyle practiced before the Zuider Zee was cut off from the North Sea.

TULIPS FOR SALE IN THE SPING

The final drive takes us back to Amsterdam. Along the way you can stop to visit the old fishing towns of Volendam, Marken and Monnickendam. Then it's back to Amsterdam to overnight in a campground or turn in that rental rig and consider the flight home.

Because the driving distances are so short in this tour it would be easy for you to shorten it by bypassing any city listed. For additional destinations and campsites see our second Europe camping book – *Traveler's Guide to European Camping*.

Roads and Driving

The Netherlands and Belgium have very good autobahn systems, they are free but often crowded. While distances are short in these countries you will find yourself on the autobahns if you want to make any kind of decent progress. International highways use the "E" prefix, national freeways use "A", and major secondary roads are designated as "N" roads.

There are really no toll roads in the Netherlands or Belgium. Some bridges, dikes, and tunnels, however, do charge tolls.

The speed limits in Belgium and the Netherlands are similar. Generally, limits are as follows unless otherwise marked: in towns and built-up areas 50 kph, on highways 80 to 100 kph as marked, and on limited-access expressways 120 kph.

Belgium and especially Holland are great for bicycle trips. There are often separated bike paths along the roads with their own traffic signs. Be alert since riders sometimes seem oblivious to automobiles, often because they have the right-of-way.

The Netherlands and Belgium have different phone numbers for emergency help. In The Netherlands emergency police, fire, and ambulance numbers are all 112. In Belgium the emergency phone number for the police is 101, fire is 100, and ambulance is 100. To call for emergency services from a mobile phone dial 112.

Camping and Campgrounds

Both of these countries have a good selection of campgrounds. Many are holiday parks with lots of amenities. Many also have large contingents of permanently-located caravans used primarily as weekend country retreats by city dwellers. You'll be impressed by the gardens in the yards of some of these. Usually the permanent units are in separate areas and do not really affect the overall atmosphere of the campground for tourists.

The Camping Card International is generally not required in the Benelux countries, but it is appreciated and often will get you a discount. Without one you may have to leave your passport at the office overnight.

Energy seems to be at a premium in these countries, particularly the Netherlands. Electricity is often metered or expensive, showers are likewise often metered and often not quite as hot as one would like. Electrical outlets in the parks are often euro-style, but in the Walloon area of southern Belgium you'll often find the French style. Electrical amperage usually falls into the medium category, from 5 to 10 amps.

Free camping is not allowed in Holland, fines are often levied and it is difficult to be inconspicuous. Belgium also restricts free camping.

Practical Tips

Belgium and the Netherlands combine to form a relatively small land area of about 65,000 square miles, about the same size as the states of West Virginia or North Carolina. They have a large population for their size, 26 million people, or about one tenth the population of the U.S. Despite the large number of people in such a small area there is lots of countryside although it is definitely not being wasted. Every spare square meter seems to be well tended and under cultivation.

The Netherlands and Belgium are also called the Low Countries, they're so low that parts are below sea level. The Netherlands (often called Holland) is very flat, some of it on land reclaimed from the sea. Dutch is spoken, of course, but English is also very widely understood, especially by the younger people. You'll probably have fun with the Dutch language. It is considered closer to English than any other European language but is different enough to seem very bizarre to an English speaker. Much of the coast is parkland composed of sand dunes and there are many good campgrounds along the North Sea.

Belgium is split ethnically with Walloon and Flemish areas speaking respectively French and Dutch. The landscape is low and flat like Holland in the north, more hilly in the south, especially in the Ardennes region. In this chapter you'll often find three versions of town names, the first is English, the second Flemish (Dutch) and the third Walloon (French).

These are thoroughly modern countries with good supermarkets and wide use of credit cards and cash machines. Prices are toward the high side of the European scale, not as high as Scandinavia nor as low as Greece or Portugal. Both are members of the EU and use the euro.

You'll find many medium-sized supermarkets but very few large hypermarkets in these countries. Supermarkets are sometimes hard to find, especially in the Netherlands, because many are tucked into residential areas away from the highways and often don't have much in the way of signs. The best way to find one is to ask at the campground or on the street.

Service stations in these countries are modern and easy to find on the expressways, sometimes not so easy off them. It is likely that you'll usually fill up somewhere along the motorways. In Belgium, particularly in the Walloon areas, you'll find some service stations associated with large French hypermarkets, they can be the least expensive place to buy fuel. Most service stations accept credit cards.

THE TOUR – BENELUX

TOUR 3 GATEWAY CITY – AMSTERDAM, THE NETHERLANDS
Population 740,000

Amsterdam is the first city visited by many travelers to Europe from North America and it is a great introduction to the Continent's charms. Schiphol Airport is an important entry point, fortunately there's easy-to-use train service to Amsterdam from the airport because taxis are extremely expensive. The central city is the perfect size, not so large that it is intimidating but large enough to keep you busy for many days. The quiet streets along canals and the residential central city area with walking streets and bicycles are unlike anything you're likely to have seen at home but are a great preview to the best European cities.

Amsterdam's central area is arranged in a half-circle fronting on the Central Railroad Station. Half-rings of canals define the city's shape. This layout was initiated in 1585 and is an excellent example of early city planning. While most of the sights are within walking distance of each other there are so many things to see that the good tram, bus, and subway system is a lifesaver. Making the whole thing even better is the fact that most Dutch people seem to speak fluent English (and other languages too).

While in Amsterdam there are several must-see museums. First on the list is the **National Museum (Rijksmuseum)** with its unsurpassed collection of Dutch mas-

TOUR BOAT NEAR CENTRAL STATION IN AMSTERDAM

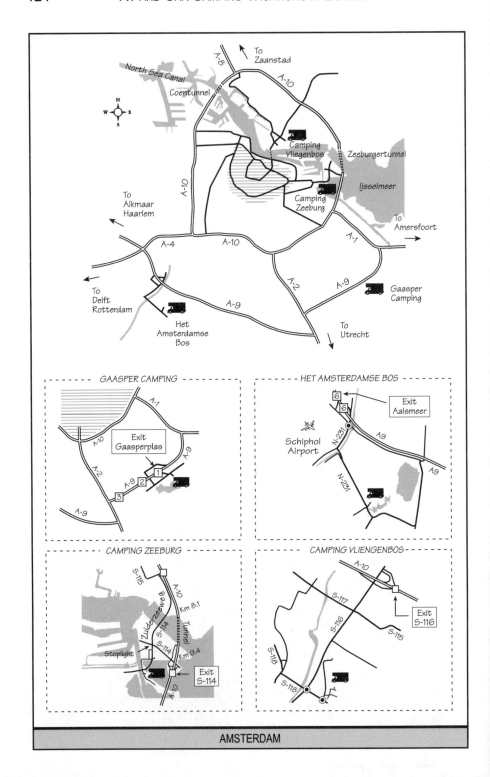

AMSTERDAM

ters. Next stop is the **Van Gogh Museum (Rijksmuseum Vincent Van Gogh),** which has the best collection anywhere of paintings by this popular artist. Other interesting museums include **Ann Frank's House (Anne Frank Huis),** the **Jewish Historical Museum (Joods Historisch Museum),** **Rembrandt's House (Rembrandthuis),** the **Stedelijk Modern Art Museum (Stedelijk Museum),** and even the **Netherlands Maritime Museum (Nederlands Scheepvaart Museum).**

If you're sick of museums you can take the popular **Heineken Brewery (Heineken Brouwerij) Tour,** visit a **diamond-cutting workshop,** or stroll through the strange **red light district** just southeast of the Central Station.

Shopping is lots of fun in Amsterdam. There are several large department stores like De Bijenkorf on Dam Square but you can also walk the Kalverstraat and Nieuwendijk pedestrian shopping streets and have as much fun watching the people as buying things. From there take a short side trip to the flower market barges on the Singel Canal. There are a number of English-language bookstores on Kalverstraat.

Amsterdam Campgrounds

▲ GAASPER CAMPING AMSTERDAM

Address:	Loosdrechtdreef 7, NL-1108
	AZ Amsterdam
Telephone:	020 6967326
Fax:	020 6969369
Website:	www.gaaspercamping.nl
GPS:	N 52° 18' 45.7", E 004° 59' 24.6"

March 15 - Nov 1 (Varies)

Gaasper Camping is a large, modern campground located south of Amsterdam at the end of the metro line. Quick, easy access to central Amsterdam and good (although sometimes almost overzealous) management make this our favorite Amsterdam campground.

The campground is a very large grass field somewhat broken up by hedges. Some parts have paved access roads and numbered sites, others are large grassy fields intended for tent camping. Most sites are grass but there are a few paved ones for winter use. Sites are assigned at the reception desk and the manager will lead you to your assigned space. There are a large number of permanent resident rigs here with landscaped yards, they are isolated from the remainder of the campground and do not dominate it. Electrical outlets are provided for individual sites (Euro, 10 amp). Some sites also have gray-water drains and there is a dump station. The shower/toilet buildings are modern but Spartan, showers are warm, not hot, and require purchased tokens (pushbutton, preset), bathroom sinks are cold water only and hot water for dishwashing requires a purchased token. There is a restaurant and a grocery shop but they are open only in summer. The campground is adjacent to a large park area with bike trails, a swimming lake, and playgrounds.

Gaasper Camping is at the far south end of the easternmost fork of the Amsterdam metro line (Gaasperplas Station). The subway station is about 500 meters from the campground and the ride to the Amsterdam Central Station takes no more than 20 minutes.

CAMPERS AT GAASPER CAMPING

The campground is just south of the A9 expressway south of Amsterdam. It is on the section of A9 between the A2 and the A1 expressways. Take the Gaasperplas exit and follow the campground signs a very short distance to the gate. Park outside and walk in to register.

▲ KAMPEERTERREIN HET AMSTERDAMSE BOS

Address:	Kleine Noorddijk 1, NL-1432 CC Aalsmeer
Telephone:	020 6416868
Fax:	020 6402378
Website:	www.campingamsterdamsebos.nl
E-mail:	camping@dab.amsterdam.nl
GPS:	N 52° 17' 38.6", E 004° 49' 24.0"

April 1 - Oct 15

This is a very large campground in the Het Amsterdamse Bos park near Schiphol International Airport. There is convenient bus service into Amsterdam and a large wooded area next to the campground for walking and biking.

Het Amsterdamse Bos has over 400 campsites, they are located on several fields of various sizes and separated by hedges so the feeling is of a smaller campground. This is a popular stop for the camping-bus tours visiting Amsterdam. There are quite a few resident rigs here but they are concentrated in an area away from the tourist campers and don't affect the atmosphere of the campground. The campsites are on grass with a few paved spots for the winter use of vehicle campers. They are unmarked and unassigned, the reception person will usually assign you a general area but not a space. Electricity (Euro, 5 or 10 amp) is available to about a third of the sites. A new shower/toilet building has been built in the rear area of the campground. It has hot showers with high-tech 5-minute timers as well as hot water for dishes. Older shower/toilet buildings are scattered around the grounds. The campground has a grocery store and small restaurant. There is a good supermarket about 2 km (1.2 miles) from the campground, ask at the reception desk for directions.

Access to Amsterdam is by bus. The Number 171 bus leaves from a stop about 300 meters from the campground and connects with the Number 172 bus at the Amstelveen station to continue in to Amsterdam's Central Station. Bus 199 from Schipol airport passes near the station, tell the driver you are going to the campground.

Take the Aalsmeer exit (No. 6) from Highway A9 near Schiphol. This exit is just southeast of where A9 meets A4. Head south on N231 along the canal and then turn left and cross the canal following the Aalsmeer direction signs. After 1.5 kilometers (.9 miles) you'll see the campground sign pointing to your left near a set of traffic lights. Het Amsterdamse Bos is about 100 meters back along the access road.

▲ CAMPING ZEEBURG AMSTERDAM

Address: Zuider IJdijk 20, NL-1095 KN Amsterdam
Telephone: 020 6944430
Fax: 020 6946238
Website: www.campingzeeburg.nl
E-mail: info@campingzeeburg.nl
GPS: N52° 21' 52.8", E 004° 57' 36.9"

Open All Year

Amsterdam's only all-year campground can get pretty full when all of the others are closed but it's a handy place to keep in mind. Since it sits on the shore of the Markermeer it can get a little chilly here during the winter months, but in summer the waterside location is pleasant. You can make reservations on the website, a good idea in winter for RV's since this is the only Amsterdam campground open in the middle of the winter.

Tent campers here have a large area along the shore. The RV area is nearer the back of the campground, sites have electricity (Euro, 10 amp). A group of buildings around a brick plaza house the reception with a grocery area, a restaurant/bar, hot showers, dishwashing area with hot water, and a laundry area. Other restroom facilities are scattered around the grounds. Access by bus is via the Molenwijk Bus 37 from the Central Station, get off at the Flevopark stop.

To reach the campground by vehicle take Exit S114 (Zeeburg), drive 0.8 km (.5 miles) toward the city center, turn left on Zuiderzeeweg and then immediately right to access a side road. Campground signs will help, it's harder to explain than to drive. Turn left to parallel Zuiderzeeweg, drive 0.3 km (.2 miles), turn right and follow a small access road that circles to the left and arrives at the campground in another 0.6 km (.4 miles).

▲ CAMPING VLIEGENBOS

Address:	Meeuwenlaan 138, NL-1022 AM Amsterdam-Noord
Telephone:	020 636 88 55
Fax:	020 632 27 23
Website:	http://www.vliegenbos.com
GPS:	N 52° 23' 24.0", E 004° 55' 35.0"

April 1 - Sept 30

With only 19 sites with electricity and a high price this north Amsterdam campground will probably appeal to few RV campers but for tenters it's a good choice. And the showers are free, unusual in the Netherlands.

The 19 sites with electricity are near the entrance. They form a small tight loop of back-in sites. Tents are pitched in large grassy fields. The reception building also houses a store and restaurant. Restrooms are almost new with fancy electronic units that sense your presence in the shower and start automatically. They're not adjustable, however. There's a bus stop on the main road outside the campground entrance. From the Central Station take bus 32 or 36. You can also use the Adelaars-Weg ferry behind the Central Station and walk about 1.5 km (.9 miles) to the site.

By vehicle take Exit S-116 from the A-10 north of Amsterdam and head toward the center of town. Get off the S-116 at the S-118 which is about 2.3 km (1.4 miles) south but the exit is sooner. Watch for campground signs and make sure you get off because if you don't you'll enter the tunnel and end up in central Amsterdam. Head east on S-118 for 0.3 km (.2 miles) to the traffic circle and turn left. Then after less than 100 meters turn right and quickly left following camping signs to enter the entrance road for the campground.

DRIVE 1 – AMSTERDAM TO DELFT
70 Kilometers (42 Miles), .75 Hour

Along The Way – The quickest route to Delft from Amsterdam is via the A4 expressway. It's 46 kilometers (29 miles) from the intersection of the A4 and A9 on the southwest side of Amsterdam to its intersection with the A13 (Exit 10) near The Hague. Continue south on A13 for about 5 kilometers (3 miles) to Exit 9 for the Delft campground.

In the spring (late March to late May) there's a can't-miss stop en route. That's Keukenhof Gardens. These are the largest gardens in the world and, as if that weren't enough, they're situated right in the middle of the Dutch tulip fields. The gardens themselves also feature tulips of course. Take Exit 4 from the A4 and go north on N207 toward Lisse. When the gardens are open you'll find lots of signs taking you on the preferred route to the parking areas.

DELFT AND THE HAGUE (DEN HAAG), THE NETHERLANDS
Population of Delft 95,000, Population of The Hague 450,000

Delft is most famous for **Delftware porcelain** which is white with blue patterns.

The town is a popular daytrip from other cities in Holland, as a camper you can beat the crowds by staying just outside of town and spending the mornings and evenings wandering the very attractive streets with their canals and old houses. Delft has many of the most attractive features of Amsterdam.

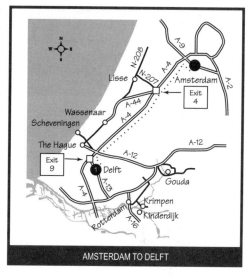

AMSTERDAM TO DELFT

Delftware was actually a copy of examples of Chinese Ming porcelain captured by Dutch pirates from a Portuguese ship in 1604. Porcelain manufacturers in Delft quickly began producing Delftware to meet the huge demand created when the limited cargo was auctioned in Amsterdam. Delft was also the home of the famous Dutch painter of quiet interiors, Jan Vermeer.

Visits to several porcelain works are possible, the reception desk at the campground can steer you in the right direction or maybe even arrange tours. The shops and sights around the central **Markt** or square are worthwhile and Delft offers an exceptionally large number of restaurants.

Delft is centrally located for visits to several interesting cities. **The Hague** and **Rotterdam**, close by but in opposite directions, are easy to reach by train or bus from Delft.

Rotterdam is a giant modern city, often thought of as Holland's Manhattan, but this is a newer town than Manhattan since most of it has been rebuilt since World War II. Consider taking a **harbor tour**, Rotterdam has the world's largest commercial harbor. You could take the nine-hour version but there is also one that takes about an hour and a quarter. The boat pier is near the Leuvehaven Station of the Metro's blue line.

The Hague is the center of government in The Netherlands although Amsterdam is nominally the capital. Parliament meets in the **Binnenhof**, the building dates from 1248. The area around the Binnenhof is the old section of town. Don't miss the **Royal Picture Gallery** in the **Mauritshuis** with its excellent collection of Dutch master paintings. **Madurodam**, north of The Hague, is a 1/25 scale model of a Dutch city complete with moving airplanes and cars. Along the ocean near The Hague is the resort town of **Scheveningen.** Take the bus to The Hague and then a tram to the beach.

There is a very popular campground located about 7 kilometers (4 miles) north of The Hague in the town of Wassenaar. This is Camping Duinrell, it is located on the grounds of a large water park. It is a great place to stay if you have kids along and is open all year. It's a possible alternate to the campground we describe below.

The well known cheese town of **Gouda** is about 25 kilometers (15 miles) east of Delft. Drive north on A13, jog northwest on A4 for a couple of kilometers, then take

A12 east to Gouda. There's a cheese market every Thursday morning in July and August. There are also some traditional Dutch windmills at the edge of town. For more windmills you can make your way about 20 kilometers (12 miles) southwest from Gouda to Krimpen. Just south of Krimpen at **Kinderdijk** is the largest collection of windmills in Holland. They are actually put into operation each Saturday afternoon in July and August.

Delft Campground

▲ Cᴀᴍᴘɪɴɢ Dᴇʟꜰᴛꜱᴇ Hᴏᴜᴛ

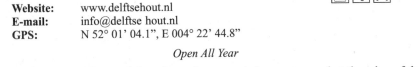

Address:	Korftlaan 5, NL-2616 LJ, Delft
Telephone:	015 2130040
Fax:	015 2131293
Website:	www.delftsehout.nl
E-mail:	info@delftse hout.nl
GPS:	N 52° 01' 04.1", E 004° 22' 44.8"

Open All Year

This is a very nice, and therefore often crowded, campground at the edge of the village of Delft. It makes a good place to stay for visiting Rotterdam and The Hague, not to mention Delft.

Camping Delftse Hout is a large campground with lots of amenities and good modern facilities. There are many permanently-located rigs here, over 200 tourist sites are located in an area separated from them. Campsites are mostly on grass, some have brick driveways. High hedges break the campground into small friendly group-

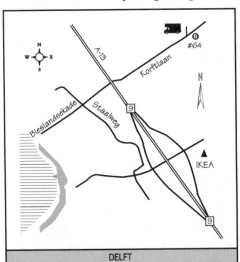

ings. Electrical outlets (Euro, 10 amp) are conveniently located near each site. The shower/toilet facilities are in the main building near the campground entrance and are modern and clean. Free hot water is provided for showers, bathroom sinks, dishes and laundry. There is also a restaurant, a grocery shop, a recreation room that sometimes shows English language movies (Dutch subtitles), and a small swimming pool. The campground is located next to a large park with a lake and many walking and biking paths. Rental bicycles are available.

The campground is close enough to central Delft to allow you to stroll to the central square in 20 minutes. Bus 64 from the Delft rail station runs right by the campground. Bus and train service to The Hague and Rotterdam from central Delft is quite convenient.

Heading south on Highway A13 take the Delft/Pijnacker exit (Exit 9) and follow campground signs as they take you north along the west side of the freeway and then right on Korftlaan to pass under the freeway. In 0.5 km (.3 miles) after passing under the freeway you'll see the campground on your left.

DRIVE 2 – DELFT TO ANTWERP
120 Kilometers (75 Miles), 1.5 Hours

A long The Way – The direct route to Antwerp is quick and easy. Just head south on A13 from Delft, jog to the east on A20 for a few kilometers, and then join A16 to the south. A16 becomes A1 once you cross the border into Belgium. As you approach Antwerp be sure to follow signs for R1, not R2. This route will take you around the east and south side of town for the best approach to the campground. See the campground write-up for directions.

DELFT TO ANTWERP

ANTWERP (ANTWERPEN OR ANVERS), BELGIUM
Population 460,000

Although Antwerp is Belgium's second largest city you can make it actually seem almost intimate by staying at Camping De Molen. The campground is located in a quiet suburb yet you can be right in the middle of the interesting and friendly old center of town with only a short walk. This is an easy way to take advantage of the lively night life that the city offers.

Antwerp became an economic power in the late fifteenth and early sixteenth century under Charles V of Spain. At that time the Zwyn estuary at Brugge was silting up and traders transferred their business to Antwerp. For a time the city was the economic capital of Europe. Antwerp quickly declined under Philip II, Charles' son, as a result of the struggles of the inquisition. Today the city acts as the unofficial capital of Flemish Belgium and is an important port even though it is located some 80 kilometers (50 miles) from the North Sea.

To tourists the town of Antwerp is synonymous with the prolific painter **Peter Paul Rubens**. You can visit his home and workshop, called the **Rubens' House (Rubens Huis),** and see his paintings in the **Royal Art Gallery** or Belgium's largest cathedral, the **Onze Lieve Vrouwe Kathedraal**. Antwerp is also a diamond-trading town, you can watch the action on **Pelikaanstraat** in the Jewish Quarter near the Central Station or visit the **Diamond Museum**. Antwerp also has a good centrally-located **zoo**.

Antwerp Campground

▲ CAMPING DE MOLAEN

Address:	Antwerpen-Strand, Thonetlaan,
	St. Annastrand, B-2020 Antwerpen
Telephone:	03 2196090
Fax:	03 2169117
GPS:	N 51° 14' 00.9", E 004° 23' 33.1"

April 1 - Sept 30

Camping De Molaen will surprise you with how close it is to downtown Antwerp. Located on the left bank of the Scheldt River it is seemingly far from the bustle and noise of the city. Yet if you stroll along the water for 10 minutes, then cross the river through an underwater pedestrian tunnel, you'll find yourself near the center of town.

This is a medium-sized campground on a grassy plot in the St. Annastrand district of Antwerp on the west side of the river. There are a few resident caravans here, but also room for quite a few tourists. Camping is on numbered grass sites that are assigned at the reception office. Electricity (10 amp) is convenient to most sites, they'll issue you a special connection cord and take a hefty deposit for it (25 euros). The shower/toilet building is modern and showers are hot and free. There is also hot water available in bathroom sinks and for washing dishes. You'll find a small supermarket near the metro station less than a kilometer away.

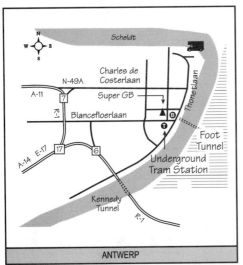

To reach downtown you can take a bus from near the campground entrance or walk about 10 minutes south to reach either a metro station or a pedestrian walkway that will take you under the river to central Antwerp. Bikes are allowed in the underground tunnel and there are escalators and bicycle elevators at each end. Backpackers can reach the campground by taking the metro # 3 Line toward Linkeroever (stop is Frederik Van Eeden Plein) and then proceeding north on Thonetlaan about 1.3 km (.8 miles) to the campground.

To find the campground driving take the first exit west of the Kennedy tunnel where the R1 ring road becomes the A14 (E17). The exit is labeled Antwerpen-Linkeroever and is Exit 6 from the east on R1. From this direction you will come to a stop light at a T, the cross street is Blancefloerlaan. Turn right and proceed 1.8 km (1.1 miles) to another T. Turn left and the campground is on your right in 1.5 km (.9 miles).

ANTWERP CASTLE

DRIVE 3 – ANTWERP TO BRUGGE
100 Kilometers (62 Miles), 1.25 Hours

Along **The Way** – It's another short driving day as you head for Brugge. Just follow A14 to the west. About 50 km (31 miles) from Antwerp turn northwest onto A10 and in another 39 km (24 miles) you'll spot Exit 8 for Brugge.

A good stop en route is the old city of **Ghent** at the intersection of the A14 and the A10. The town centers around a chain of squares and historic buildings including St. Baaf's cathedral, the Belfry, St. Nicholas' Church and Gravensteen Castle. Inside St. Baaf's cathedral is the huge painting by Jan van eyck called *Adoration of the Lamb*. It's one of the earliest oil paintings and is probably the most famous painting in Belgium. Also in Ghent is the Museum voor Schone Kuntsten with a collection of Flemish masters from the 16th and 17th centuries.

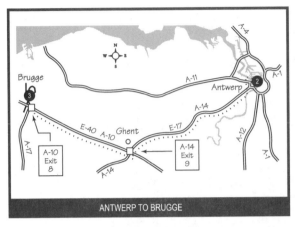

ANTWERP TO BRUGGE

Although small, Brugge is probably Belgium's most popular tourist town. The popularity stems from the town's medieval buildings and streets dating from an extremely prosperous period in the fourteenth and fifteenth centuries. The old town was preserved because the Zwijn estuary silted up in the early sixteenth century cutting the town off from the sea and stalling the economy. Today the river is filled with pleasure boats and the town with visitors. A ring of water circles the center of town, you can wander at will on foot, boat, bike, or horse-drawn cab with little chance of becoming seriously lost.

BRUGGE STREET SCENE

The **Burg** and **Markt**, two squares, are at the center of town. The **Belfry** next to the Markt is a good place to climb for the view while the buildings around the Burg are genuinely medieval. The cluster of museums a few blocks south of the squares includes the **Memling Museum** and the **Groeninge Museum** , both with Flemish masterpieces.

Brugge Campground

▲ CAMPING ST. MICHIEL

Address:	Tillegemstraat 55, B-8200 St. Michiel, Brugge
Telephone:	050 380819
Fax:	059 806824
Website:	http://www.campingbrugge.be
E-mail:	campingbrugge@hotmail.com
GPS:	N 51° 10' 50.7", E 003° 12' 13.6"

Open All Year

This large campground has a convenient location. It is about 2 kilometers from the center of Brugge and convenient to the freeway. Brugge itself is convenient because it is on the direct route between the cross-channel ferry ports (Zeebrugge is only 15 kilometers away) and Continental destinations to the east. This is the first night's stop for many British campers headed south on holiday.

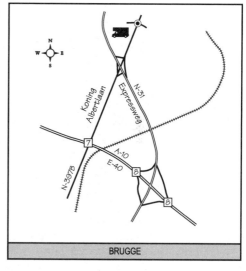

BRUGGE

The campground is a large grassy plot with most individual sites separated by hedges. While there are quite a few permanently-located caravans there are also a lot of sites reserved for tourist campers. Parking is on grass and electrical outlets (Euro, 10 amp) are conveniently located. The toilet/shower building is large (perhaps even a little damp and dark) but the water in the showers (preset) and sinks is hot. Coin-operated washers and dryers are available. The campground also has a grocery shop (in summer) and a good restaurant. There are two clay tennis courts.

You can easily reach town by walking or riding a bike, the distance is about 2 kilometers and takes about 30 minutes to walk. Bus service is also available (Number 7).

To find the campground take Exit 8 from A10 (E40). Follow the signs north towards Brugge on the N31 Espressweg for 2.4 km (1.5 miles) . Turn right at the intersection onto Koning Albertlaan. In another 0.4 kilometers (.2 miles) you will see the campground on the left. Proceed to the next intersection to make the sharp left into Tillegemstraat. Just past the restaurant turn left into the campground entrance, there's a gate so you'll have to stop and go inside to sign in.

Drive 4 – Brugge to Brussels
100 Kilometers (62 Miles), 1.25 Hours

A long The Way – It's another short drive from Brugge to Brussels. Enjoy it because the next one is the longest of this tour. Just follow A10 for 81 kilometers (50 miles) to the Brussels ring road R0 and then follow it to the left for both Brussels campgrounds.

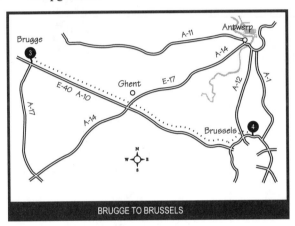

BRUGGE TO BRUSSELS

Brussels (Brussel or Bruxelles), Belgium
Population 980,000

Brussels is both a modern and a medieval city, home to the European Community, NATO, and an attractive 15th-century old town. Visits to the old city center around the **Grand' Place**, a large square lined with medieval **Guild Halls**. Just a few blocks away you'll find the **Manneken Pis**, the statue of a small peeing boy that must be the top tourist attraction in town. Also interesting are the narrow streets filled with cafes and shops, some in glass-covered galleries to protect shoppers from the often inclement weather.

Just southeast of the old city you'll find the **Parc de Bruxelles** with the **Palais Royal** on one end and the **Palais de la Nation** on the other. From this higher area you have views over the old town and are near several good museums including the **Musée d'Art Moderne** and the **Musée Royale d'Art Ancien**.

Napoleon was finally defeated by combined English and Prussian forces in June 1815 at the village of Waterloo which is just south of Brussels. Follow the RO ring road south along the east side of Brussels to Exit 23 for Waterloo. There are several sites and museums relating to the battle in the area. You can climb the **Lion's Mound (Butte du Lion)** for a view of the battle area.

Beersel Castle, dating from the thirteenth century, is an impressively restored castle located just southwest of the city. Take Exit 14 from the A7 freeway running around the west side of Brussels.

About 12 kilometers (7 miles) east of Brussels in the town of Tervuren is the **Royal Museum of Central Africa (Musée Royal de l'Afrique Centrale)**. This museum is the legacy of Belgium's days as an imperial power controlling what was then called the Belgian Congo. It has an excellent collection of African art.

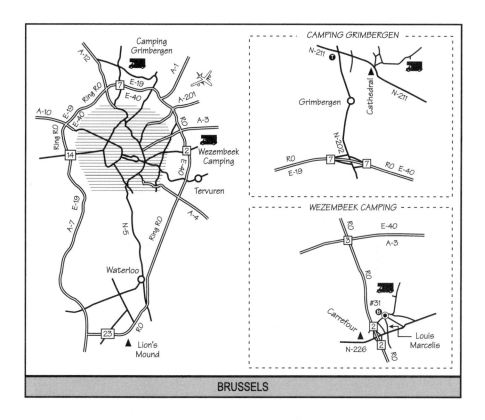

BRUSSELS

Brussels Campgrounds

▲ CAMPING GRIMBERGEN

Address:	Veldtkanstraat 64, B-1850 Grimbergen
Telephone:	02 2709597
Fax:	02 2701215
GPS:	N 50° 56' 05.9", E 004° 22' 57.0"

April 1 - Oct 31

This campground is modern and has decent facilities for both tent campers and those with rigs. There is good bus service to central Brussels from the center of Grimbergen, a distance of 2 km (1.2 miles) from the campground. This is a pleasant place to stay while visiting Brussels.

For tents and vehicle camper overflow there is a large grassy field. Normal vehicle sites are back-ins, they are numbered with some on gravel and some on grass, electrical outlets (Euro, 10 amp) are near the sites. Restroom have hot water for showers, bathroom basins, and dishes. Next door is the city swimming pool and rental bicycles are available.

To reach the campground start on E19, the Brussels ring road, north of the city. Take Exit 7 for Antwerpen/Grimbergen N202 and head north. After 2 km (1.2 miles) you will reach an intersection with the town train station to the left. Turn right here on N211 toward Vilvoorde. After 0.7 km (.4 miles) at the second traffic light turn left and in another 0.7 km (.4 miles) you will see the campground entrance on the right.

▲ Wezembeek Camping   €€ △ ☖ ⑪ ▦

    Address: Warandberg 52, B-1970 Wezembeek, Belgium   🐕 ▣ ℄ ▤

    Telephone: 02 7821009

    GPS: N 50° 51' 25.7", E 004° 29' 03.5"

April 1 - Sept 30

This is a well-tended medium-sized site operated by the Belgian Camping Club in the Brussels suburb of Wezembeek. Trees and shrubs provide shade and some separation between rigs. Access to downtown Brussels is not difficult and you don't have to brave the city traffic to reach the campground.

There are many permanently-located caravans here but about 30 sites are set aside for tourist rigs. These sites are numbered and assigned when you check in, the surface is grass, some have gravel wheel pads, all are relatively flat. Electricity (Euro, 6 amp) is available, you may need a longer cord for some sites. The campground has hot showers (push valve, not adjustable) and two clean toilet buildings, hot water is available in the shaving sinks but not for dishwashing. An area for hand washing laundry and hanging clothes to dry inside is also provided. A clubhouse building provides inside seating and some snacks.

The Kraainem metro station is about 3 kilometers (2 miles) from the campground. You can reach it by taking the local bus, Number 31, from a stop that is about one-half kilometer from the campground. Using the combination of bus and metro you can reach downtown in about 45 minutes, we found that even by walking to the metro station we could be there in under an hour. There is a shopping center with two large supermarkets about 2 kilometers (1.2 miles) from the campground in the direction of the metro station.

To find the campground take Exit 2 from the Brussels ring road just south of the point where Highway E40 intersects. Turn east towards Wezembeek and then almost immediately take the first possible left turn after the freeway on-ramp, it is marked with an inconspicuous camping sign and is Rue Louis Marcelis. About 0.3 km (.2 miles) from the turn you will come to a large circle around the central square of a small town, go around it counter-clockwise to a T. Then turn right. Take the left fork of the Y that you will soon come to and 0.4 km (.2 miles) after the Y you will see the campground entrance on the left. There are inconspicuous campground signs all along this route. The gate is closed from noon to 2 pm and there is nowhere to park and wait so keep this in mind.

Drive 5 – Brussels to Arnhem
210 Kilometers (130 Miles), 2.5 Hours

A long **The Way** – From Brussels drive north toward Antwerp on either A1 or A12. The one you choose will probably depend upon which campground you chose to use while visiting Brussels, it's about 35 km (22 miles) on either one. From Antwerp continue north on A1 for about 45 km (28 miles) where you join A27 (signed Utrecht). Be aware that just 6 km (4 miles) after getting on to A27 you must exit again at another intersection, again it's signed A27 Utrecht. Stay on A27 for approximately 72 km (45 miles) (that's both sections) until you reach southern Utrecht where you should join A12 which will take you east for 47 km (29 miles) to Exit 25 (signed Oosterbeek) for the Arnhem campground.

ARNHEM, THE NETHERLANDS
Population 135,000

BRUSSELS TO ARNHEM

Arnhem is a modern Dutch city mostly rebuilt after heavy damage in World War II. The town is interesting because of it's World War II history and because it is near the Hoge Veluwe, the largest Dutch national park.

BIKERS IN HOGE VELUWE NATIONAL PARK

Arnhem was the scene of the disastrous World War II Operation Market Garden described in Cornelius Ryan's book *A Bridge Too Far*. The World War II sites to see are the **Airborne Museum** in Oosterbeek and the **Airborne Cemetery** nearby.

The **Hoge Veluwe** is a double attraction. The **Kröller-Müller Museum** in the park is one of Europe's most important museums with many Van Gogh paintings and a great outdoor sculpture garden. The park itself is a very large natural area with miles of bike paths and free bikes for the use of visitors. You may even see a red deer or two.

The Arnhem area is home to two other well known attractions. The **Burgers Zoo** is the largest in Holland and has very well-designed natural enclosures. **Nederlands Openlucht Museum** is one of the ubiquitous European open-air museums with preserved traditional buildings, costumes, and demonstrations.

Arnhem Campground

▲ Campeercentrum De Hooge Veluwe

Address: Koningsweg 14, NL-6816 TC Arnhem
Telephone: 026 4432272
Fax: 026 4436809
Website: www.dehoogeveluwe.nl
E-mail: info@dehoogeveluwe.nl
GPS: N 52° 01' 52.5", E 005° 51' 59.4"

March 31 - Oct 28 (Varies)

Campeercentrum De Hooge Veluwe is a very large holiday campground. You won't find many of these in this book but this one has a very good location at the

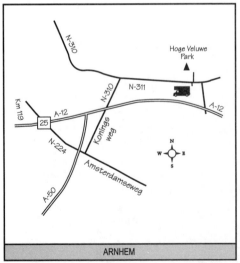

south entrance to the Hoge Veluwe park. You can walk across the street and into the park, the bicycle racks aren't far beyond.

This extremely large campground gets five stars from the rating agencies, it has everything they like. Parking is on grass with convenient electrical outlets (Euro, 16 amp), either in smaller areas encircled by hedges at the front of the park or in a large field at the back. Restrooms are modern and have hot water for showers, lavatory sinks, and dishes. There is a good grocery shop, a restaurant, and a swimming pool. If you wish to visit Arnhem from the campground Bus 92 passes the campground every half-hour.

The campground is located just south of Hoge Veluwe park, about six kilometers (4 miles) northwest of central Arnhem.

Easiest access is from Exit 25 of the A12 autoroute. After the exit head southeast on N224 for 1.4 km (.9 miles), then turn left on Koningsweg (N310). At the junction in another 2.3 km (1.4 miles) turn right onto N311, still called Konignsweg, and you'll see the campground on the right in another 2.2 km (1.4 miles).

DRIVE 6 – ARNHEM TO ENKHUIZEN
130 Kilometers (81 Miles), 1.75 Hours

Along The Way – From Arnhem drive north on A50 for 35 kilometers (22 miles) to the exit for N309, signed for Epe and Nunspeet. Now follow N309 to the northwest. It will lead north to Elburg and then across Flevoland, the last Dutch province drained from the sea, it was opened to settlement only in the late 50s and early 60s. You'll pass Dronten and enter Lelystad.

Lelystad has two interesting museums, both located on the coast just west of the point where the N302 starts across the Ijsselmeer. The first is the **Nieuw Land Erfgoedcentrum** which tells the story and techniques of draining the polders. The second is just next door, the **Batavia Werf.** It's a marine museum with a replica of the Batavia, a Dutch East India Company frigate. There's also a factory outlet mall at the same location.

After visiting the museums join N302 as it crosses the Ijsselmeer to Enkhuizen, 26 kilometers (16 miles) away across the water.

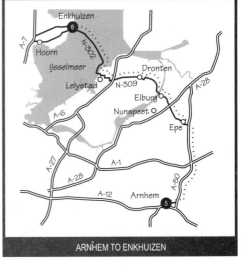

ARNHEM TO ENKHUIZEN

ENKHUIZEN, THE NETHERLANDS
Population 17,000

With its canals and old houses Enkhuizen feels a lot like a town from the past. While the town and setting are nice the reason to come here is really the **Zuiderzeemuseumu**. There are two parts. Right next to the campground is an open-air museum showing life in a typical village of the area about 100 years ago. It's very authentic, and fascinating. It's called the **Buitenmuseum**. After touring the outdoor museum you can take a short ferry ride to visit the **Binnenmuseum,** a more traditional-style museum with exhibits about the economic activities of the region at the turn of the century.

Enkhuizen Campground

▲ ENKHUIZER ZAND

Address:	Kooizandweg 4, NL-1601 LK Enkhuizen
Telephone:	0228 317289
Fax:	0228 312211
GPS:	N 52° 42' 36.6", E 005° 17' 42.2"

April 1 - Oct 1

Enkhuizer Zand is located on the coast of the Ijsselmeer and right next to the Zuiderzee outdoor museum. That alone makes this a must-visit Dutch campground. An added attraction is the easy stroll into town.

The campground has many permanent units in a central area along the water and

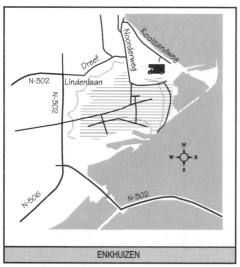

ENKHUIZEN

many other sites in large grassy fields back from the water. Parking is on grass, some sites have electrical outlets nearby (Euro, 4 amp). Restroom are located throughout the campground, some are basic portables and some more sophisticated permanent units with hot water for dishes and showers. There is a sand beach near the campground entrance that is open to anyone as well as a swimming pool, a voucher for pool use is part of the campground fee.

To find this campground start at the point where N302 makes a 90-degree bend when the roads from the A7 to the west and the dike to the south meet. Go east on Lindenlaan and then Dreef for 1 km (.6 mile), turn left at the T and enter the large recreation area to the right in another 0.2 km (.1 mile). Circle around to the right and then southeast along the water to reach the campground.

DRIVE 7 – ENKHUIZEN TO AMSTERDAM
75 Kilometers (45 Miles), 1.25 Hour

A long The Way – It's a short drive south to Amsterdam but there are several interesting stops along the way. From Enkhuizen follow N302 west to the A7 autobahn. In just 4.5 km (3 miles) exit at Exit 7 and follow N247 south to Edam, Volendam, Marken, and Monnickendam. These four towns are former fishing ports, now tourist towns. Edam is famous for it's cheese, Volendam is a port for the short ferry ride out to Marken and the center of tourist activities, and Monnickendam is quieter. The whole area is a destination for tourist busses from Amsterdam, but it's still an interesting place to visit with lots of photo opportunities.

From Monnickendam you can continue south along the dike at the water's edge to Amsterdam's ring road, a distance of 19 km (12 miles).

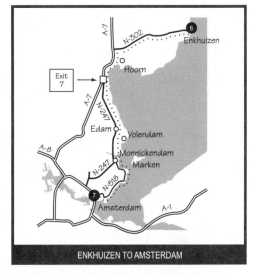

ENKHUIZEN TO AMSTERDAM

Information Resources

See our Internet site at www.rollinghomes.com for many links to information sources.

Netherlands Board of Tourism, 335 Lexington Ave., New Your, NY 10017, (212 370-7360). In Canada contact Netherlands Board of Tourism, 25 Adelaide Street East, Suite 710, Toronto, ON, M5C 1Y2 (416 363-1577).

Belgian Tourist Office, 780 Third Avenue, Suite 1501, New York, NY 10017 (212 758-8130). In Canada contact Office Belge du Tourisme, P.O. Box 760, Succursale NDG, Montreal, Quebec H4A 3S2 (514 484-3594).

Luxembourg National Tourist Office, 17 Beekman Place, New York, NY 10022 (212 935-8888).

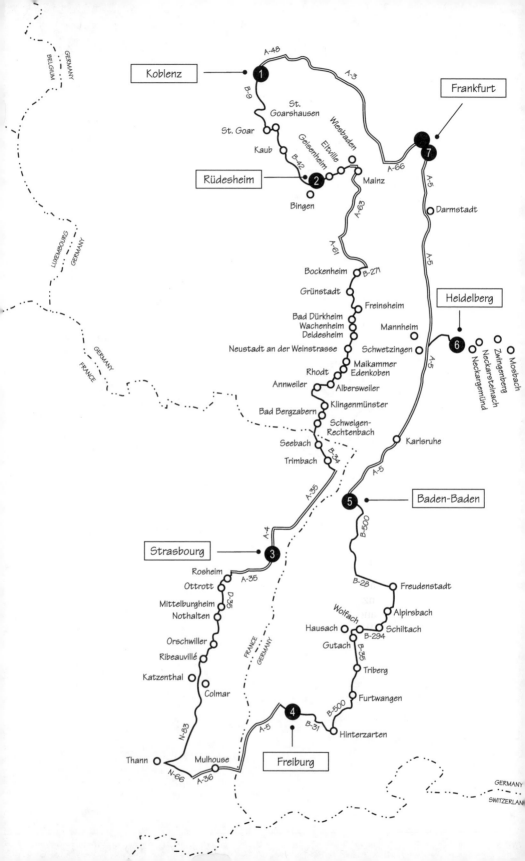

Koblenz **1**

Frankfurt **7**

St. Goarshausen

Wiesbaden

Eltville

St. Goar

Geisenheim

Kaub

Rüdesheim **2**

Mainz

Bingen

Darmstadt

Bockenheim

Grünstadt

Freinsheim

Heidelberg

Bad Dürkheim
Wachenheim
Deidesheim

Mannheim

Neustadt an der Weinstrasse

Schwetzingen

6

Mosbach

Rhodt

Maikammer
Edenkoben

Zwingenberg

Neckarsteinach

Annweiler

Albersweiler

Neckargemünd

Klingenmünster

Bad Bergzabern

Schweigen-
Rechtenbach

Seebach

Karlsruhe

Trimbach

Baden-Baden **5**

Strasbourg **3**

Rosheim

Ottrott

Freudenstadt

Mittelburgheim

Alpirsbach

Nothalten

Wolfach

Schiltach

Hausach

Orschwiller

Gutach

Ribeauvillé

Triberg

Katzenthal

Colmar

Furtwangen

Freiburg **4**

Hinterzarten

Thann

Mulhouse

GERMANY
BELGIUM

LUXEMBOURG
GERMANY

GERMANY
FRANCE

FRANCE
GERMANY

GERMANY
SWITZERLAND

Chapter 7

Tour 4

Rhine Valley

Top Attractions

- ❖ Frankfurt
- ❖ Romantic Rhine Valley and Castles
- ❖ Rüdesheim's Drosselgasse
- ❖ Deutsche Weinstrasse
- ❖ Strasbourg
- ❖ French Route du Vin
- ❖ Black Forest
- ❖ Heidelberg

General Description

This tour covers a long stretch of the Rhine River, both in the Romantic Rhine Valley between Koblenz and Bingen and along the much wider upper Rhine Valley as it separates Germany and France in the regions known in Germany as the Rhineland-Palatinate and Baden-Wurttemberg and as the Alsace in France. The total distance is 1,075 km (667 miles) making it one of the shorter tours in the book.

The gateway city for this tour is Frankfurt. This is one of Germany's most modern and successful cities, a great introduction to today's Germany. It's also an easy fly-in destination with a good selection of rental automobiles and RVs.

From Frankfurt the first drive leads to Koblenz on the Rhine River. The Moselle (Mosel) River flows into the Rhine in Koblenz and the campground sits right at the junction of the two rivers.

The next drive runs south along the most scenic stretch of the Rhine, the Romantic Rhine Valley. You'll see lots of castles and have the opportunity to watch the river

CROSSING THE RHINE ON THE FERRY AT ST. GOAR

traffic as you drive. You'll even cross the river on a small ferry. The night is spent in Rüdesheim, a town along the river known for it's restaurants and wine.

Drive three is a tour of Germany's wine road, the Deutsche Weinstrasse. You'll follow small roads through vineyards and can stop to eat, taste wine, and perhaps buy a bottle or two. Before the end of the drive you'll cross into France and spend the night in Strasbourg, a city known for it's cuisine.

Drive four is similar to drive three, a wine road, but in France instead of Germany. This one is known as the Route du Vin. At the end of the drive you'll cross the Rhine River and reenter Germany. The evening is spent in Freiburg, gateway to Germany's Black Forest.

And the Black Forest is the next driving route. We've detailed many interesting stops. At the end of the drive you'll stay in a campground with bus service to Baden-Baden.

From Baden-Baden to Heidelberg is a short drive on the autobahn. That should give you plenty of time to tour this popular destination.

The final drive brings you back to Frankfurt, again on the autobahn. It's an easy drive giving you lots of time to return that rental vehicle and either catch a flight or resume your exploration of Frankfurt.

You can easily modify this tour by bypassing a town or even using the autoroutes/ autobahns to whisk you quickly to your next destination instead of following back roads. You can also easily connect with the next tour in this book of the Central European cities or perhaps the Alps Tour to extend your trip to three or more weeks. For many more destinations and campgrounds not listed in this book see our second European camping guide – *Traveler's Guide to European Camping*.

Roads and Driving

Most of this tour is spent in Germany with only one destination in France in the city of Strasbourg. For roads and driving information related to France take a look at the introductory section of Chapter 11.

Generally, speed limits in Germany are as follows unless otherwise marked: in towns and built-up areas 50 kph, on highways 100 kph. Germany is well known for its autobahns and the fact that many have no speed limits. You'll be smart to stay well to the right and keep an eye on your rear-view mirror, the speed differential between an RV and a powerful Mercedes, BMW, or Porsche coming up behind can easily be more than 50 miles an hour. Don't let this intimidate you however, you'll have lots of company in the right lanes in the form of thousands of trucks traveling across the country, just like in the U.S. Many sections of the autobahns do have speed limits, a 120 kph (75 mph) limit is quite common. One of the best thing about the German autobahns is that they have no tolls.

On the maps and highway signs autobahns have an "A" prefix and often also an alternative "E" or international prefix. Secondary roads have a "B" prefix and in Germany they are usually good. Most are wide and have shoulders but off the beaten track and in the eastern part of the country the standards are not as good. Since autobahns are so common and are used for most long-distance travel you'll find that secondary roads tend to run through towns instead of bypassing them. Germans have lots of cars so you'll usually have plenty of company on the highway. Roads smaller than the "B" roads are labeled as "L" roads, smaller ones are "K" roads.

The general emergency phone number in Germany for police, ambulance and fire is 112.

Camping and Campgrounds

For information about France see Chapter 11 about Camping and Campgrounds in France.

Germany has plenty of campgrounds, about 3,500 of them. Facilities are gener-ally of good quality and clean with hot water and electricity available. You will find that many campgrounds meter electricity and charge by the amount used, some have coin-operated meters and in others an attendant reads the meter before you hook up and when you leave. The CEE17 or Euro plug is the most common plug but the older German style is also used. In Germany more than anywhere else in Europe you will find many campgrounds full or nearly full of semi-permanent resident caravans. Many are used only on weekends or during the July and August summer holiday. The camp-grounds listed in this guide tend to cater to tourist campers, but many of them also have a large resident population with tourist sites intermixed with those occupied by permanent caravans. Often no English is spoken by the reception person at German campgrounds, especially if he or she is older, but this is no problem, sign language always proves adequate. Campground reception offices are often closed for a couple of hours during lunch. Most campgrounds have a coin-operated washing machine and clothes dryers.

An International Camping Card is not required in Germany, but you can sometimes get a discount if you have one.

Practical Tips

Again, because most of this tour is spent in Germany with only one night in France the practical tip section here only covers Germany. For Practical Tips related to France take a look at the introductory section of Chapter 11.

Germany may feel more like home to people from the United States or Canada than most places in Europe. The country is prosperous and organized. There are many people, yet much of Germany is not overly crowded. Roads are good, signage and traffic lights are similar to ours, and drivers are generally skillful and not overly aggressive, except on the autobahn. You'll find that Germans are outdoors enthusiasts so there are many campgrounds and natural areas with miles of bike and hiking trails. Many of the large German cities were destroyed during World War II and have been rebuilt so they often have a modern appearance. Efficient public transportation and traffic-free central areas are common. In western Germany, at least, English is widely spoken.

As a rich modern country you will find that Germany has plenty of shops and lots of variety. Supermarkets tend to be smaller than those in France and Great Britain but generally offer a good selection. A real problem in Germany is that opening hours in stores are restricted by law. Things are gradually getting better but evening hours are restricted and most stores are closed on Sunday except those in railroad stations. You will find some mini-markets at gas stations with longer hours but only a few items.

Germany uses the euro as currency. Debit and credit cards are widely used, particularly Master Card, Visa, American Express and Diners Club. Our experience has been that Master Card is more widely used than Visa in this country. Cash machines are widespread, even in small towns. Most gas stations now accept credit cards.

THE TOUR – RHINE VALLEY

TOUR 4 GATEWAY CITY – FRANKFURT A.M., GERMANY
Population 650,000

Your overwhelming impression of Frankfurt will probably be how modern and well-off it is. This is the business capital of Germany. The skyscrapers and the newness of the central area are the result of two bombing raids during World War II, the old town was practically leveled. Frankfurt has obviously recovered, this is arguably the busiest and most productive of German cities (Munich and Hamburg residents might not agree) and much of the resulting resources have gone into making the city a showplace.

Frankfurt has many museums, maybe more than any other German city, and that's saying a lot. A few of the best are the **Goethe Haus** (the house where Goethe was born and also a museum), the **Städel Museum**, and the **Museum of Modern Art**. Many museums are located on the southern bank of the Main River, the area is known as the Museum Embankment. When your museum visits are finished the place to seek refreshment is the **Sachsenhausen** area a few blocks south of the Main River.

Frankfurt Campground

▲ CITY CAMP FRANKFURT AM MAIN

Address:	An der Sandelmühle 35 b,
	D-60439 Frankfurt am Main
Telephone:	069 570332
Fax:	069 57003604
Website:	www.city-camp-frankfurt.de
E-mail:	City-Camp@t-online.de
GPS:	N 50° 09' 46.9",
	E 008° 38' 59.1"

Open All Year

There are several campgrounds around Frankfurt but this is the closest to the city. The location is not very scenic, but the convenient access to the U-Bahn makes up for a lot.

The campground is medium-sized with many permanent residents and also room for quite a few tourist rigs. While facilities are adequate the campground seems a little run down. The management is friendly and helpful. Many of the folks staying here appear to be Germans with business interests in town. The campground can be crowded so the manager

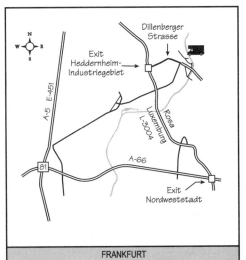

will probably assign you a place to park. Most camping sites are not clearly marked. There is an older shower/toilet building in the center of the site, hot showers require a token, shaving and dishwashing sinks have free hot water. There is another portable-type toilet building near the entrance to the campground, it has no showers but is convenient to the front area of the campground where most tourist rigs park. You can swim in the nearby off-site pool.

Access to central Frankfurt is where this campground shines. The Heddernheim stop on the U-1,2 and 3 lines is about 300 meters from the campground. The trip to central Frankfurt takes about 15 minutes.

To reach the campground start on the A5 autobahn which runs north and south to the west of Frankfurt center. Take the A66 towards the east for 4.5 kilometers (2.8 miles) and then take the Nordweststadt exit. Following the signs toward Nordweststadt will put you on another elevated expressway heading north, this is Rosa Luxemburg Str. After another 3.8 kilometers (2.4 miles) take the Heddernheim-Industriegebiet exit and turn to the right onto Dillenberger Strasse. You'll see the first campground signs here and can follow them to the park. In another 1.2 kilometers (7 miles), just before the Dillenberger Strasse crosses the Nidda River you'll exit to the right and pass under the bridge to the left and to the campground.

Dʀɪᴠᴇ 1 – Fʀᴀɴᴋꜰᴜʀᴛ ᴛᴏ Kᴏʙʟᴇɴᴢ
128 Kilometers (79 Miles), 1.5 Hours

A long The Way – The first day's drive is easy to accomplish after picking up your rental car or RV in Frankfurt. It takes you northwest to Koblenz at the confluence of the Rhine and Mosel Rivers.

Head west from Frankfurt on either the A3 or A66 autobahn, then north on the A3. After about 71 kilometers (44 miles) join A48 which leads 20 kilometers (12

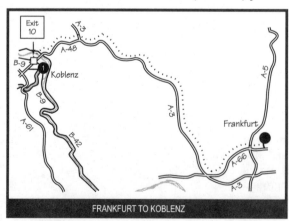

FRANKFURT TO KOBLENZ

miles) west to Koblenz. Take Exit 10 and then go left on B9 toward Koblenz for 3.1 kilometers (1.9 miles). Take the off-ramp and turn left on Eifelstrasse. Follow signs on city streets for 3 kilometers (1.8 miles) to the campground.

Kᴏʙʟᴇɴᴢ, Gᴇʀᴍᴀɴʏ
Population 110,000

Koblenz's origins are Roman. It was founded in 10 BC. The city was heavily damaged in WWII so the center is modern. Sights include the **Deutsches Eck** statue of Kaiser Wilhelm II at the point where the rivers join. Also impressive is the **Ehrenbreitstein**, a fortress on the opposite side of the river constructed during the 19th century.

Koblenz Campground

▲ CAMPINGPLATZ RHEIN-MOSEL

Address:	Schartwiesenweg 6, D-56070 Koblenz
Telephone:	0261 82719
Fax:	0261 802489
GPS:	N 50° 21' 57.7", E 007° 36' 14.7"

April 1 - Oct 15

This large campground sits on a much-photographed site at the confluence of the Rhine and Mosel Rivers. This is a large campground. Most parking is on grass or gravel with a few paved sites (Euro, 16 amp). The restrooms have free hot water for showers, basins, and dishwashing. There is a small restaurant. In summer there is a convenient walk-on ferry running across the Mosel to central Koblenz.

The campground sits on the west bank of the Rhine and the north shore of the Mosel. Access is complicated but if you start on B9 north of Koblenz there are campground signs that will lead you east to the site.

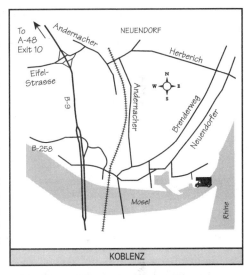

DRIVE 2 – KOBLENZ TO RÜDESHEIM
68 Kilometers (42 Miles), 1.5 Hours

A long The Way – This drive is an easy one. From Koblenz follow B9 south along the west bank of the Rhine for 33 kilometers (20 miles) to St. Goar. There take the ferry across the river and continue south on the east bank of the river on B42 for 31 kilometers (19 miles) to Rüdesheim.

You'll be traveling along an extremely scenic and historical section of river. Flowing from north to south the Rhine is passing through a range of hills. Headed upstream the barges here have to fight their way because the current is swift, going downstream they're traveling almost too fast for safety. In times past this was a strategic traveling route, that's evidenced by the castles standing along both sides of the river.

In **St Goar**, before you cross the river you can easily stop and tour one of the castles. It's called **Burg Rheinfels** and you'll spot it high above the town. Fortunately, there's a road up the hill so you don't have to climb it on foot.

Once you've ferried across the river from St. Goar to St. Goarshausen you'll find yourself driving right along the river around a rocky bluff. This bluff is the **Loreley**, a spot where legend has it that mariners were lured to their doom as they tried to pass on the river.

About 8 kilometers (5 miles) farther along, in the village of Kaub, you'll see the

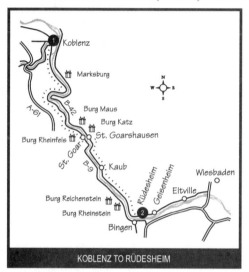

KOBLENZ TO RÜDESHEIM

Pfalzgrafenstein on an island in the river. Chains were strung from this little castle to the shore on both sides of the river to stop boats and extract tolls.

From Kaub it's another 21 km (13 miles) along the busy river to Rüdesheim.

RÜDESHEIM, GERMANY
Population 11,000

There is a cluster of towns situated near the point where the Rhine enters the Taunus Mountains: Wiesbaden, Eltville, Geisenheim, Bingen, and Rüdesheim. Rüdesheim is a wine town and a tourist town and makes a great base for exploring. This area, the **Rheingau**, is famous primarily for its wine, Riesling.

In Rüdesheim itself you'll probably spend at least one evening in the **Drosselgasse**, a narrow Weingasse or wine alley full of restaurants. You can combine your interests in wine and castles by visiting the **Schloss Brömserburg**, home of the **Weinmuseum in der Brömserburg**, a wine museum located in a castle. High above Rüdesheim is the **Niederwald Denkmal**, a statue and memorial to united Germany dating from 1883 which offers great views of the river below. There's a chair lift from the center of town up to the memorial or you can walk or drive.

Rüdesheim Campground

▲ RICHTER CAMPINGPLATZ AM RHEIN

Address:	D-65385 Rüdesheim Rhein
Telephone:	06772 2528
Fax:	06772 406783
Website:	www.campingplatz-ruedesheim.rwu.de
GPS:	N 49° 58' 41.4", E 007° 56' 15.3"

May 1 - Oct 3

Campingplatz am Rhein is one of the nicest campgrounds in the region and it is well worth your time to spend at least one night here if you are nearby. An added benefit is that many Rhine tour boats leave from Rüdesheim and you could leave your rig in the campground while you cruised the river. Unfortunately there are several islands offshore here and most of the river traffic passes on the other side, too far away to really enjoy it.

This large campground is a grassy field on the banks of the Rhine. There is a tree-covered promenade between the river and the campsite. Most sites are on grass although there is also an attractive brick paved area. Many sites are not marked but a warden will guide you to a parking spot. This is a tourist campground with no resident campers. Electrical service boxes (Euro, 10 amp) are on scattered poles, this is another campground where you will want to have a long electrical connection cord. The shower/toilet building near the entrance is an attraction in itself, both men's and women's sides are large with vines growing along the ceiling, displays showing the region's attractions, and even an old wine keg. The token-operated show-

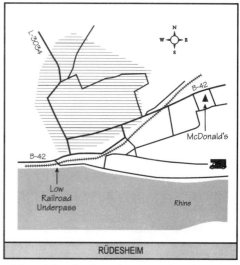

ers have hot water, shaving sinks and dishwashing sinks also have hot water but don't require a token. There is a small grocery store. A good-sized supermarket is about 1 kilometer away, ask at the reception kiosk for directions. Toward town along the river are tennis courts and a large swimming pool.

Access to central Rüdesheim is by foot, the 1 kilometer walk along the Rhine is

PFALZGRAFENSTEIN IN THE ROMANTIC RHINE VALLEY

scenic and interesting. The tree-shaded pathway runs past the docks for several of the Rhine cruise boats.

To find the campground head east from central Rüdesheim along the river. The road will run inland and almost immediately a campground sign will point toward the water. You may take this route if you're rig is less than 2.8 meters high (there is a low railroad underpass), otherwise you may want to take the next right by the McDonald's and work your way towards the river, then left to the campground.

DRIVE 3 – RÜDESHEIM TO STRASBOURG
256 Kilometers (159 Miles), 4 Hours

A long The Way – This drive's route heads upriver from Rüdesheim to cross the Rhine near Mainz, then follows autobahns south to the German Wine Road. For 90 kilometers (56 miles) it runs through vineyards and small German wine towns until it again it reaches the French border and re-joins the autoroutes on the way to Strasbourg.

RÜDESHEIM TO STRASBOURG

From Rüdesheim drive east on B42 for 21 km (13 miles) until you reach A643 and the bridge over the Rhine. Cross the river on A643, join A60 to bypass Mainz, and then drive south on A63. After 35 km (22 miles) on A63 exit and join A61 as it continues south for another 18 kilometers (11 miles) to the Worms-Nord/Mörstadt exit.

Drive east to B271 and then follow it south to Bockenheim and the beginning of the German Wine Road. Bockenheim is about 12 km (7 miles) from the autobahn.

The German Wine Road (**Deutsche Weinstrasse**) runs through Bockenheim, Grünstadt, Freinsheim, Bad Dürkheim, Wachenheim, Deidesheim, Neustadt an der Weinstrasse, Maikammer, Edenkoben, Rhodt, Albersweiler, Annweiler, Klingenmünster, Bad Bergzabern and Schweigen-Rechtenbach. It has official signs showing a bunch of grapes to show you the way. You can stop and taste wine at places labeled Weinprobe, don't overdo it. Perhaps a better idea is to stop for lunch and pick up a bottle or two for the evening.

When you reach Schweigen-Rechtenbach you've also just about reached the French border. Continue south on D34 through Seebach and Trimbach to reach the A35 autoroute. Follow the A35 southeast to the A4 and then drive south on the A4 into Strasbourg.

STRASBOURG, FRANCE
Population 425,000

Strasbourg, located just a short distance from the Rhine, is in a much-disputed area, the Alsace. Both France and Germany have controlled the city at various times, and the influence of the two cultures on the town is what makes it unique. The Alsace is an important wine-growing region, and as you would expect Alsatian cuisine is outstanding.

The tourist center of the town is the **Cathédral Notre-Dame** with its one lacy tower and pink sandstone. Surrounding the cathedral and its square is the old town, which is in turn surrounded by water. The Ill River separates and runs on both sides of Strasbourg. The old town is full of museums and pedestrian shopping streets. Don't forget to stroll through the small **Petite France** section which has cobblestone streets and restaurants along the river.

Strasbourg Campground

▲ CAMPING MONTAGNE VERTE

Address:	2 Rue Robert Forrer, F-67000 Strasbourg
Telephone:	03 88302546
Fax:	03 88271015
Website:	www.fuaj.org
E-mail:	strasbourg camping@fuaj.org
GPS:	N 48° 34' 31.2", E 007° 42' 52.6"

March 14 - Oct 30 and Nov 24 - Jan 5

Camping Montagne Verte is located in the suburb of Montagne Verte just southwest of Strasbourg. The walk to the old city takes 40 minutes, there's also convenient and frequent bus service.

The large campground has sites arranged on grass off paved driveways that circle around a field with scattered trees, some quite large. Individual sites are numbered and assigned at the reception office. Electricity is available at widely scattered boxes (Euro, 6 amp). The two shower/toilet buildings are modern and clean with plenty of facilities for the size of the campground. Hot showers are free (pushbutton valves, not adjustable). Hot water is also available in bathroom basins and dishwashing sinks. The campground has coin-operated washers and dryer. It also has a small kiosk selling limited groceries and meals, tennis courts, a playground, and a volleyball court.

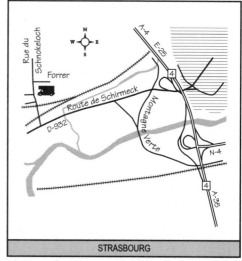

To reach the city from the campground you must walk about 500 meters to the main street running through Montagne Verte. Catch the 3 or the 23 bus. Alternately you can walk the 4 kilometers (2.5 miles) in to town, the route has good sidewalks the entire distance.

Finding the campground is not difficult if you know that it is located in the suburb of Montagne Verte just southwest of the city. This is right about where A4 from the north becomes A35, it is also where N4 from the east joins A4/A35. Both the A35 highway and N4 highway have off-ramps for Montagne Verte but have no campground signs until you leave the autoroute. Once you leave the autoroute (Exit 4 from A35) you should see campground signs that will lead you directly to the site.

DRIVE 4 – STRASBOURG TO FREIBURG
208 Kilometers (129 Miles), 3 Hours

A long The Way – Today's route takes you east to the Route du Vin, then south along it to a point west of Mulhouse. There you'll pick up the autoroutes and autobahns which will take you quickly northeast to Freiburg. The Route du Vin is France's version of the Deutsche Weinstrasse you saw yesterday. An officially designated wine route, it primarily follows D35 and N83 but there are deviations. You can stay on the route by following the many Route du Vin signs along the way.

From Strasbourg head west on A35 and A352 to Exit 11B, then jog south 1.5 km (.9 miles) on D500 to pick up the north end of D35 and the **Route du Vin**. It will lead you south some 100 km (62 miles) through little wine towns filled with places to taste wine and eat Alsatian specialties, until it meets N66 near Thann. Follow N66 southeast 14 km (9 miles) to reach the A36 autoroute.

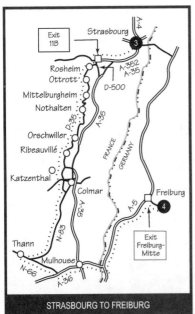

STRASBOURG TO FREIBURG

Once on the autoroute it will take you east across the Rhine and into Germany, where you join the A5 autobahn heading north. Follow A5 north 35 km (22 miles) to the Freiburg-Mitte exit and then follow the directions in the campground write-up below to reach Hirzberg Camping.

FREIBURG, GERMANY
Population 200,000

Freiburg is a university city and the gateway to the Black Forest. It was heavily damaged during WWII but has been restored, the most important sight in town is probably the Münster. The **Münster** or cathedral is a combination of Romanesque and Gothic that took three centuries to build and is sometimes called the finest in Europe. The medieval area around the Münster is also a good place to try some of the local Black Forest food specialties. Note the little streams set into the streets, these are called Bächle. They were used to deliver water

TOURIST RESTING AFTER A DAY OF TOURING FREIBURG

to the residents of the town (not for drinking). It's fun to ride the cable car to **Schauinsland** peak overlooking the town or to walk up if you feel up to it.

Freiburg Campground

▲ HIRZBERG CAMPING

Address:	Kärtauserstrasse 99, D-79104 Freiburg
Telephone:	0761 35054
Fax:	0761 289212
Website:	www.freiburg-camping.de
E-mail:	hirzberg@freiburg-camping.de
GPS:	N 47° 59' 32.1", E 007° 52' 25.8"

Open All Year

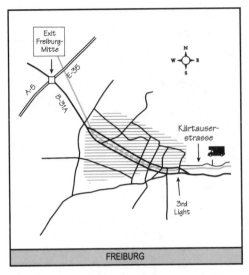

This small campground slopes from a treed hillside down to the street in front. The reception people will lead to your slot up the hill. These are back-in spaces with convenient electricity (Euro, 10 amp) and some shade. The reception building near the entrance houses restrooms and most facilities. There's a restaurant with a beer garden next to the entrance. There's also a small building housing a internet setup and library.

This campground is located about 1.5 km (.9 miles) east of central Freiburg. If you are approaching from the A5 autobahn to the west take the Freiburg Mitte exit and head east on B31A. After 4.5 km (2.8 miles) at the third stoplight turn left. At the second stoplight turn right on Kärtauserstrasse and after another 1.5 km (.9 miles) you'll see the campground entrance on the left.

DRIVE 5 – FREIBURG TO BADEN-BADEN
210 Kilometers (130 Miles), 3.5 Hours

Along **The Way** – Today's drive takes you through Germany's famous Black Forest. From Freiburg drive east on B31 for 23 km (14 miles) to the intersection with B500 near Hinterzarten. This section of road is known as the **Höllental** (Hell's Valley). At Hinterzarten turn north on B500. In another 25 km (16 miles) you'll reach Furtwangen.

In Furtwangen you'll find a good introduction of what is to come, the town is home of the **Deutsches Uhrenmuseum** (German Clock Museum). It's definitely worth a stop.

Leaving Furtwangen continue north 14 km (9 miles) to Triberg. Set in a deep valley Triberg is home to the **Gutach Waterfall**, about 500 feet tall. Also in Triberg is the **Heimatmuseum**, an excellent Black Forest cultural museum. More importantly, however, at least to the tourists, this is cuckoo-clock land. There are plenty of places to buy one, and there are even two different clocks claiming to be the world's largest.

From Triberg continue north, this time on B33. Twenty-five km (15 miles) north is the village of Hausach. It has two attractions. First, 4 km (2.5 miles) south of town along the B33 near Gutach is an excellent open-air museum called the **Schwarzwälder Freilichtmuseum** which shows off traditional farming life in the region. Second, in town is an old monastery, now home to a Black Forest traditional costume museum called the **Trachtenmuseum**.

In Hausach turn east onto B294 and almost immediately you will be in Wolfach.

There's another stop here, this time for the **Dorotheenhütte**, a glassblowing workshop and museum.

From Wolfach it's 12 km (7 miles) east on B294 to cute little Schiltach, probably the most traditional Black Forest-looking village of them all with many mural-painted half-timbered houses.

Next stop, 9 kilometers (6 miles) to the north and still on B294 is Alpirsbach. Here you'll find the **Klosterkirch St Benedict**, a beautiful Romanesque basilica (now a Protestant church) that was once part of a monastery.

From Alpirsbach continue north on B294 along the Kinzig Valley to Freudenstadt, a distance of 18 km (11 miles). This town is known as the capital of the eastern Black Forest, it's the largest town in the area. Worth a look is the huge central market square which is Germany's largest.

From Freudenstadt drive west on B28 and then north on B500. This 60 km (37 mile) stretch of road leads all the way north to Baden-Baden, it's known as the **Schwarzwald-Hochstrasse** (Black Forest Highway). It's a very scenic road that runs along ridgelines with views to the east and west. You'll probably be happy to hear that there are no cuckoo-clock stops along this section of the route.

The Baden-Baden campground is south of town. You can reach it easily by passing through Baden-Baden, still on B500, to the A5 autobahn west of town. Follow it south 8 km (5 miles) to the exit for Camping Adam.

BADEN-BADEN, GERMANY
Population 50,000

A popular health spa, Baden-Baden can also be considered the gateway to the Black Forest. The town is located near the Rhine and the French city of Strasbourg, and the forest rises to its south and east. Baden-Baden is the premier German resort with more millionaires per square acre than Palm Springs. Shopping and restaurants are excellent, of course, but could strain the budget.

FREIBURG TO BADEN-BADEN

While you're in Baden-Baden you might visit one of the baths. The two best choices are on Römerplatz near the old Roman bath ruins, naturally called the **Römische Badruinen**. Rather than touring the old baths, take a bath yourself. The **Friedrichsbad** will run you through a two hour series of showers and baths while the **Caracalla-Therme** just gives you the run of their pools and saunas. While the Caracalla is considerably cheaper you might base your decision on another factor. The Friedrichsbad allows no clothes on some days while the Caracalla always requires a bathing suit.

Besides the baths you may want to take advantage of the many hiking trails that run through the hills surrounding the town. There's also the casino.

Baden-Baden Campground

▲ ADAM CAMPING

Address:	Campingstrasse 1, D-77815 Bühl-Oberbruch
Telephone:	07223 23194
Fax:	07223 8982
Website:	www.campingplatz-adam.de
E-mail:	info@campingplatz-adam.de
GPS:	N 48° 43' 35.9", E 008° 05' 00.6"

Open All Year

This large campground makes a handy place to stop when traveling north and south on A5 since it's not far off the autobahn. It's also about the best place to stay while visiting Baden-Baden.

This large campground has lots of permanent and long-term campers but also a

THIS CAMPING RIG AT ADAM CAMPING IS CUTE AS A BUG

large paved area with electrical boxes (Euro, 10 amp) and grassy tent area for travelers. Folks pulling trailers don't even have to unhitch. Restrooms are decent with hot showers, basins, and dishwashing sinks. In summer the lake in the middle of the campground is great for swimming. To reach Baden-Baden by bus take Bus 268 from the Seestrasse stop in Oberbruch to the Bühl station and then another bus from there.

To reach the campground take the Bühl exit (Exit 52) some 5 km (8 miles) south of the point where B500 meets A5. Head west 1.3 km (.8 miles) and at the far side of Oberbruch turn left, almost immediately you'll see the campground entrance on the right.

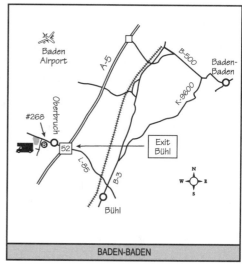

BADEN-BADEN

DRIVE 6 – BADEN-BADEN TO HEIDELBERG
105 Kilometers (65 Miles), 1.25 Hours

A long The Way – After three days of threading your way through the German and French countryside on small roads you may be relieved to find that today's drive is a short one, all on the autobahn. It should give you the time to make a relaxed departure and arrive near Heidelberg in time to look around.

From the campground join the A5 autobahn heading north. Stay on it for 86 kilometers (53 miles) until you reach the B535/Heidelberg/Schwetzingen exit. Follow Speyerer Strasse northeast through Heidelberg to the south bank of the Neckar River and then drive along it on B37 for 7 kilometers (4 miles) until you reach the town of Neckargemünd. Follow the directions in the campground write-up to find the campground.

BADEN-BADEN TO HEIDELBeRG

HEIDELBERG, GERMANY
Population 140,000

Heidelberg is the oldest university town in Germany, the university dates from 1386. The town also has a **castle**, a very interesting **old town** area, and is full of students and tourists. The scenic location on the Neckar River is an added attraction. When you walk around town and see the foreign tour groups you will know that you are truly on the tourist road.

A favorite pastime in Heidelberg is just wandering around the old town. Heidelberg did not sustain damage in World War II so what you see is not reconstructed. It is a great place to take pictures, you'll see many people doing just that. The walk up the hill to the castle is worthwhile, if the idea of a lot of stairs bothers you there is a funicular railway that will take you to the top.

Schwetzingen, 8 kilometers (5 miles) southwest of Heidelberg, has an impressive 18th-century palace and gardens. This is also Germany's asparagus center, something to bear in mind in the late spring and early summer.v

The **Castle Road (Burgenstrasse)**, formally begins in Mannheim, but Heidelberg is where it really gets serious. If you follow the Neckar Valley upstream you'll find castles in or near the towns of Neckargemünd, Neckarsteinach, Zwingenberg, and Mosbach; and that's only the first 45 kilometers (28 miles), the Castle Road now runs all the way to Prague.

Heidelberg Campground

▲ CAMPINGPLATZ AN DER FRIEDENSBRUCKE

Address:	Falltorstrasse 4, D-69151 Neckargumünd
Telephone	
and Fax:	06223 2178
Website:	www.campingamneckar.de
E-mail:	j.vandervelden@web.de
GPS:	N 49° 23' 44.8", E 008° 47' 39.7"

April 1 - Oct 15

To visit Heidelberg and stay in a campground it is necessary to stay outside the city. This campground is located in Neckargemünd, a town about 8 kilometers (5 miles) upstream along the Neckar.

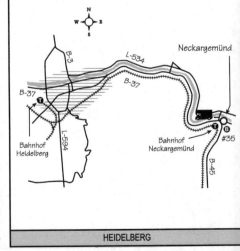

The campground sits on the south bank of the river just west of the bridge. Campsites are on grass (Euro, 12 amp). The restroom building has hot showers (payment required), hot water in basins, and hot water for dishwashing. Bus service to Heidelberg is on the main street a short walk from the campground.

It's easy to find this campground. Just follow the highway eastward from Heidelberg along the south bank of the river. Even if you miss the campground signs in the small town of Neckargumünd you can easily find the campground, just look under the bridge.

DRIVE 7 – HEIDELBERG TO FRANKFURT
100 Kilometers (62 Miles), 1.25 Hours

A long The Way – Today's drive is even shorter than yesterday's. It gives you the chance to make an early arrival in Frankfurt to turn in your vehicle and do a little more looking around.

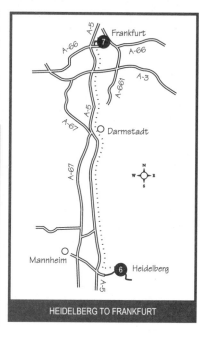

From the campground drive west along the river to reach the A5. Frankfurt is 76 kilometers (47 miles) to the north.

Information Resources

See our Internet site at www.rollinghomes.com for many links to information sources.

German National Tourist Office, Chanin Building, 52nd Floor, 122 East 42nd Street, New York, NY 10168-0072 (323 655-6085). In Canada, PO Box 65162, Toronto, Ontario M4K 3Z2 (416 968-0372).

For information sources for France see the end of Chapter 11.

HEIDELBERG TO FRANKFURT

ONE OF MANY CAMPING SITES WITH A TERRIFIC RHINE RIVER VIEW

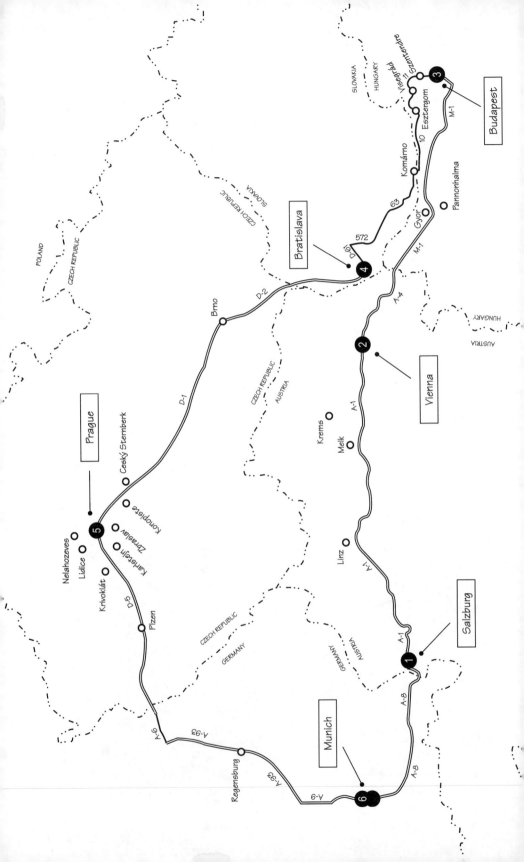

Chapter 8
Tour 5

Great Cities
of Central Europe

Top Attractions

❖ Munich
❖ Salzburg
❖ Vienna
❖ Budapest
❖ Bratislava
❖ Prague

General Description

The countries included in this tour are the new hot destinations for European visitors. They aren't just for backpackers any more. That doesn't mean you should hesitate to visit, they're fun and less expensive than the countries farther west. Total driving distance for this tour is 1,613 kilometers (1,000 miles). There are 6 driving days rather than the 7 days in all of the other tours in this book.

This tour uses Munich as a gateway. It's one of Europe's great cites and a favorite with travelers. It's also conveniently close to the Central European capitals and a good place to rent an automobile or RV.

The first driving day takes you to Salzburg via autobahn. It's an easy drive and not far, but it means moving from Germany to Austria. On this tour you'll cross a border almost every driving day.

The second drive takes you on to Vienna. There's no border to cross and the route is via autobahn again. You might want to break your trip by stopping to visit the fabulous abbey at Melk. Vienna needs no introduction, it's another of Europe's great cities, there are several to come.

The third driving day crosses into Hungary. The destination is the ancient city of Budapest.

On the fourth drive you travel north to pass through the Danube Bend region of Hungary and then cross the Danube into Slovakia. You'll spend the evening in Bratislava, a surprisingly enjoyable city, but surprising only because it hasn't yet been discovered by the international tourist industry.

After leaving Bratislava you travel northwest and enter the Czech Republic. Your destination, of course, is the best known of the Central European cities – Prague.

The sixth drive takes you from Prague back to Munich. Along the way you may want to pay a visit to the mother city of beer – Plzen, or perhaps stop and take a look at Germany's Regensburg.

You'll note that there are only five destination cities in this tour rather than the six in most other chapters. That's to give you extra time in whichever one of these extraordinary cities strikes your fancy.

This tour can easily be combined with the several of the other tours in this book if you have several weeks. The most obvious are the Alps Tour and the Rhine Valley Tour. For lots more destinations and campgrounds you can check out our other European camping guide – ***Traveler's Guide to European Camping***.

Roads and Driving

The tour in this chapter involves driving in five different countries: Germany, Austria, Hungary, Slovakia, and the Czech Republic. We've already talked about Germany in the previous chapter, we'll discuss driving in the other four here.

First of all, every one of these countries has a toll program modeled after the Swiss system. That means that if you are going to drive on their autobahns you must buy a vignette or sticker that you place on your windshield. You buy these vignettes either at the border or at the first gas station you can find. If you delay you'll probably get ticketed and regret it. None of the stickers really costs much, they're all much cheaper than Switzerland and you can often buy them for very limited periods.

For this tour you should make sure to obtain an International Driver's License as described in Chapter 2 in the Visas and Other Documents section. Several of the countries on this tour either encourage or require their use and your rental company may require you to have one.

Speed limits vary a little from country to country. Generally, speed limits are as follows unless otherwise marked (the format is towns and built-up areas/highways/limited access highways and expressways): Germany – 50/100/130, Austria – 50/100/130, Hungary – 50/90/130, Slovakia – 60/90/130, Czech Republic – 50/90/130. These speeds are in kilometers per hour of course.

The road systems vary a little between countries, here are the details.

Austria has a modern system with a numbering system like that in Germany. On the maps and highway signs autobahns have an "A" prefix and often also an alternative "E" or international prefix. Secondary roads have a "B" prefix. Roads smaller than the "B" roads are labeled as "L" roads, smaller ones just have a four-digit number. In Austria the emergency telephone numbers are 133 or 112 for police, 122 or 112 for fire and 144 or 112 for ambulance.

Hungary has a very limited autobahn system, largely limited to the road from Austria to Budapest and other approaches to the capital. On maps these autobahns are labeled with an "M" prefix. Most roads are two-lane highways, these have two digit numbers with no letter prefix. Emergency numbers in the Hungary are as follows: police, 107; fire department, 105; ambulance, 104.

Slovakia also has a very limited autobahn system, here they receive a "D" prefix. The many secondary roads are labeled with a number with no letter prefix. The emergency telephone numbers are as follows: police, 158; fire, 150; ambulance, 155.

The Czech Republic uses the same highway numbering system as Slovakia. Not surprising since until fairly recently they were both part of the same country. The emergency numbers are the same too.

Camping and Campgrounds

You'll find that there is not a lot of difference between the campgrounds in these countries and those farther west. The campgrounds in this book are all traveler's campgrounds, there aren't a lot of permanently-situated holiday caravans in them.

Most campgrounds are older, there is a lot of variation in the types of amenities from one to the next. Campgrounds often have older German- or French-style outlets, electrical amperage tends to be in the medium range. Hot showers are available at almost all campgrounds, the Bratislava campground is the only exception listed in this chapter.

Throughout these countries the camping carnet is usually not required but may get you a 10% discount. Generally a passport is required for identification and may be held to insure that you pay when you leave. Customs are not uniform in this regard.

In the Czech Republic, Slovakia, and Hungary camping outside campgrounds is not allowed. Even where camping outside campgrounds is either not prohibited or seems to be the practice regardless of the rules it is good to remember that break-ins are frequent, as is vehicle theft. If you plan to leave your vehicle parked anywhere outside a campground you should make sure that it is being watched over by a responsible party.

Practical Tips

The **Czech Republic** has an area of 78,864 square kilometers and a population of about 10.2 million people. The Czech Republic, then called the Czech and Slovak Federal Republic, underwent a "velvet revolution" in 1989 and had free elections in 1990. In 1992 the country split into the Czech Republic and Slovakia. The Czech Republic has been one of the most successful of the formerly Communist countries in terms of tourism and economics. The capital of the country, Prague, is currently one of the top European visitor destinations.

Slovakia has an area of 48,845 square kilometers and a population of about 5.4 million people. Slovakia split from the Czech and Slovak Federal Republic on December 31, 1992 to become a separate country, this split largely reflected the different cultural and ethnic makeup of the two areas.

Hungary has an area of 93,030 square kilometers and a population of about 10.1 million people. Hungary's Communist government fell in 1988 and the first free elections were held in 1990.

Germany and **Austria** use the euro and it is only to be expected that the Czech Republic, Slovakia, and Hungary will adopt the euro as soon as they are allowed, and that will mean rising prices. Until that time, however, most of these Central European countries are inexpensive destinations when compared with Western Europe.

The currency of the **Czech Republic** is the koruna, abbreviated Kè, CZK or even CSK. One euro is equal to approximately 32.76 Kè at the time of publication. Prices here have been rising, particularly in tourist areas. Prague is no longer the really good deal it once was, but it's still better than farther west.

Slovakia's currency is also called the koruna (or crown) and is abbreviated SKK. One euro is worth approximately 40.83 SKK at the time of publication. Slovakia's prices are among the lowest of the five countries covered here.

Hungary's currency is called the forint, it is abbreviated as HUF. One euro is equal to approximately 268 HUF at the time of publication. Hungarian prices are generally quite reasonable.

Large supermarkets, particularly England's Tesco, are rapidly appearing in the Czech Republic, Slovakia and Hungary. They make shopping for supplies easier than in Germany and Austria.

Cash machines are readily available throughout the region. Machines are located at bank locations, of course, but also at the larger supermarkets. Credit cards are widely accepted at gas stations, restaurants, and shops as well as in larger grocery stores.

Both diesel and gasoline are readily available in mostly familiar brands in all five countries. GPL (propane) is also available along motorways and in some larger stations except in Slovakia.

THE TOUR – GREAT CITIES OF CENTRAL EUROPE

TOUR 5 GATEWAY CITY – MUNICH (MÜNCHEN), GERMANY
Population 1,300,000

Munich is pretty well known around the world as a fun town. Most people have heard of the Oktoberfest celebration which attracts beer lovers from everywhere for a two-week party. There is also the Fasching or Carnival before Lent. Some people think there's a little bit of the Italian in every Bavarian, something must be responsible for the personality difference between this part of Germany and all of the rest.

For orientation purposes you can consider the center of town to be the **Fussgängerzone**, a long stretch of pedestrian shopping streets and squares starting in the west near the Hauptbahnhof and running for two kilometers to the southeast. This is the center of shopping, eating, and tourism in Munich. Toward the east end you'll find the **Marienplatz** overlooked by the **Neues Rathaus** with its famous **Glockenspiel**. A few blocks off this end of the Fussgängerzone you'll also find the **Hofbräuhaus beer hall**.

Munich is, of course, famous for its beer. There are many breweries in town and the famous **Hofbräuhaus** is just one of a large number of beer halls, beer cellars, and

SIDEWALK PAINTING NEAR THE MARIENPLATZ IN MUNICH

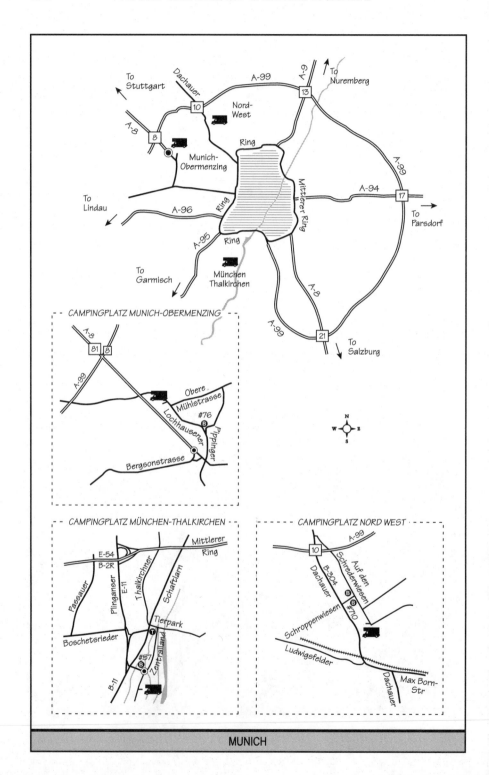

MUNICH

beer gardens. The biggest party, the **Oktoberfest**, is really mostly in September, it runs for two weeks and always ends on the first Sunday in October. While there are people having a good time all over town the center of the action is the **Theresienwiese**. You can reach it easily on the subway, there's a Theresienwiese stop on the U4/U5 subway line. Large beer hall pavilions are set up as well as circus rides and everything else it takes for literally millions of people each year to have a good time.

For 750 years until 1918 Munich and Bavaria were ruled by monarchs, the Wittelsbachs. The most famous member of this family is probably **Ludwig II**, not because he was a good king but because he wasted a lot of money building the ridiculously expensive castles that are now some of Bavaria's top tourist attractions. Ludwig wasn't the only Wittelsbach builder, Munich is full of their palaces and government buildings. These include their town palace complex, the **Residenz** and their summer palace complex, the rococo Versailles-like **Schloss Nymphenburg**. During their long reign the Wittelsbachs had time to collect a great deal of art so Munich has some great museums. The **Alte Pinakothek** is considered one of Europe's best painting galleries, full of Italian, Dutch, and German masters. Across the street is the **Neue Pinakothek** with a more modern selection.

While there are other well-known art museums that are well worth a visit probably the most popular museum in Munich is the **Deutsches Museum**, located on Museum Island, a short walk from the Fussgängerzone. This is a huge science and technology museum full of such things as a walk-through submarine, airplanes and rockets, cars and trains, science experiments that allow you to participate, a planetarium and an IMAX theater. In all there are 30 different departments. No kid under the age of 90 will want to miss it. You may also be interested in the **BMW Museum** (Munich is BMW's home); the **German Hunting and Fishing Museum (Deutsches Jagd-und Fischereimuseum)** near the Michaelskirche on the Fussgängerzone; or the **Marstallmuseum** at Schloss Nymphenburg with its royal carriages and Nymphenburg porcelain.

Other interesting offerings in Munich are the **Englischer Garten**, the Continent's largest city park; the **Olympiapark**, site of the 1972 Olympic games.

Munich has an excellent subway. It also has a good bike path system, you can pick up a bike path guide at the tourist office.

Just 20 kilometers (12 miles) northwest of Munich is **Dachau**, the first Nazi concentration camp. It is one of the few that have been preserved in Germany. You'll find the walls, a museum, one of the dormitory buildings (and the foundations of the others), and the crematorium. To drive there from Munich take the autobahn toward Stuttgart and then the Dachau exit. Drive toward Dachau and watch for signs. There is a large parking lot. You can also easily reach Dachau from Munich on the S-2 suburban rail line.

Munich Campgrounds

▲ Campingplatz Munich-Obermenzing

Address:	Lochhausener Str. 59, D-81247 München
Telephone:	089 8112235
Fax:	089 8144807
E-mail:	campingplatz-obermenzing@t-online.de
GPS:	N 48° 10' 28.6", E 011° 26' 46.7"

March 15 - Oct 31

Obermenzing is probably the easiest Munich campground to find. It's located near where the A8 from Stuttgart arrives in Munich. Thalkirchen, on the south side of town is more difficult to find if you don't know exactly how to get there. Obermenzing has good facilities and is much quieter.

This is a large campground set on a heavily treed plot in the western outskirts of Munich. There are no resident campers. The A8 Stuttgart Autobahn runs just next door so there is a little traffic noise. There is a large area with numbered sites for trailers (drive-throughs!) and motor coaches with the sites separated by high hedges. Tent sites are located in a separate area and there is also more room for more wheeled campers to park around the outside of that area. The reception person does not usually assign sites letting you park where you wish unless the campground is crowded. Individual electrical outlets are conveniently located next to many of the sites, they are metered (Euro, 10 amp), requiring you to deposit coins. The shower/toilet building is older and a little grim but clean, hot showers require a token, free hot water is available in shaving sinks and for washing dishes and clothes. The campground has a coin-operated washer and dryer, a small grocery shop, and a tavern that offers snacks.

There is a bus stop about 1 km (.6 mile) from the campground for the No. 76 bus that will take you to the Pasing S-Bahn station. From there it is clear sailing on in to central Munich.

The driving route to the campground begins at the roundabout before the beginning of the Stuttgart autobahn. Don't start westward down the autobahn, the first U-turn exit is 10 kilometers (6 miles) away. Turn north at the first turn east of the roundabout onto Pippinger Str. The campground signs are poor here at the roundabout but are fine once you make this critical turn, you'll reach the campground in about 1.4 kilometers (.9 miles) as the signs gradually lead you back towards the north side of the autobahn on Lochhausener Str. From the other approaches to Munich follow signs toward the Stuttgart Autobahn, they'll lead you to that last roundabout where you can reverse and proceed to the campground.

▲ Campingplatz München-Thalkirchen

Address:	Zentralländstr 49, D-81379 München
Telephone:	089 723170 7
Fax:	089 7243177
GPS:	N 48° 05' 28.1", E 011° 32' 41.9"

March 15 - Oct 31

Thalkirchen is one of the best-known campgrounds in Europe, almost everyone passes through at one time or another, many during Oktoberfest. Its large size, decent facilities, and very convenient location make it Munich's best place to stay. Much of the summr and fall you can count on it being overcrowded and noisy, that's part of the experience.

The campground is a large, partly-shaded field located in the Isar Valley Conservation Area about 4 kilometers (2.5 miles) from the center of Munich. Individual sites are of many kinds, most of those for wheeled vehicles are numbered and usually separated by low pipe fences. Tents are pitched in large grassy areas, generally away from the owner's cars. Bus tour companies love this campground and there are often large areas covered with their identical small backpacking tents. The reception staff does not generally assign individuals camping sites, they just assign you a general area. Electrical outlets are widely spaced (Euro, 10 amp). Several shower/toilet buildings of various ages and quality service the campground, hot water always requires a token or coin. There is a grocery shop, a snack bar, and a laundry room.

The Thalkirchen U-Bahn subway stop on the U3 line is about 2 kilometers (1.2 miles) from the campground. The number 57 bus does nothing but make a circuit from a stop 400 meters from the campground to the subway station with the entire circuit taking about 20 minutes including a 5-minute stop at each end. The driver always seems polite but bored.

Finding Thalkirchen is a challenge despite numerous campground signs posted all over the city. If you lose the thread while following the signs head for the B11 that leads south on the west side of the Isar River. The campground is well signed from this road about 1.8 km (1.1 mile) south of E54/B2R Mittlerer Ring.

▲ CAMPINGPLATZ NORD WEST

Address:	Schrederwiessen 3, D-80995 München
Telephone:	089 1506936
Fax:	081 3121978
GPS:	N 48° 11' 56.6", E 011° 29' 49.3"

Open All Year

This is a medium-sized campground with grass-covered sites. It has many resident rigs, tourists with motorhomes are usually parked in small sites along the outside fence. Electrical boxes are widely spaced and metered, the manager will read the meter before you hook up and when you check out to determine your usage. The shower/toilet building is small but clean and heated in the winter. Showers are nice and hot. There is a nearby stop for Bus 710 which will take you to the Moosach S-bahn station.

To find Campingplatz Nord West proceed northwest on Dachauer Str (B304) from Munich. This is a major arterial that runs northwest from the Hauptbahnhoff or railway station in the central part of town. After about 7 kilometers (4 miles) the street comes to a T and bears left to circle around a railway yard, just after this you'll see a campground direction sign pointing to the right.

DRIVE 1 – MUNICH TO SALZBURG
146 Kilometers (91 Miles), 1.5 Hours

A long The Way – The route from Munich to Salzburg is a good one for your first day on the road. It follows the autobahns for the entire distance.

From Munich head south from the city on the A8 autobahn. This highway leads directly to Salzburg, a distance of about 140 kilometers (87 miles).

The border between Germany and Austria is just west of Salzburg. It is marked but there is no required stop, at this point the autobahn name changes from A8 to A1. As explained in the introductory material in Austria you are required to have a toll vignette on your window indicating that you have paid the highway toll. Stop at the kiosk next to the road at the border to get one if you don't have a current one on your window already. If the kiosk is not open you should pull off at the first available service station to buy one to avoid receiving a fine.

To reach the Salzburg campground take the Salzburg-Nord exit from the Munich-Vienna A1 autobahn north of Salzburg and follow the driving instructions in the individual campground description below.

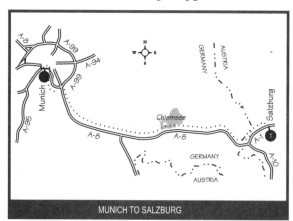

MUNICH TO SALZBURG

SALZBURG, AUSTRIA
Population 145,000

Salzburg is a friendly-sized city with a beautiful location. The green glacial-colored Salzach River runs through the middle of the city and the **Hohensalzburg Castle** looks down from above the old town on the south bank. There are great views of the town from the castle. Mountains rise in almost every direction.

This is the town made famous in America by the movie The Sound of Music. Probably the most popular activity is the ***Sound of Music Tour*** which visits places seen in the movie, including some in the nearby Salzkammergut lake region to the east. You'll also want to see the baroque **Mirabell Palace** and visit **Hellbrunn Castle** just south of town with its gardens and trick fountains.

There's an outstanding beer hall and huge beer garden in Salzburg. Don't miss the **Augustiner Bräustübl**, you can buy the fixings for a snack to go with your beer from the stands along the hall inside.

Salzburg is also a good place to take a salt mine tour. The **Durrnberg Salt Mines** in Hallein are about 12 km (7 miles) south of Salzburg.

East of Salzburg only a few miles is a district of lakes and mountains known as the **Salzkammergut**. Today the region is known for its beauty, in earlier times salt was more important. The salt found here was so valuable that for many years the entire area was closed to visitors. In German the word Hall means salt and you'll see it in many of the names in the area.

The Salzkammergut is not a particularly large area. If you include Salzburg it makes a square that is 60 kilometers in each direction. In the north the lakes are shallower and warmer, the mountains are smaller. In the south the mountains get steeper and higher, the lakes deeper and colder.

You can easily do a driving tour of the region. **St. Gilgen** is on the north shore of the Wolfgangsee while **Fuschl** is just 6 kilometers (4 miles) north on the smaller **Fuschlsee**. About 20 kilometers (12 miles) north from Fuschl by roundabout small roads is the **Mondsee** (Moon Lake), warmest of the lakes for swimming. On the north shore is the town of Mondsee, the abbey church here was the setting for the wedding in **The Sound of Music.**

The largest lake in the region, the **Attersee**, is just east of the Mondsee. From **Steinbach** on the east shore of the Attersee you can follow a small road 25 kilometers (15 miles) east to **Gmunden** on the north shore of another large lake, the **Traunsee**.

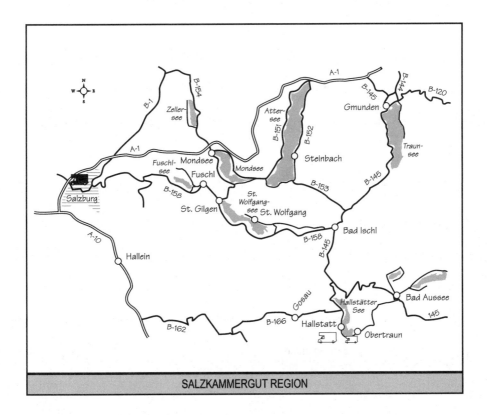

SALZKAMMERGUT REGION

Gmunden is the largest town in the area after Salzburg and has its own double castle, the **Schloss Orth** with one castle on the shore and another on a connected island. Lake cruises are possible and there's a cable car up the **Grünberg** for the view. From Gmunden you can head south for Bad Ischl and Hallstatt, a distance of 50 kilometers (31 miles).

Salzburg Campground

▲ Panorama Camping Stadtblick

Address:	Rauchenbichlerstrasse 21, A-5020 Salzburg
Telephone:	0662 450652
Fax:	0662 458018
Website:	www.panorama-camping.at
E-mail:	panorama.camping@utanet.at
GPS:	N 47° 49' 43.1", E 013° 03' 08.8"

March 20 - Nov 5 (Varies)

This is a very pleasant small campground overlooking Salzburg. It is easy to get to because it is just off the autobahn and has a good bus connection to central Salzburg. There are three campgrounds in the general area of the Salzburg Nord autobahn exit so you'll have some other choices if this campground happens to be full.

The campground sits under tall trees at the top of a grassy slope. The camping sites are terraced so many have a great view of Salzburg and the Hohensalzburg Castle. There are no resident rigs here. The sites are either grass or gravel. Electrical outlets are widely spaced (Euro, 10 amp). All of the facilities are in one building overlooking the campground. Free hot water is available for showers (adjustable), bathroom sinks and dishwashing. There are coin-operated washers and dryers, TV room, restaurant, and small grocery shop. About 1 kilometer from the campground toward town is a medium-size supermarket. Two hundred meters below the campground along a stream is a bike path and small city park with playground equipment for children.

SALZBURG

The city bus stop is about one-half kilometer from the campground. The No. 51 bus runs frequently, this stop is the end of the line for the bus so it waits for a few minutes every circuit. If you would like to ride your bike into Salzburg there is an excellent bike path that follows a small stream down to the Salzach River and then along it to the old part of town. The distance is about 4 kilometers (2.5 miles).

From the east/west Munich-Vienna A1 autobahn take the Salzburg Nord exit. You want to head south toward Salzburg. Almost immediately take a sharp right and follow a camping sign up a small lane to the top of the hill and the campground.

DRIVE 2 – SALZBURG TO VIENNA
285 Kilometers (177 Miles), 3.5 Hours

Along The Way – From Salzburg the A1 autobahn leads directly east 285 kilometers (177 miles) to Vienna. There are no borders to worry about but there is an interesting stop about 210 kilometers (130 miles) from Salzburg. This is the **Stift Melk**, a fantastic baroque fortified Benedictine abbey that overlooks the Danube River. It's one of the top baroque masterpieces in Europe, you shouldn't pass by without stopping.

To reach the abbey take Exit 80 which is marked B3A/Melk. Head north and follow signs to the abbey parking lot, there's lots of room. Plan on at least 2 hours to see the place, you don't have to take a tour but be sure you don't miss the interior of the church.

As you approach Vienna you must decide which campground you will use. The first, Camping Wien West, is easiest to find since it is located near where A1 enters the city. The second, Donaupark Camping Klosterneuburg, is located north of the city near the Danube. It's a nicer campground but not quite so convenient. From A1 take Exit 41 and follow B19 27 kilometers (17 miles) north to Tulln, a small town on the south shore of the Danube River. From there follow B14 along the river east to Klosterneuburg, another 21 kilometers (13 miles). See the individual campground descriptions for final driving directions.

SALZBURG TO VIENNA

VIENNA (WIEN), AUSTRIA
Population 1,650,000

Vienna is one of the great cities of Europe. It is best known for its history: baroque architecture, coffeehouses, music, and the monuments of the Habsburgs.

The layout of the city is simple, especially the central area where most of the sights are located. In the 19th century the city walls were demolished and a ring road, the **Ringstrasse** was built. This ring road is a boulevard, not an expressway, it circles the central district on all sides except the northeast where the border of the city is formed by the Danube Canal.

The central city inside the Ringstrasse is full of walking streets, churches and coffeehouses. Many of the sights of Vienna are located here and walking tours are rewarding. The most centrally-located sight is the very unusual **St. Stephen's Cathedral (Stephansdom)** with its multicolored tile roof where you can climb or take an elevator up the **steeple (Steffel)** for an orientation view of the city. Coffeehouses are a big part of a visit to Vienna and the best are located in this district. Try the recently-restored **Café Central**, one of the city's most historic and one of Vienna's must-visit sites. The popularity of coffee in Vienna dates from 1683 when the city was introduced to the bean by a besieging Turk army.

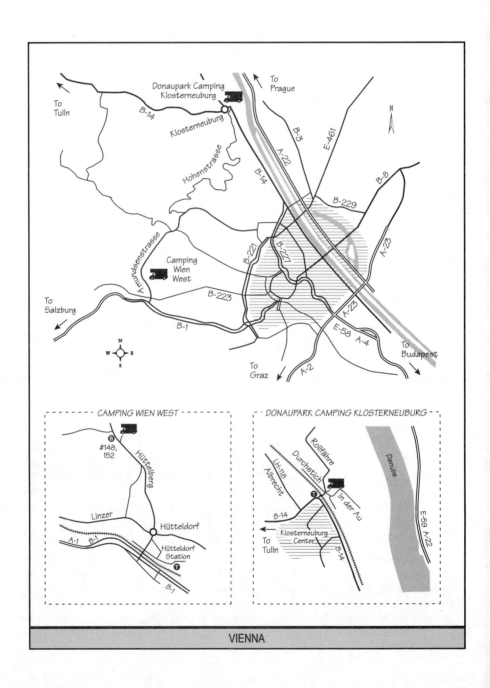

VIENNA

The second major area of interest in Vienna is the Ringstrasse itself. Many majestic buildings were built along the street, the most impressive is probably the **Hofburg** or Royal Palace. It is really a group of buildings and houses many of the city's most popular attractions including the **Spanish Riding School (Spanische Reitschule)**, the **Grand Hall of the National Library (Hofbibliothek Prunksaal)**, and the **Imperial Apartments**. The **Kunsthistorisches Museum** is nearby and slightly farther out from the center is the **Belvedere Palace** which houses another museum with the works of nineteenth and twentieth-century Austrian artists like Gustav Klimt and Egon Schiele.

An important Viennese destination is farther outside the Ringstrasse. This is **Schönbrunn Palace** which is located in the western suburbs most easily reached by using the U4 subway line and getting off at either the Schönbrunn or Hietzing stop. This is the Habsburg's Versailles-style palace, built to outshine the original. The tour of the interior is a must but don't miss the gardens behind the palace. These gardens also house what is said the be the world's oldest zoo, the **Tiergarten**, founded in 1752.

A boat trip on the Danube makes a good side trip. You can travel up the river to Krems, Melk, or Linz.

A VIEW OF VIENNA FROM THE TOP OF ST. STEPHEN'S CATHEDRAL

Vienna Campgrounds

▲ CAMPING WIEN WEST

Address:	Hüttel-bergstrasse 80, A-1140 Wien
Telephone:	01 9142314
Fax:	01 9113594
Website:	www.wiencamping.at
E-mail:	camping.west@verkehrsbuero.at
GPS:	N 48° 12' 50.9", E 016° 15' 01.4"

March 1 – Feb 1

This is one of two city campgrounds sitting near each other in the western suburbs of Vienna. Wien West 1 is only open during July and August. Wien West 2 is an all-weather campground and stays open most of the year. Using a bus/subway combination you can conveniently reach the center of Vienna in about half an hour from these campgrounds.

Wien West 2 is a large campground with lattice brick or earth-surfaced campsites for vehicles located around an oblong access road. Individual sites are marked and assigned at the reception desk. There are two grassy tent areas. This is a tourist campground with no permanent rigs. Electrical connections are widely spaced (Euro, 12 amp). The showers and toilets are in a modern two-story building at the center of the campground. Showers are hot (pushbutton valve, adjustable) and there is hot water in the bathroom sinks. Dishwashing with free hot water and cooking facilities including hotplates are available in the reception building. There is a grocery store and restaurant kiosk with a covered seating area located in the central building

The Hütteldorf subway station (U4 line) is a five-minute bus ride from the camp. Two busses, Nos. 148 and 152, provide service every half-hour or so. Once you know the route this also makes a nice walk. The U4 subway line will take you directly to the convenient Karlsplatz station near the center of things.

Easiest access to the campground is from the A1 autobahn eastbound. At the end of the autobahn at the Aushof go straight, turn left at the first lights. Go straight through the next lights into Hüttelbergstrasse and follow this road up the hill to the campground which will be on your right after 1.8 km (1.1 miles). The route is well signed from the autobahn.

▲ DONAUPARK CAMPING KLOSTERNEUBURG

Address:	A-3402 Klosterneuburg bei
Telephone:	02243 25877
Fax:	02243 25878
Website:	www.campingklosterneuburg.at
E-mail:	campklosterneuburg@oeamtc.at
GPS:	N 48° 18' 38.2", E 016° 19' 38.0"

March 1 - Oct 31

Donaupark is a first-class campground that is located west of Vienna on the south shore of the Danube in the small town of Klosterneuburg. You'll have decent access to Vienna with a base that offers small town amenities and bike trails along the Danube.

The campground is a large field that is mostly unshaded. The sites are marked and assigned when you check in. This is a tourist campground with no permanent residents. There is a special tent area set aside for cyclists biking along the Danube. The site surfaces are grass. Electrical outlets are convenient and numerous (Euro, 6 amp). The shower/toilet buildings are modern, heated and clean. Hot water is provided for showers (pushbutton, adjustable), bathroom sinks, and dishwashing. Hotplates are available in the same room as the dishwashing sinks. Coin-operated washers and dryer are available. The campground has a restaurant and a small grocery shop and offers Vienna tours. There's even a large swimming park next door. In town, about 400 meters from the campground, is a grocery store.

During the summer it is easy to visit Vienna, the campground runs a shuttle bus. During the rest of the year it is not much more difficult, a suburban train station is less than 250 meters from the campground, the trip to Vienna's Heiligenstadt subway station takes only 15 minutes, and from there the green line will drop you at the Karlsplatz which is very convenient for starting your walking tour of Vienna. You can also ride your bike the 10 kilometers (6 miles) or so in to town. There is a bike trail along the river, part of the extensive Lower Danube Bike Route. For the first few kilometers the route is on back roads, then on a paved bike path.

The campground is easily reached from Highway B14 which follows the south bank of the Danube west of Vienna. Near the southeastern edge of Klosterneuburg next to the railway station you'll see a campground sign pointing northeast toward the river. The road is easy to recognize because it immediately dives under a railway trestle and also because there's a campground sign. The campground is less than 200 meters down this road on the right.

DRIVE 3 – VIENNA TO BUDAPEST
250 Kilometers (155 Miles), 3.25 Hours

A long The Way – The drive from Vienna to Budapest is a straight shot on the autobahn, the distance is about 250 kilometers (155 miles). Follow A1 out of Vienna to the east and, at the border with Hungary, the same highway becomes the M1. The region between Vienna and Budapest is known as the Transdanubia.

The Hungarian border is about 85 kilometers (53 miles) east of Vienna. You will need a new toll vignette to drive Hungarian roads. Check at the border for a kiosk to purchase one, if there is not one open then be sure to stop at the first available gas station and pick one up.

If you want to get off the highway and stretch your legs you can visit the **Pannonhalma Abbey** south of Gyor in Hungary. It must be visited on a tour, they are run at 11 am and 1 pm during the summer. To reach the abbey leave the highway 53 kilometers (33 miles) east of the border crossing at Gyor and follow highway 82 south for 11 kilometers (7 miles) to Pannonhalma.

M1 approaches Budapest from the west. Follow signs toward the center until you reach the river, then turn north along the west side. See the campground description for final driving instructions.

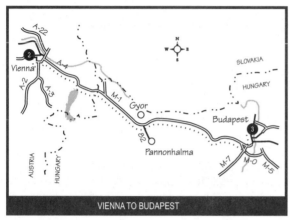

VIENNA TO BUDAPEST

BUDAPEST, HUNGARY
Population 1,800,000

Larger even than Vienna, Budapest is a world-class tourist city. It is located just 230 km (143 miles) east of Vienna and 190 km (118 miles) east of Bratislava so it's easy to get there. This is by far the largest city in Hungary, a fifth of the population of the country lives here.

Budapest straddles the Danube with Pest on the left bank (facing downstream) and Buda on the right. Buda is the old city, it occupies several hills and looks out over the much larger but almost completely flat modern Pest.

Tourist sights in Buda are largely up on Castle Hill. There's a funicular to carry you to the top. When you arrive you'll see the **Royal Palace** on your left. It houses both the **National Gallery** and the **Budapest History Museum**. North a bit you'll find **Matthias Church** with its patterned interior walls and tiled roof. On the separate **Gellért Hill** to the south is the **Citadella**, the best views of Budapest are from here.

Crossing the **Chain Bridge** from the base of the Castle Hill funicular you can work your way eastward to the foot of **Andrássy út**. This elegant boulevard runs northeast to **City Park**, under it is the yellow metro line, the city's first. Before heading toward the park, however, you might want to visit **St Stephen's Basilica** where you can climb to the dome for more great views.

Pest has several excellent museums, tops are the **National Museum** and, on Heroes Square, the **Museum of Fine Arts**.

Budapest Campground

▲ Római Camping

Address:	1031 Budapest Szentendrei út 189, H-1031 Pest	
Telephone:	06 1 3686260	
Fax:	06 1 2500426	
E-mail:	romai@message.hu	
GPS:	N 47° 34' 29.9", E 019° 02' 58.7"	

Open All Year

Budapest offers many campgrounds but we like this one because it has convenient metro access to the central area as well as decent but older facilities.

Sites in this large campground are not marked, you park where you wish under huge spreading trees. Electrical outlet boxes (German, 6 amp) are scattered about and usually require a long cord. Restroom buildings are older and maintenance is not great but hot showers are available as well as coin-operated washers and dryers. There is a good restaurant with nice outdoor seating and take-away food as well as a small grocery store. Across the street is a swimming park and about a kilometer behind the campground is the river with several cafes along a waterside walk. Motorhomes can dump at the campground in an unmarked (ask at the reception desk) manhole. The metro HEV line runs on the street outside the park, tickets are available at the reception desk, the stop is called Rómaifürdö.

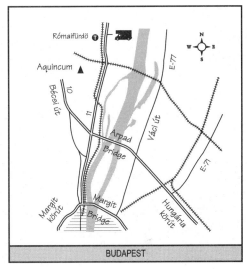

The campground is located on the west (Buda) side of the river along Hwy 11 to the north of the central part of town. If you follow Hwy 11 north you'll pass the Roman Ruins and then see the campground entrance sign on the right about 5 km (3 miles) north of the Margaret Bridge.

DRIVE 4 – BUDAPEST TO BRATISLAVA
217 Kilometers (135 Miles), 3 Hours

A long The Way – On today's route you'll stay away from the big highways. The route runs north and passes through the lovely **Danube Bend** area. Crossing the Danube at Komárno you'll then follow Highway 63 north toward Bratislava across the Slovakian countryside. There are several worthwhile stops en-route.

Follow Highway 11 north from Budapest for 14 kilometers (9 miles) to **Szentendre**. Stop here to take a look at the old center of town with its churches and galleries. This is a favorite day-trip destination from Budapest.

Continuing north on Highway 11 in 21 kilometers (13 miles) you'll reach **Visegrád**. Again, it's worthwhile to stop and look around. The view of the Danube Bend area from the **Citadel** is great.

Driving east just 21 kilometers (13 miles) there's another important stop, Esztergom. Take a look at the **Esztergom Basilica**, Hungary's largest church, which overlooks the Danube.

The route continues westward on Highway 11 and then Highway 10 for 50 kilometers (31 miles) to cross the Danube at Komárno. This is another border crossing and, while you won't reach a toll road for a while you had better start looking for a gas station to pick up another toll vignette.

From Komárno follow Highway 63 and then Highways 572 and 503 north to

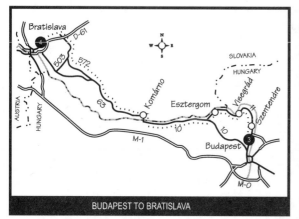

BUDAPEST TO BRATISLAVA

intercept the D61 expressway, then follow it in to Bratislava. Entering Bratislava watch for the large Tesco supermarket on your left, when you see it make a U-turn and follow the directions in the campground write-up to the campground.

Bratislava, Slovakia
Population 440,000

Bratislava has been the capital of Slovakia since it split from the Czech Republic in 1992. Keeping in mind the relatively small size of this city it has a surprising number of attractions. Perhaps the most important one of these for many is the reasonable prices in this world-class city located just 60 km from Vienna. It's hugely popular with the Austrians who visit for reasonably-priced cultural attractions, not to mention the inexpensive restaurants. Since Slovakia joined the European Union in 2004 and will probably join in the use of the euro as soon as possible thereafter there's no time to lose in planning your visit, the prices are bound to rise within the next few years.

The old center of town is largely a walking area. In the summer there are probably more outdoor restaurants here that in any similarly-sized city in Europe. Sights in the area include a number of museums including the **Slovak National Museum**, the **Slovak National Gallery**, and the **Municipal Museum**. The area also houses the **Slovak National Theater** and the **Reduta Palace** concert hall.

Overlooking the old town is the **Bratislava Castle**. The castle itself has been extensively rebuilt in modern times but from the hill there are great views of the old city, the Danube River, and the soaring Novy most suspension bridge.

Probably the most-visited attraction outside the city is the ruined **Devin Castle**. It overlooks the Danube about 10 km west of Bratislava. There are bike paths and restaurants in the area as well as the castle, it's a good place to get into the countryside. Busses make access easy.

Bratislava Campground

▲ Zlaté Piesky

Address:	Senecká Cesta c. 2, SK-82104 Bratislava
Telephone and Fax:	02 44257373
Website:	www.intercamp.sk
E-mail:	kempi@netax.sk
GPS:	N 48° 11' 18.1", E 017° 11' 12.9"

May 1 - Oct 15

The only real campground for Bratislava is a mixed bag: good access to town but poor facilities. It is worth trying to make the best of it however, since Bratislava is such a great town to visit.

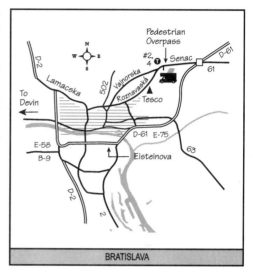

BRATISLAVA

The campground is part of a large park north of town. In addition to the campground facilities there is a lake (really a large gravel pit) for swimming, water sports and fishing. There are also restaurants, rental rooms, playgrounds, a water slide, and even mini-golf. All of this means that there are lots of people wandering around, you are issued a slip when you check in warning you to make sure all valuables are checked at the reception desk to avoid theft. Campsites are grass and mostly you camp where you wish within the bounds of the camping area. Some sites have convenient electric outlets (French, 16 amp). Restroom facilities are very old and although there is supposed to be hot water available we found none when we visited. A room with inadequate cooking and dishwashing facilities is available, you're probably going to have to wait in line to wash dishes. There is an upscale restaurant on the grounds as well as many kiosks with outdoor seating. Limited supplies are available at these kiosks but there is a large new Tesco just to the south of the campground. Access to town is by tram, the campground is located at the end of Lines 2 and 4.

The campground is located about 7 km northeast of town along Hwy 61 which becomes E75 to Zilina. If you come from the south on highways through town it is best to follow signs for Zilina. From that direction when you see a large Tesco on the right with a huge parking lot you are getting close. You'll see a pedestrian crossing ahead, turn into the campground entrance just before the crossing and then follow signs to the camping area entrance. Southbound on 61 just watch for the Tesco and then do a U-turn.

DRIVE 5 – BRATISLAVA TO PRAGUE
337 Kilometers (209 Miles), 3.5 Hours

A long The Way – This day's drive fairly long, but it's on some of the best roads of Slovakia and the Czech Republic. Follow D2 for 131 kilometers (81 miles) to the Czech city of Brno, then D1 on to Prague.

You'll cross the border into the Czech Republic 71 kilometers (43 miles) north of Bratislava. The Czech Republic too has a vignette program so you'll have to search out a place to pick one up before proceeding.

To find your campground in Prague follow the instructions given in the individual campground descriptions below.

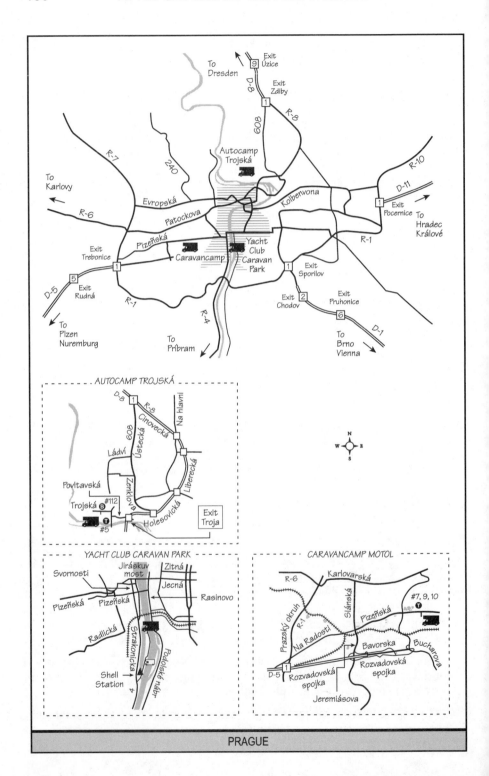

PRAGUE

PRAGUE, CZECH REPUBLIC
Population 1,200,000

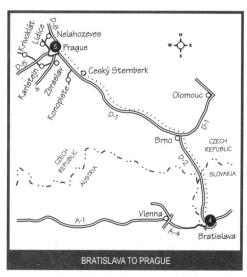

This city is an extremely popular tourist destination. The attractions are many. There are excellent facilities including hotels, restaurants and some rather unusual campgrounds. Until recently the city was spared the extremes of 20th-century development because it was sheltered from the modern world behind the Iron Curtain. Prague is no high-rise city, the friendly scale and historic Gothic and Bohemian baroque facades along the city's streets make a visit a pleasure. Finally, the price is right. Even though prices are rising you'll find them much lower than in more western European countries. Add to all of this the fact that the Czech Republic is home to the world's best beer and it is no wonder that the city is popular.

Prague is bisected by the wandering Vltava River. On the west bank is Little Town (Mala Strana), the original settlement. Overlooking Little Town is the **Hradcany (Prague) Castle** where you'll find **St. Vitus Cathedral** and the **Royal Palace**. Below

HRADCANY CASTLE AS SEEN FROM CHARLES BRIDGE

the castle is an outstanding example of Bohemian baroque architecture, the **Church of St. Nicholas**.

Across the **Charles Bridge** with its sidewalk vendors, street performers, and thirty 18th-century statues is **Old Town**. This section of Prague centers around the **Old Town Square** which is surrounded by narrow medieval streets filled with shops and restaurants. In the square itself is the **Clock Tower** where you can watch the 16th-century mechanism toll the hour. This area of town is also home to the historic **Jewish Quarter (Joseph's Town)**, with its **Old Jewish Cemetery**.

Wenceslas Square (actually a boulevard) leads from the edge of the Old Town into the **New Town**, the bustling center of modern Prague. The square and streets off its lower end form a pedestrian shopping area and at the top of the square is the **National Museum** with a statue of St. Wenceslas overlooking the bustling activities below.

Prague has an excellent system of subways and trams so it is easy to get around. If you stick to the Old and Little towns you'll really only need the public transportation to travel from your campground. You'll also find that Prague has English-language movies with Czech subtitles.

Tours of the castles in the countryside surrounding Prague are very popular. You can do this in your own vehicle. Some of the most popular (in alphabetical order) are **Ceský Sternberk** (45 kilometers southeast), **Hrad Karlstejn** (28 kilometers southwest), **Hrad Krivoklát** (45 kilometers west), **Konopiste** (45 kilometers southeast), **Nelahozeves** (30 kilometers north), and **Zbraslav** (15 kilometers south). Most have interesting exhibits.

The town of **Lidice** is 20 kilometers (12 miles) northwest of Prague. It is infamous because the Nazis razed the entire town in 1942 and either killed or shipped the inhabitants to concentration camps This was done as punishment for the assassination of Rheinard Heydrich, the Nazi official in charge of the so-called "final solution to the Jewish question". There is now a new village and a monument.

Prague Campgrounds

▲ AUTOCAMP TROJSKÁ

Address:	Trojská 375/157, CZ-17100 Praha 7
Telephone:	02 83850487
Fax:	02 33542945
Website:	www.autocamp-trojska.cz
E-mail:	autocamp-trojska@iol.cz
GPS:	N 50° 07' 01.3", E 014° 25' 39.5"

Open All Year

North of Prague, near the north bank of the Vltava where D8/E55 crosses, there is a cluster of small campgrounds. Many are situated behind residences under fruit trees. They make a good place to stay because they are pleasant and very convenient. Autocamp Trojská is one of the smallest, others include Sokol Troja, Dana Troja and Autocamp Hajek.

Autocamp Trojská is a small campground with about fifteen spaces. The sites are

on grass beneath apple and walnut trees, access to the campground is carefully moni-
tored and sites are informally assigned. There are no resident rigs. Electricity (both
Euro and German, 10 amp) is available. The showers and toilets are clean, modern,
more than adequate for the number of campers. Hot water is free and available to
showers, bathroom basins, and dish and clothes washing areas. There are covered
picnic areas and a limited snack bar and grocery shop. Bread and beer are both available.

Access to downtown Prague is extremely easy. You can either take the bus (No.
112) which stops beside the campground driveway and runs to the north metro station
or you can walk about one-half kilometer and take the tram (No. 5) directly in to
town. The tram takes about 15 minutes and tickets are available at the campground
reception desk. You'll find public transportation in Prague to be very reasonably priced.

The campground is accessible from Highway D8/E55 north of town. If you're
starting in central Prague follow signs toward Teplice. From the highway take the exit
for Troja and then proceed west, you'll soon see a number of campground signs. Take
your pick.

▲ YACHT CLUB CARAVAN PARK

Address: Císarská Louka 599, CZ-15000 Praha 5-Smíchov
Telephone: 02 57318681
Fax: 02 57318387
Website: www.volny.cz/convoy
E-mail: convoy@volny.cz
GPS: N 50° 03' 44.4", E 014° 24' 49.2"

Open All Year

Císarská Louka is an island in the Vltava River that sits about three kilometers
above (to the south of) the old town. There are two good campgrounds on the island,
the Yacht Club Caravan Park is on the north end. The quiet location is nice and a small
private walk-on ferry giving easy access to the subway system makes it even better.

The campground is medium-sized and occupies a well-drained grass field next to
the river. There are no permanently-located rigs. Campsites are unmarked and electrical services (Euro, 10 amp) are far apart. The shower/toilet building is a prefab portable but is relatively new and well maintained. It has hot-water showers, hot water in
the bathroom sinks, hot water for dishwashing and a laundry room. There is also a
restaurant.

The yacht club operates a small ferry that runs to the left bank every hour. The
charge is 10 koruna, about a third of a euro. From the ferry landing it is a short five-
minute walk to the Smíchovské Nádrazi subway stop on the yellow metro line.

There is only one bridge onto the island. It is on the south end and can only be
accessed from the northbound lanes of Highway 4 on the west or left bank of the river.
You must watch carefully for the road to the bridge, it is marked but easy to miss if
you are traveling too fast. About 1.2 kilometers (.7 miles) after passing the large
Barrandov Bridge interchange you'll see a Shell gas station coming up on the right
side. The island road is just **before** the station. Don't miss it! Turn right, cross the
small bridge, and follow a small paved road north past another campground on the

right to the Yacht Club Campground at the end of the road.

▲ CARAVANCAMP MOTOL   €€ ☐▲ ‖‖ 🛒
                                                         🐕 (🚐

Address: Pizeňská 279, CZ-15000 Praha 5-Motol
Telephone: 02 57215084
Fax: 02 57215084
Website: www.travelguide.cz
E-mail: caravancamp@volny.cz
GPS: N 50° 04' 05.7", E 014° 20' 58.7"

April 1 - Oct 31

This campground is older and not very well maintained, but it is located outside the busy central area to the west of the city.

Caravancamp is a large campground in a poorly clipped grassy field located next to a major Prague arterial. Road noise is noticeable but not a big problem, especially later in the evening. Camping sites are on grass, they are not individually marked and campers choose their own sites. Electrical connections are widely spaced (German, 10 amp). The centrally-located services building contains everything: reception, washrooms, dishwashing, and restaurant. Showers have free hot water (adjustable), only cold is available for dishes.

You can easily reach the Prague central area in about 15 minutes on Trams 7, 9, or 10 which stop just in front of the campground at a stop called Hotel Golf. Tickets are sold at the campground reception desk.

The easiest approach to this campround if you are approaching on D1 is to circle around the city to the west using the outer ring roads. When you reach D5/E50 head inward. Just as the autobahn ends campground signs will take you on a 270 degree loop and send you north. After 1 kilometer (.6 mile) take the off-ramp following signs for Centrum. This will put you on Plzeská heading east and in another 1.2 kilometer (.7 mile) you'll see the campground on your right. The entrance is another 50 meters or so towards town.

DRIVE 6 – PRAGUE TO MUNICH
378 Kilometers (234 Miles), 4.25 Hours

A long The Way – The last drive is a long one. You can stop for an hour or so in Plzen to tour the brewing museum and perhaps the brewery.

From Prague head west on D5 to Plzen, a distance of about 85 kilometers (53 miles). If you're a beer drinker this is an important stop. **Plzen** (or Pilsen) is the home of Pilsner beer. You can visit the Brewery Museum and, only at 12:30 pm on weekdays, tour the Pilsner Urquell Brewery.

Continuing west on D5 you'll reach the German border about 70 kilometers (42 kilometers) to the west. You'll be pleased to hear that you won't need to buy a vignette to travel the German autobahns.

At the border D5 becomes A6 and continues on to meet the A93 autobahn. Turn south on the A93.

If you didn't stop in Plzen perhaps you have time to stop in **Regensburg**. The A93 runs through Regensburg about 120 km (74 miles) north of Munich. The town is known as one of the country's most attractive cites, the most impressive sight is probably the Gothic Dom St. Peter.

When you leave Regensburg follow the A93 and then the A9 south to Munich.

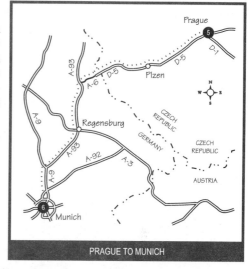

PRAGUE TO MUNICH

Information Resources

See our Internet site at www.rollinghomes.com for many links to information sources. Before you go you can call or send for information from these offices. If you mention that you will be camping they may send additional information.

German National Tourist Office, Chanin Building, 122 East 42nd Street, 52nd Floor, New York, NY 10168-0072 (323 655-6085). In Canada, PO Box 65162, Toronto, Ontario M4K 3Z2 (416 968-0372).

Austrian National Tourist Office, P.O. Box 1142, New York, NY 10108-1142 (212 944-6880). Use the same office from Canada.

Hungarian National Tourist Office, 150 East 58th St., 33rd Floor, New York, NY 10155-3398 (212 355-0240). Use the same office from Canada.

Slovakia does not maintain foreign tourist offices.

Czech Tourist Authority, 1109-1111 Madison Ave., New York, NY 10028. In Canada, Czech Airlines, 401 Bay St., Suite 1510, Toronto, Ontario M5H 2Y4.

TENT CAMPERS AT THALKIRCHEN IN MUNICH

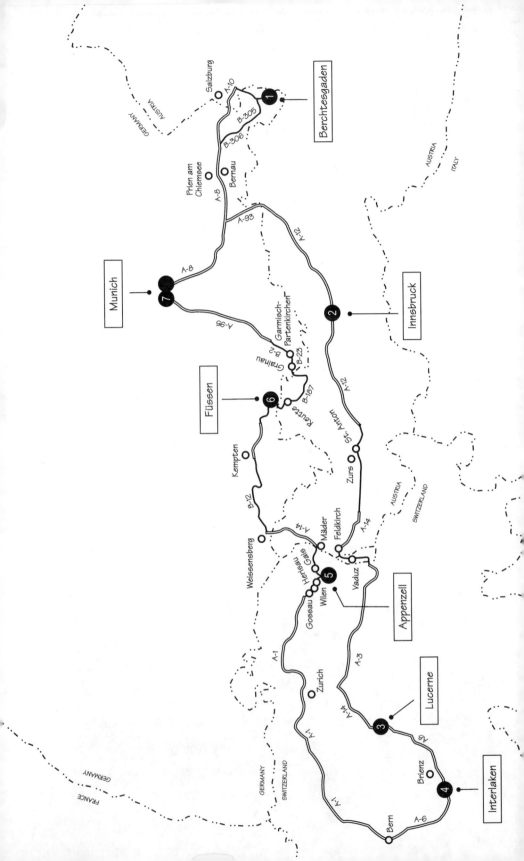

Chapter 9

Tour 6

The Alps

Top Attractions

- ❖ Munich
- ❖ Königssee
- ❖ Hitler's Eagle's Nest
- ❖ Schloss Herrenchiemsee
- ❖ Arlberg Pass
- ❖ Lucerne
- ❖ Jungfrau Region
- ❖ Bern
- ❖ Neuschwanstein Castle
- ❖ Zugspitze

General Description

This tour offers a great introduction to some of the most interesting sites in the northern Alps. Total driving distance is 1,207 kilometers (810 miles).

The gateway city is Munich. The prior tour, that of Central European Capitals, also uses Munich as a gateway. You could easily do both of these tours on the same visit if you have the time. Munich is a fun city with lots to see and do. It also has decent air travel connections and is a good place to rent an automobile or RV.

After picking up your vehicle the first driving night is spent in the German alpine resort of Berchtesgaden. The campground there has an excellent location just a quick walk from the Königssee.

The second drive takes you into Austria. Your destination, Innsbruck, is a popular visitor destination and the campground has grocery shopping nearby.

The third drive takes you across (or under) the Arlberg Pass and into Switzerland. The end of the day will find you in beautiful Lucerne on the shores of Lake Lucerne. From the campground you can stroll the lakeshore into town.

Drive four takes you farther into Switzerland, the destination is our favorite, the fun-packed Jungfrau and Interlaken.

The next driving day you'll head north again. Your final night in Switzerland is spent in the very traditional Appenzell region.

Drive five brings you back into Germany. Your destination is Füssen, home of Neuschwanstein. Pictures of this castle must grace more posters and book covers than any other sight in Europe.

The last drive is only 152 kilometers (94 miles). Along the way you can visit Germany's highest peak, the Zugspitze.

This tour can easily be combined with the several of the other tours in this book if you have several weeks. The most obvious are the Central European Cities and the Rhine Valley Tour. For lots more destinations and campgrounds you can check out our other European camping guide – *Traveler's Guide to European Camping*.

Roads and Driving

The roads covered by this chapter are in three countries: Germany, Austria, and Switzerland. Austria and Switzerland are covered below, for information about the German road system see Chapter 7.

Switzerland has an excellent expressway system. This is a toll system but tolls are not collected at booths. Instead you pay an annual fee and receive a vignette (sticker) that must be placed on your windshield. All users must have the vignettes, even visitors. You can buy the vignette at border crossings or gas stations near the border crossing. If you can't find a place to buy your vignette at the border just go to a post office, and stay off the autobahns until you do. The cost of the vignette at publication is 40 Swiss Francs, the fine for not having one on an autobahn is at least 100 Swiss Francs and you must also buy the vignette. A separate sticker is required for a trailer. Rigs over 3.5 metric tons pay on a different scale, it's more expensive but can be paid for shorter terms (periods less than a year) so motorhome drivers with heavy rigs actually will probably get off cheaper than those with lighter ones. There are additional tolls in some of the big tunnels.

Swiss secondary roads are good, but the mountains sometimes make driving a challenge. You can run into snow and ice at almost any time of the year. Many high mountain passes are closed to vehicles pulling trailers. When driving in the mountains remember to pull off to let faster traffic pass. On narrow roads uphill traffic has the right-of-way over downhill traffic.

The highway numbering system in Switzerland is simple with autobahns designated as "A" roads. International routes have an additional "E" designation and secondary roads are numbered with no letter prefix.

Austria has several excellent autobahns. The country has recently initiated a fee system like that in Switzerland using windshield vignettes. Vignettes can be purchased for 10 days or two months. There's a special two-month, two-trip ticket (called a Kombi) that can be used to transit the country on important trans-Europe routes like the Brenner Pass. Buy vignettes at border crossings, gas stations near border crossings, and post offices, just as in Switzerland. Austrian roads, both autobahns and secondary, are well maintained but the mountainous character of the country means that many have steep grades with high passes and tunnels.

Austria has a numbering system like that in Germany. On the maps and highway signs autobahns have an "A" prefix and often also an alternative "E" or international prefix. Secondary roads have a "B" prefix. Roads smaller than the "B" roads are labeled as "L" roads, smaller ones just have a four-digit number.

Speed limits vary a little from country to country. Generally, speed limits are as follows unless otherwise marked (the format is towns and built-up areas/highways/

CAMPING IN THE SHADOW OF THE ALPS IN INNSBRUCK

limited access highways and expressways): Germany – 50/100/130, Austria – 50/100/130, Switzerland – 50/80/100. These speeds are in kilometers per hour of course.

The telephone numbers for emergencies in Switzerland are 117 for police, 118 for fire, and 144 for ambulance. In Austria the emergency telephone numbers are 133 or 112 for police, 122 or 112 for fire and 144 or 112 for ambulance.

Camping and Campgrounds

Campgrounds in Germany, Austria and Switzerland are excellent. Standards of cleanliness and quality of the improvements both tend to be very good.

Swiss campgrounds use an electrical plug type that is entirely different than any other country. It has three prongs set on a diamond-shaped base. You should probably wait until you reach Switzerland to try to find one, most campgrounds and hardware stores can provide a compact adapter.

Free camping in Germany, Switzerland and Austria is generally allowed as long as you don't set up camping equipment outside the vehicle. In other words, be discrete. Some localities do not, however, allow free camping so you should check. Make sure to get permission if you camp on private property.

The Camping Card International is not required in these countries but often will get you a discount at the campgrounds.

Practical Tips

Please see the Practical Tips section of Chapter 7 for more information about Germany.

Prices in Austria and particularly Switzerland are high. Austria uses the euro while Switzerland has its own extremely strong currency called the Swiss Franc. In fact, we think that Switzerland is prohibitively expensive for travel if you aren't on a camping vacation.

In Switzerland many gas stations are closed on weekends. Many have automatic dispensers that can be used while they are closed. Some accept credit cards and many accept Swiss ten and twenty franc notes.

The credit card situation in Austria and Switzerland is much like Germany and France. They are widely accepted and cash machines are easy to find.

THE TOUR – THE ALPS

TOUR 6 GATEWAY CITY – MUNICH (MÜNCHEN), GERMANY

See Chapter 8, which also starts in Munich, for information about the city.

DRIVE 1 – MUNICH TO BERCHTESGADEN
144 Kilometers (89 Miles), 1.5 Hours

A long The Way – From Munich follow the A8 autobahn south and then east. At 45 kilometers (28 miles) you'll see the A93 autobahn branching off to go to Innsbruck and Italy over the Brenner Pass. Don't take that road, continue on A8 past the Chiemsee to the Austrian border.

At the Austrian border, one hundred and fifteen kilometers (71 miles) from Munich, you will have to buy a toll vignette for the short time you'll be on the Austrian toll autobahns today and the much longer time tomorrow. If there is no kiosk along the highway be sure to stop at the first possible service station to buy one.

As you cross into Austria the name of the autobahn changes to A1. Two kilometers (1 mile) from the border go south on A10. Seven kilometers (4 miles) from the A1/A10 junction take the exit for Berchtesgaden. Go to the right (south), toward Berchtesgaden, you'll cross back into Germany and arrive in Berchtesgaden in 30 kilometers (19 miles). Follow signs for Königssee and they'll take you another 4 kilometers (2 miles) up the valley to the campground. See the instructions in the campground write-up for more details.

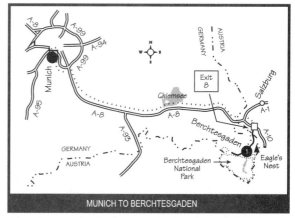

MUNICH TO BERCHTESGADEN

BERCHTESGADEN, GERMANY
Population 8,000

Berchtesgaden is a popular German resort that is located in a valley almost surrounded by Austria. If you've heard of Berchtesgaden it may be because this is the site of the **Eagle's Nest**, Hitler's alpine redoubt. Much of it has been destroyed but there's still a lot to see, with the bonus of a great view and good hiking. It's best to take the bus from Berchtesgaden since this is a steep road and you would have to park and take a bus for the last portion of the trip anyway. Another interesting destination is the **Salzbergwerk**, an operating salt mine which offers underground tours including a ride on an small underground railway and on a boat across an underground lake.

Munich's Wittelsbachs had a palace here too, the **Schloss Berchtesgaden** is now a museum.

The **Berchtesgaden National Park** to the south of town is one of only a few German national parks. You can cross the beautiful **Königssee** on an electrically-driven excursion boat and then hike another kilometer or so to another lake, the **Obersee**, with its **Rothbachfall** waterfall. There are many other hikes in the park. The campground below is within easy walking distance of the Königssee shore and docks.

Berchtesgaden Campground

▲ CAMPING GRAFENLEHEN

    Address: D-83471 Konigssee
    Telephone: 08652 4140
    Fax: 08652 690768
    GPS: N 47° 35' 42.9", E 012° 59' 10.9"

Open All Year

This is a large campground with about 150 spaces. Parking is on grass in numbered and assigned back-in spaces (Euro, 16 amp). The one central restroom building is clean and modern and has free hot water for showers, bathroom basins, and dishwashing. There's a restaurant on site and a shop, in nearby Königssee you also have a large selection of restaurants. There's a hiking and bike path that leads down the valley toward Berchtesgaden, also many hiking trails in the area. The tourist town of Königssee is about 500 meters from the front gate. There you'll find the dock for electric boats up the lake as well as for busses to all the sights downvalley.

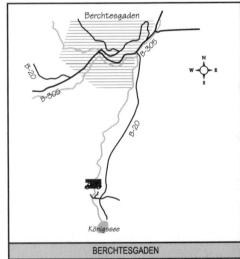

To find the campground just head for Königssee, just before the gates to the parking lot turn right into the campground access road.

DRIVE 2 – BERCHTESGADEN TO INNSBRUCK
203 Kilometers (126 Miles), 2.5 Hours

Along The Way – Rather than backtrack today we'll take a new route to reach the A8 motorway as we travel back to the west before heading south toward Innsbruck.

From the campground drive back down the valley to Berchtesgaden, then turn

TOURING THE IMPRESSIVE INTERIOR OF THE SCHLOSS HERRENCHIEMSEE

left and follow B305 and B306 west and then north to the A8 autobahn, a distance of about 48 kilometers (30 miles) on scenic country roads. Head west when you reach the A8.

Since this is a relatively short driving day there's an enjoyable side trip in this area. This is **Schloss Herrenchiemsee**, one of mad king Ludwig's three castles. This one sits on an island in the middle of the usually placid Chiemsee, you reach it using one of the frequent ferries from the town of Prien am Chiemsee. To drive there take the exit just 22 kilometers (14 miles) from where you joined the autobahn, it is marked for Bernau A. Chiemsee and Prien A. Chiemsee. Drive north toward Prien, about 6 kilometers (4 miles), follow signs to the ferry dock, find a place to park, and enjoy your voyage to the island and castle.

Back on the autobahn continue west for 21 kilometers (13 miles) and turn south on A93 for Innsbruck. You'll reach the city 100 kilometers (62 miles) from the inter-section of A8 with A93. Follow the instructions in the campground write-up to reach Camping Innsbruck-Kranebitten.

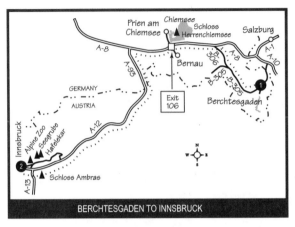

BERCHTESGADEN TO INNSBRUCK

INNSBRUCK, AUSTRIA
Population 120,000

Innsbruck straddles the most direct route from Germany to Italy, the Brenner Pass. From Innsbruck the autobahn immediately begins its steep climb to the south, but Innsbruck is at a low altitude in the broad Inn Valley with peaks rising impressively all around. Innsbruck has a lot to offer and is a great central location for day trips into the surrounding Alps.

Most of the sights in Innsbruck itself are in the central **Old Town (Altstadt)** area. You'll want to see the **Olympic Museum's** famous **Golden Roof**, the **Imperial Palace (Hofburg)**, and the **Hofkirche** with Maximilian's mausoleum (he is actually buried near Vienna, against his wishes). You can also take the **Hungerburgbahn** funicular up the hillside to the north of town to see the **Alpine Zoo** or even higher to the lookouts at **Seegrube** or **Hafelekar**.

Schloss Ambras is just outside Innsbruck to the southeast and can actually be easily reached by bus from the city center. It is a popular castle dating from the 11th century and was rebuilt in the 16th century. You'll find an arms museum at the castle.

Innsbruck Campground

▲ CAMPING INNSBRUCK-KRANEBITTEN

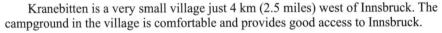

Address:	Kranebitten Allee 214, A-6020 Innsbruck
Telephone and Fax:	0512 284180
Website:	www.camping innsbruck.com
E-mail:	campinnsbruck@hotmail.com
GPS:	N 47° 15' 48.4", E 011° 19' 34.6"

Open All Year

Kranebitten is a very small village just 4 km (2.5 miles) west of Innsbruck. The campground in the village is comfortable and provides good access to Innsbruck.

Camping Kranebitten is a medium-sized campground placed on a south-facing hillside just above the Inn Valley. About half the campground is terraced to provide flat sites for four-wheeled vehicles and the other half slopes and has lots of shade, perfect for tents and trailers. All site surfaces are grass and are unnumbered and unassigned. Electrical outlets (Euro, 6 amp) are widely-spaced. Shower/toilet facilities are in a building on one side of the campground, the building is older but in good repair and clean. Hot showers are free (mostly premixed with a foot-operated pressure valve), and there is also hot water in bathroom and dishwashing sinks. The laundry room with a coin-operated washer is located in the women's washroom. There is a nice restaurant and a kiosk-style grocery shop. There is also a large playground on the hillside just above the campground. You'll find a major shopping center 2 km (1.2 miles) from the campground on the south side of the autobahn, watch for the McDonald's arches.

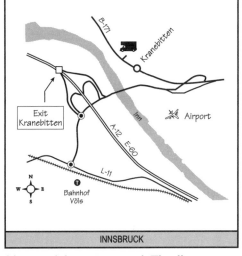

INNSBRUCK

Innsbruck is 4 km (2.5 miles) to the east of the campground. There is a good bike route which runs along the road for 3 kilometers (1.9 miles) and then cuts over to the river. The stop for the most frequent bus route is a five-minute walk from the campground, ask at the reception desk for directions.

From Highway A12 just west of Innsbruck near the airport take the Kranebitten exit and follow signs for Kranebitten and the campground. The distance from the autobahn to the campground is only 1.5 km (.9 miles).

DRIVE 3 – INNSBRUCK TO LUCERNE
300 Kilometers (186 Miles), 3.5 Hours

A long The Way – From Innsbruck drive west on A12. This highway will carry you smoothly west up the Inn Valley. When you meet the mountains at the end it goes under them, the tunnel here is called the Arlberg Tunnel and is 14 km (7 miles) long. Above are the ski towns of **St. Anton** and (just off the main road) **Zurs**. If you want to take the **Arlberg Pass** route rather than the tunnel just take Exit 145, Signed St Anton and Arlbergpass. Follow S16 and B197 over the Alberg Bundesstrasse. Tak-

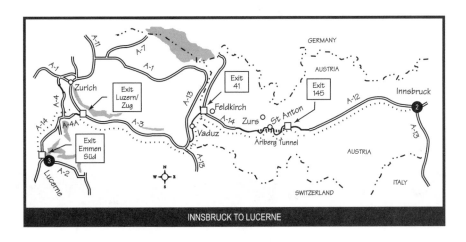

INNSBRUCK TO LUCERNE

ing the pass rather than the tunnel will add just a few kilometers to the drive and save the tunnel toll.

Back on the autobahn (which soon becomes the A14) continue west until you reach Exit 41, marked Feldkirch. Follow signs for Vaduz southeast into **Liechtenstein**. Vaduz is the capital of the country. Twenty-one kilometers (13 miles) of driving will take you the length of the Liechtenstein and out the other side.

Head south again on the A13 autoroute for just a 4 kilometers or so and join A3 toward Zurich. A3 will take you south of Lake Wallen and then Lake Zurich. After 73 kilometers (45 miles) on the A3 take the exit marked Luzern and Zug. This will take you west on the Zugerstrasse for 11 kilometers (7 miles) to the A4A autobahn which connects with the A4. At the A4 follow signs south toward Lucerne. The signs will take you onto the A14 in a few kilometers and you'll soon be approaching Lucerne. Exit at the Emmen Süd sign and follow signs for the campground south to the lakeshore. See the campground write-up for directions on how to reach Camping Lido.

LUCERNE (LUZERN), SWITZERLAND
Population 60,000

In direct contrast to nearby Zurich, Lucerne is undeniably a tourist town. There's lots to keep you occupied.

The old section of town with its pedestrian streets, shops, and restaurants is on

A PICTORIAL PANEL UNDER THE ROOF OF THE KAPELLBRÜCKE

the east side of the River Reuss, the outlet to Lake Lucerne (the Vierwaldstätter See), which is straddled by the town. The 14th-century **Chapel Bridge (Kapellbrücke)** across the river and adjoining **Water Tower (Wasserturm)** are popular attractions, the tower must be photographed since it is the city's premier landmark. Boats ply the lake and will take you almost anywhere. If you're interested in an effort-free view there's a cog railway up **Mt. Pilatus**. Near the campground is the **Swiss Transport Museum (Verkehrshaus)**, one of Switzerland's top tourist attractions.

Lucerne Campground

▲ CAMPING LIDO LUCERNE

Address:	Lidostrasse 8, CH-6006 Luzern
Telephone:	041 3702146
Fax:	041 3702145
Website:	www.camping-international.ch
E-mail:	luzern@camping-international.ch
GPS:	N 47° 02' 59.8", E 008° 20' 16.1"

March 15 - Oct 31

Camping Lido Lucerne is a large campground with a very good location for visitors to Lucerne. All sites are small without anything to separate them. Motorhomes and vans are parked in a separate area from trailers, and tents also have their own area. A warden will lead you to the proper area and usually let you choose your own site. Electricity (Swiss, 10 amp) is metered, 1 franc buys you 2 kilowatt hours. The shower/toilet buildings can be heated during cooler weather, hot showers and hot water for dishwashing cost a half franc while hot water in the bathroom basins is free. The campground has laundry facilities with coin-operated machines and a grocery kiosk with some take-away meals (broiled chickens). The Lido (beach) is across from the campground and the well-known Swiss Transport Museum is right next door.

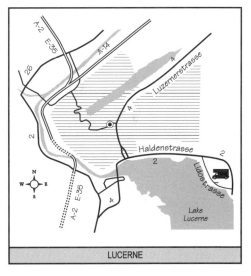

Bus service to Lucerne is very good with busses at least every quarter of an hour from outside the campground. You can also easily walk the 1.5 km along the lake in about 20 minutes. It is even possible to travel in to town by steamer from a dock nearby.

Find the campground by following the road that runs along the north shore of Lake Lucerne out of town to the east. The campground is well signed and is on the right after 1.5 kilometers (.9 miles). There's an access road that also serves the beach and transport museum.

DRIVE 4 – LUCERNE TO INTERLAKEN
69 Kilometers (43 Miles), 1 Hour

A long The Way – This day's drive is short and that's a good thing. There's so much to do in the Interlaken region. From the Lucerne campground work your way west along the waterfront and across town to the A8 autobahn and head south following signs for Interlaken. Six kilometers (4 miles) south follow the Interlaken signs through a short tunnel and onto A8. Interlaken is 60 kilometers (37 miles) to the south. See the write-up below to decide where in this area you'd like to spend your time and the campground write-ups for driving directions.

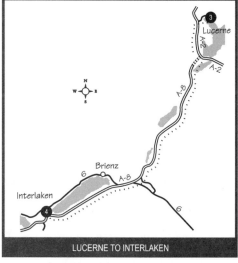

LUCERNE TO INTERLAKEN

INTERLAKEN AND THE JUNGFRAU REGION, SWITZERLAND

The draws in the Jungfrau Region near Interlaken are the mountains to the south: the Eiger (Ogre), Jungfrau (Virgin), and Mönch (Monk); the foothills and valleys below these peaks; and Lake Brienz (Brienzer See) and Lake Thun (Thuner See) on either side of Interlaken. The area is chock full of alpine railways, lifts of various sorts, hiking trails and boat routes on the lakes.

Interlaken (population 5,000) is the gateway to the Jungfrau Region. It is also an excellent base for your visit. Like all of the towns and villages in the Jungfrau Region Interlaken's business is tourism, you will be well taken care of. Supplies, banking, restaurants and diversions are all easy to find. Interlaken has been popular for years with the English, the town is often referred to as a Victorian resort town and was one of the first alpine resorts.

While the surrounding lakes and mountains are the prime attractions you will find some worthwhile sights in Interlaken itself. The oldest part of town is on the north side of the Aare River. You'll find the **Marktplatz** there, as well as the **Schloss Unterseen** and the **Stadthaus**. The **Touristik-Museum der Jungfrau Region** is a good introduction to the tourist industry in the region. Back on the south side of the river the **Höhematte Park** is the place for a nice stroll. You might also enjoy the demonstration of traditional Swiss cheese making at the **Chäs-Dörfli.** Finally, you'll find that Interlaken has its own **Casino**.

Interlaken has seven campgrounds. All of the them are numbered and there are signposts with the numbers all around town. The campgrounds with their numbers are as follows: Camping Manor Farm (1), Camping Alpenblick (2), Camping Hobby (3), Camping Lazy Rancho (4), Camping Jungfrau (5), TCS-Camping Sackgut (6), and

Camping Jungfraublick (7). In addition to these campgrounds there are also some in surrounding small villages. Camping Alpenblick (2) is described below as **Interlaken and the Jungfrau Region Campground No. 1 - Interlaken**.

Interlaken covers the flat plain between the **Brienzer See** (Lake Brienz) and the **Thuner See** (Lake Thun). Both of these lakes are served by graceful lake steamers making circuits to places of interest on the shores. The Brienzer See stops include **Iseltwald** where you can take a beautiful hike to the **Gliessbach Falls** and **Brienz**. **Brienz** has a famous woodcarving school where you can actually learn to carve small figures, and is the terminus for a cog railway up the **Rothorn**. Nearby is the **Ballenberg** open-air museum with 80 different traditional structures set in a 200 acre park. The Thuner See has even more, stops include **Spiez, Thun, Hilterfingen, Oberhofen** and **Beatenbucht**. Many of these towns have an interesting castle. Thun has a much-admired medieval square and unique shopping street that actually sits on the roofs of the shops of the street below. From Beatenbucht you can take a funicular up to

A LIFT CLIMBS FROM THE VALLEY IN GRINDELWALD

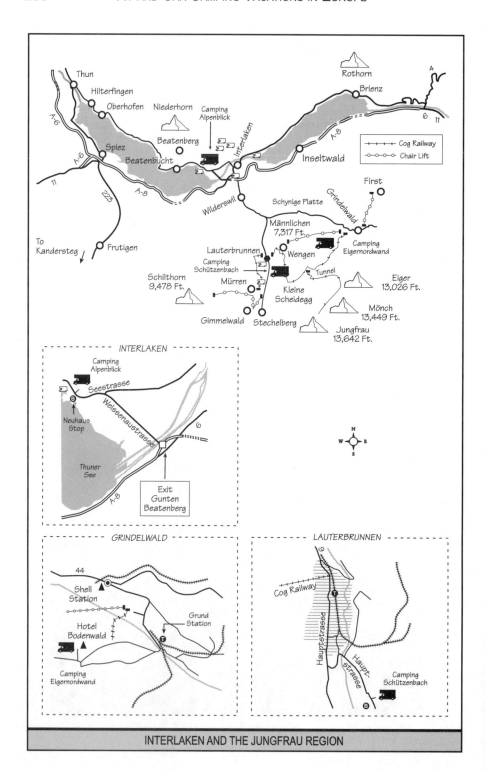

INTERLAKEN AND THE JUNGFRAU REGION

Beatenberg where trails or a chairlift will take you even higher to the **Niederhorn** and great views as far as Mont Blanc. All of the lakeside towns mentioned above are also accessible by road.

South of Interlaken the twin valleys of the Lütschine River afford access to the winter skiing and summer hiking of the high country below the Eiger, Mönch and Jungfrau. The left valley, that of the Schwartze Lütschine (Black Lütschine) climbs to the high resort town of Grindelwald. The right valley, that of the Weisse Lütschine (White Lütschine) doesn't climb as steeply so that when you reach the village of Lauterbrunnen you are surrounded by steep cliffs.

Grindelwald (population 4,000) an alpine village perched in the mountains south of Interlaken offers anything a mountain enthusiast could desire. The sophisticated village has shops, restaurants, and even a sports center. Lifts of various descriptions will whisk you into beautiful high country containing hundreds of kilometers of hiking trails, or you can climb the hills under your own power. Towering over everything is the Eiger. The valley offers several campgrounds. Most are well signed from the entrance of the village. You can stop at the information map mounted on a board in a parking area on the road into town to orient yourself.

A campground in Grindelwald is described below as **Interlaken and the Jungfrau Region Campground No. 2 - Grindelwald**.

From Grindelwald it is possible to catch a cog railway up to **Kleine Scheidegg** at an altitude of 6,762 feet and then another on up to the **Jungfraujoch** at 11,333 feet.

SWISS CAMPING AT THE EIGERNORDWAND

The second cog railway runs inside the Eiger, huge viewing galleries have been blasted in the side of the mountain and the train stops for an occasional peek on the way up. At the top is a viewing station with a restaurant and activities including dogsled rides and an ice-sculpture museum. From Kleine Scheidegg you can continue on across to the village of Lauterbrunnen or return to Grindelwald.

If you head south from Interlaken into the mountains and turn right at the fork you'll find yourself in the Lauterbrunnen Valley. Not far up the valley is the village of **Lauterbrunnen** (population 3,500). The village sits close below high cliffs on both sides of the valley, the **Staubbach Falls** make a very long drop from the top of the cliff just south of town. There are two campgrounds here: TCS Camping Schützenbach and Camping Jungfrau. Another few kilometers up the valley is another campground, Breithorn, in the even smaller village of Stechelberg. Lauterbrunnen is a good place to catch a ride up into the high country, the cog railway heads uphill away from the road from here to Wengen and Kleine Scheidegg. On the other side of the valley you can catch the more reasonably-priced funicular and train combination to Mürren and Gimmelwald and many hiking trails above and below them.

A campground in Lauterbrunnen is described below as **Interlaken and the Jungfrau Region Campground No. 3 – Lauterbrunnen**.

Interlaken and Jungfrau Region Campground No. 1 - Interlaken

▲ CAMPING ALPENBLICK

Address:	Seestrasse 135, CH-3800 Interlaken
Telephone:	033 8227757
Fax:	033 8231470
Website:	www.campinginterlaken.ch
E-mail:	goetz-castro@bluewin.ch
GPS:	N 46° 40' 47.1", E 007° 49' 02.5"

Open All Year

This is one of seven campgrounds in Interlaken. It is one of the farthest from the center of the town, but the distance is only two kilometers (1.2 miles). One indication of this region's popularity is that all of the campgrounds have fairly high prices for the facilities that they offer, Alpenblick is one of the more reasonable.

The campground is a large grassy field with scattered trees. Gravel access roads cross the campground, sites are not numbered or assigned. Many permanent resident caravans are at the rear of the campground but there are large areas for tourist campers. Electricity is available at a few boxes (Euro, German, and Swiss, 10 amp). The shower/toilet building is rustic, hot showers are free and there is hot water in some of the bathroom basins, and for dishwashing. Laundry machines are available in the reception office. There are also a few grocery items. The Camping Manor Farm and the Motel Neuhaus are across the street, they offer restaurants, groceries, and a golf course.

Bus transportation to the center of Interlaken is convenient, the bus stops just outside the campground. The 2 kilometers to town is easily accomplished on foot or on a bicycle, there are trails the entire distance.

From the A8 autobahn you can most easily reach the campground by taking the Gunten and Beatenberg exit at the west end of the tunnel. This is a spur road that runs right past the campground which will be on your right. From Interlaken itself follow the signs for Camp 2 from near the Interlaken West train station.

Interlaken and the Jungfrau Region
Campground No. 2 - Grindelwald

▲ CAMPING EIGERNORDWAND

Address:	CH-3818 Grindelwald
Telephone:	033 8534227
Fax:	033 8535042
Website:	www.eigernordwand.ch
E-mail:	camp@eigernordwand.ch
GPS:	N 46° 37' 18.8", E 008° 00' 59.9"

Open All Year

Eigernordwand is located on the valley floor below the village of Grindelwald. The Männlichen cable car passes almost over the site and views in all directions are spectacular.

This is a medium-sized site located in a slightly sloping field. All campsites are on grass and they are not separated or numbered. Electricity is available (Swiss, 6 amp) from a few widely-scattered boxes. The shower/toilet building is modern and heated, hot water is free for showers (adjustable), bathroom basins, dishwashing and hand-laundry sinks. The laundry room has coin-operated machines and a heated drying room. There is a restaurant at the Hotel Bodenwald adjacent to (and part of) the campground and a small grocery kiosk at the reception desk. There's also a dump station. Groceries are available in town at two small supermarkets about 1.5 km (.9 mile) from the campground but uphill.

As you drive in to Grindelwald you'll notice the Männlichen cable car on your right and below you. You'll probably also see the campground just beyond it. Turn right at the traffic circle just after the Shell gas station toward the Grund railway station. You'll pass it at the bottom of the valley, then the signs will take you across a small bridge to the right and along narrow roads for about a half-kilometer (.3 mile). The site is next to the Hotel Bodenwald.

Interlaken and the Jungfrau Region
Campground No. 3 - Lauterbrunen

▲ CAMPING SCHÜTZENBACH

Address:	CH-3822 Lauterbrunnen
Telephone:	033 8551268
Fax:	033 8551275
Website:	http://www.schuetzenbach.ch/sites/index.htm
E-mail:	http://www.schuetzenbach.ch
GPS:	N 46° 35' 25.6", E 007° 54' 43.1"

Open All Year

This is a medium-sized campground on flat ground just south of the village of

Lauterbrunnen. Camping sites are grass or gravel. There are quite a few permanent resident caravans here but they are located in a separate area. Sites are not numbered and are not assigned. Electricity is available in widely-scattered boxes (Swiss, 10 amp). The shower/toilet building is heated, girls upstairs and boys down. Hot showers require payment but there is free hot water in the bathroom basins. Dishwashing sinks also require payment for hot water. There is a laundry room with coin-operated machines. A cooking area is outside but covered and has a couple of gas stoves. Prepared food is available at a snack bar and there is a small grocery shop. The campground also has a playground. More complete grocery shopping is available at the Coop supermarket in Lauterbrunnen about a kilometer from the campground.

You can find the campground by staying on the main road through Lauterbrunnen. It is on the left as you leave town.

DRIVE 5 – INTERLAKEN TO APPENZELL
268 Kilometers (166 Miles), 3 Hours

Along **The Way** – From Interlaken drive east on A8 and A6 20 kilometers (12 miles) to **Bern**. Bern is the capital of Switzerland and well worth a stop.

Bern is unusual because it is one of the few larger Swiss cities that is not located next to a lake. It does have a river, however, the Aare. The river curves around the city, making the old town a peninsula. Bern is the Swiss capital and has the best-preserved historical city center in Switzerland. The central area's streets are lined with arcades and have many fountains. The city's mascot is the bear, and just across the Nydeggbrücke from the center of town are the **Bärengraben** (bear pits) where you

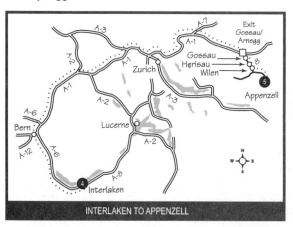

INTERLAKEN TO APPENZELL

can feed carrots to the bruin residents, they've been there since 1513. The town has several good museums including the **Swiss Postal Museum** covering the unusual Swiss postal system, the **Fine Arts Museum (Kuntsmuseum)** with a collection featuring the artist Paul Klee and others, and the **Swiss Alpine Museum**.

From Bern follow A1 northeast a full 225 kilometers (140 miles) to well past Zurich. As you approach Gossau take the exit marked Gossau/Arnegg. Follow Highway 8 south through Gossau toward and through Herisau and Wilen. At the intersection 6 kilometers south of Gossau leave Highway 8 and continue toward Appenzell, some 10 kilometers (6 miles) farther along. See the campground description below for driving instructions for finding the campground.

APPENZELL, SWITZERLAND
Population 5,000

Appenzellerland is known as the most traditional and least progressive area in Switzerland, women only began voting here in 1991. The town of Appenzell is known for it's open-air politics, the Landsgemeinde (parliament gathering) is held in the main square on the last Sunday in April. Appenzell is a cute tourist town but the real attraction is the surrounding countryside. The Alps here are lower and more rounded than farther south, but there are many walking routes and the campground perches high above the town, we have been serenaded at dusk by a local farmer across the valley playing an alphorn.

Appenzell Campground

▲ EISCHEN/KAU

Address:	CH-9050 Kau-Appenzell
Telephone:	071 7875030
Fax:	071 7875660
Website:	www.eischen.ch
E-mail:	info@eischen.ch
GPS:	N 47° 19' 21.1", E 009° 23' 15.1"

Open All Year

This campground sits high above Appenzell surrounded by grassy fields. The views are fantastic and you'll feel like you're in storybook Switzerland.

There are many permanent units in this campground, but also large areas for travelers. The travelers park in three areas: one below the restaurant, one below and behind it, and one near the entrance. Camping is on grass with very widely scattered electrical boxes (Swiss, 10 amp). Restrooms are clean and modern, hot showers require a coin but hot water for basins and dishwashing is free. The restaurant here is very good, it attracts diners from town which is saying something in view of the drive to get here. You can walk down the hill to town on trails in about 40 minutes, we find it takes a while longer to climb back up to the campground.

The road up to the campground leaves Appenzell to the southwest. Highway 448 runs east-west along the northern edge of the town and is also known as Umfahrungsstrasse. Turn south where the signs indicate onto Enggenhuttenstrasse, drive 0.3 km (.2 mile) to a T. Turn left onto Rinkenbach and drive 0.2 km (.1 mile). Now turn right on St Antonstrasse and follow it for 0.3 km (.2 mile) until you see a right turn that leads you to a rail crossing. Drive up and out of town until you reach a junction 1.9 km (1.2 mile) from the railroad tracks. Turn left here and soon you'll enter the campground. There should be a white campground sign at each of these turns.

Drive 6 – Appenzell to Füssen
160 Kilometers (99 Miles), 2 Hours

A long The Way – From the east side of Appenzell follow Highway 448 up and out of the valley and down to Mäder. You'll cross the A13, cross the border from Switzerland into Austria, and find the A14 shortly beyond. Drive north on the A14 for 32 kilometers (20 miles). You'll cross the border into Germany. Take the exit marked B12, Weissensberg/Kempton and follow B12 (signed for Kempton) east for 58 kilometers (36 miles) to the A7 autobahn. Now follow the A7 southeast to Füssen and Schwangau.

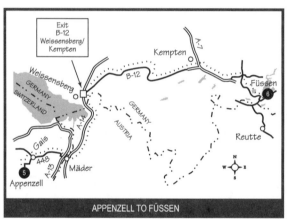

APPENZELL TO FÜSSEN

Schwangau-Füssen, Germany
Population 15,000

The real attraction in Füssen (population 15,000) isn't really in town at all. About 5 kilometers (3.1 miles) to the east are two of the most famous castles in the world, mad king Ludwig II's **Neuschwanstein** and his boyhood home **Hohenschwangau**. These castles aren't the only attractions in the area however. There is another castle in Füssen itself, the **Hohes Schloss**. There are many kilometers of trails in the mountains and along the lakes around the town, the Forggensee is good for sailing and windsurfing, and this is also an important winter sports area with downhill skiing possibilities.

We list two campground for this destination. The second is in Reutte, it's about 10 kilometers (6 miles) south of Füssen in Austria but still a convenient place to camp while visiting the area. See the individual campground descriptions for final driving directions.

Schwangau-Füssen Campgrounds

▲ Ferienplatz Brunnen am Forggensee

Address:	Seestr. 81, D-87645 Schwangau-Brunnen
Telephone:	08362 8273 **Fax:** 08362 8630
Website:	www.camping-brunnen.de
E-mail:	info@camping-brunnen.de
GPS:	N 47° 35' 45.1", E 010° 44' 20.4"

Dec 21 - Nov 5 (Varies)

Ferienplatz Brunnen is located in Brunnen on the shore of the Forggensee, a large lake. The campground is about 5 kilometers (3.1 miles) north of the castles and 6 kilometers (3.7 miles) from Füssen.

It is a large campground with few permanent rigs. All sites are on gravel and are separated from each other by rows of small trees or bushes. Electrical boxes are widely separated, you may need a long cord (Euro, 16 amp). The shower/toilet building is a strong point here. The building is modern, heated, and spacious, there are lots of showers and they are free, hot water is also provided to the bathroom sinks, dishwashing sinks and laundry sinks. There are several coin-operated washers and dryers and there are hot plates in the dishwashing room. The campground has its own small grocery shop and a playground. There is also a dump station. Swimming in the lake is popular in the summer and many people use small boats, there are sailboats for rent. There is a good restaurant near the campground and a Spar supermarket about 2 kilometers away in the town of Schwangau. This campground is very popular and can be busy, get there as early as you can. Reservations are available only in the winter.

There is only one bus stop in Brunnen so you can't go wrong. It is about 300 meters from the campground. The bus services both the castles and Füssen. You can also easily use your bike or walk to either destination. There are good bike trails all over the area. An especially nice trail follows the lake shore to Füssen. Bicycles are available for rent at the campground.

To find the campground take B17 northeast from Füssen about 4 km (2.5 miles) to Schwangau. In the middle of Schwangau you will see the signs pointing left for Brunnen or Forggensee and for camping. Follow the road, Seestrasse, 2 km (1.2 miles) to the end.

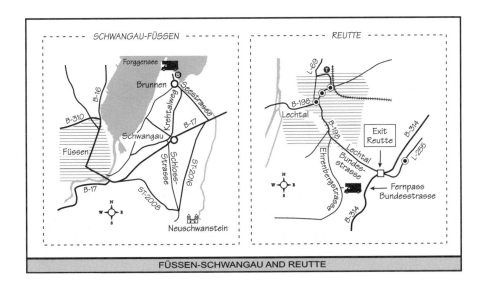

FÜSSEN-SCHWANGAU AND REUTTE

Reutte Campground

▲ CAMPING REUTTE

Address: Ehrenbergstrasse 53, A-6600 Reutte
Telephone: 05672 62809
Fax: 05672 62809 4
Website: www.camping-reutte.com
E-mail: camping-reutte@aon.at
GPS: N 47° 28' 40.0", E 010° 43' 23.1"

June 1 - April 30

High season for this campground is the winter, take a look at that interesting schedule of the months they are open.

This campground is a very large field of well-clipped grass with paved driveways. Electricity is convenient to the sites (Euro, 16 amp, metered). Restroom facilities are modern and clean with free hot water for showers, basins, and dishes. There's even a sauna. The walk in to central Reutte is less than a kilometer and there you'll find shopping of all kinds.

You can easily find the campground from the B314 Fernpass Bundesstrasse which bypasses Reutte to the east. Take the B198 exit for Reutte and travel toward town for 0.9 km (.6 mile). Turn left on Ehrenbergstrasse, the campground entrance will be on your left in 0.7 km (.4 mile).

CHURCH SITTING BELOW NEUSCHWANSTEIN CASTLE

DRIVE 7 – FÜSSEN TO MUNICH
152 Kilometers (94 Miles), 2 Hours

Along The Way – Today's drive takes the scenic route back to Munich with a great stop en route.

From Füssen drive south into Austria toward Reutte. About 16 kilometers (10 miles) south of Füssen turn onto B187 (marked Ehrwalder Bundesstrasse) which will take you east to the German border. At the border the road becomes B23. A few kilometers east near Grainau follow signs to the right to the Zugspitze parking lot.

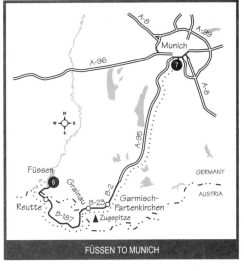

FÜSSEN TO MUNICH

The **Zugspitze** is the highest mountain in Germany. You can ride a cable car to the station on the top for what fantastic views of southern Germany and the surrounding mountains. It's an experience you won't want to miss.

Back on the highway continue east through Garmisch-Partenkirchen. B23 soon becomes B2 and then the A95 autobahn. The A95 will take you all the way back to Munich.

Information Resources

See our Internet site at www.rollinghomes.com for many links to information sources.

German National Tourist Office, Chanin Building, 122 East 42nd Street, 52nd Floor, New York, NY 10168-0072 (323 655-6085). In Canada, PO Box 65162, Toronto, Ontario M4K 3Z2 (416 968-0372).

Austrian National Tourist Office, P.O. Box 1142, New York, NY 10108-1142 (212 944-6880). Use the same office from Canada.

Switzerland Tourism, 608 Fifth Ave, New York, NY 10020 (877 794-8037). Use the same office from Canada.

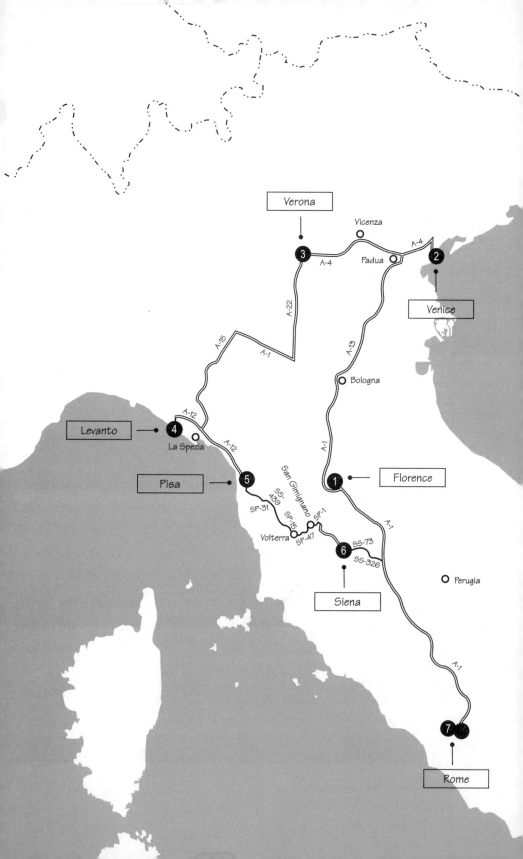

Chapter 10

Tour 7

Italy

Top Attractions

- ❖ Rome
- ❖ Florence
- ❖ Venice
- ❖ Verona
- ❖ Cinque Terre
- ❖ Leaning Tower of Pisa
- ❖ Piazza del Campo in Siena
- ❖ Duomo in Siena

General Description

This tour of Italy is a wonderful way to visit some of Italy's most interesting and popular sights. Total driving distance is 1,425 kilometers (884 miles). That's not bad since we'll be traveling on the autostradas on the long days.

The weather is mild in Italy, at least compared with that north of the Alps. Campground openings would allow you to do this tour any time from March 1 to November 15. If you skipped Verona and the Cinque Terre it could be done any time of the year. It can be fun to visit Rome, Florence and Venice when the crowds are not there. Winter camping in a tent wouldn't be fun, but with an RV you might give it a try.

Due to the distance involved and the slow nature of Italian secondary roads most driving is on the autostradas, an easy way to make sure you'll have enough time to explore these fascinating towns.

The gateway city is Rome, it can keep you occupied for many days before or after your motoring travels. It's also has decent air connections and vehicle rental outlets.

The first drive takes you north on the autostrada to Florence. The most popular campground here, Michelangelo, overlooks the central area of town which is dominated by the dome of the Duomo.

Drive two takes you northeast, again on autostradas, to the city of Venice. This is a great city to visit as a camper, access to the city from both campgrounds listed here is by boat.

On the third driving day you head west to Verona, the city of Romeo and Juliet. Verona also has a Roman amphitheater.

The following drive takes you south to the Adriatic Coast and one of Europe's most interesting hiking destinations, the Cinque Terre. The campground in Levanto offers easy access by train in just minutes to any of the Cinque Terre towns, you can plan your own hiking itinerary between them.

Drive five is a relatively short one south to Pisa. The campground is a 15-minute stroll from the leaning tower.

The next drive goes south through Tuscany to Sienna. Along the way you can stop and see two interesting Tuscan towns, Volterra and San Gimignano. The campground in Siena offers good bus service into town.

The final drive of the tour routes you east to the autostrada and south to Rome. Once there you can either catch a flight or spend several more days exploring the city.

Roads and Driving

Italian driving has a certain reputation, just as German driving does. When we picture the German driver we see a large powerful car speeding down the autobahn. When we picture Italian driving we see crowded roads with aggressive drivers in small cars honking their horns and shaking their fists. The stories about crazy Italian drivers are largely an exaggeration, but many of them are aggressive. Most Italian drivers are very good, the driving environment is just less structured than the ones most of us are accustomed to. You're likely to see Italian drivers making some maneuvers that will astound you by their audacity. On the other hand, we've found Italian drivers to be amazingly considerate when it comes to putting up with comparatively large and slow RVs. Just make sure to "check your six" for passing traffic before making any left or right turns.

Italy is also motor scooter country. They're more common here than in any other west European country and they often disregard the traffic rules. It is entirely normal for scooters and mopeds to thread through traffic ignoring lights and signs. You must never change lanes, even a little, without double checking to see if a scooter might be coming up behind you in a blind spot.

Italy has a fine system of expressways, called autostradas. Since this is a mountainous country you will see very impressive highway engineering in the form of huge bridges, viaducts, and tunnels. Autostradas are toll roads, you can expect to pay about .05 euro per kilometer for an automobile, a little more for vans and motorhomes, and cars with trailers paying a little more still. Secondary roads are also pretty good, but they are often crowded and they tend to run through many small towns. If you want to travel any longer distance in Italy you will probably soon find yourself on an autostrada, and you will be glad to be there.

On maps and signs the autostradas are designated with an "A" prefix, other state roads have a "SS" prefix with one, two, or three digits in the numeric designation. A smaller number of digits indicates a larger and better road.

Speed limits in Italy are as follows unless otherwise marked: towns and built-up areas – 50 kph, highways – 90 kph, limited-access highways – 130 kph.

It is not advisable to take your vehicle into the cities, particularly the larger ones. Traffic is heavy and roads are sometimes narrow. Parking is very difficult and even if you should find a space your vehicle will probably not be safe while you are away. Break-ins are very common. The best strategy is to leave your car or RV in a campground and use public transportation.

Camping and Campgrounds

Italy is a wonderful country for a visit. Camping is very popular here. Italians own and manufacture lots of motorhomes, their small Italian-built class C's are known for modern design, some of the nicest in Europe. There are over two thousand campgrounds in the country, almost any town or city of any size will have one.

This is not a homogenous country. In general, the farther north you are the more affluent the people. Northern Italy may remind you of Germany while southern Italy is more like Portugal or even rural Mexico. The whole country, however, offers great food and wine and many things to see. Remember that Italy was home to the Roman Empire and the Renaissance, not to mention the Catholic Church.

The overall level of quality of Italian camping facilities is somewhat uneven. There are modern campgrounds with excellent sanitation standards and there are older places where standards are barely passable. Most localities do have campgrounds, cities tend to be well serviced since many Italians use their motorhomes for business travel. A general rule with many exceptions is that the north has better and more modern campgrounds than the south.

Since temperatures are mild in southern and central Italy the shower/toilet buildings are often only partially enclosed and unheated. Continental toilets are common. Showers are sometimes preset at coolish temperatures but are usually free. Cleaning can be hit-or-miss.

Electricity is usually inexpensive. This is possible because Italian campgrounds often have very low ampere breaker settings. Three amperes is not uncommon. That's just enough to run lights and a refrigerator but nothing else. You'll find Euro (CEE17) outlets in common use with German-style outlets in the older campgrounds.

Free camping is common in Italy as long as local regulations do not prohibit it. You'll often see large numbers of people camping in public parking lots. Sometimes they've been moved out by the next day but frequently the parking lot is really a designated camping area.

A Camping Card International is not usually required in Italy but if you don't

SMALL GROCERY MARKETS ARE COMMON IN EUROPEAN CAMPGROUNDS

have one you will probably have to give up your passport for the length of your stay in the campground.

Practical Tips

You should be able to easily find large supermarkets in Italy. They are usually located in the suburbs near major arterials. In the central areas of cities the stores tend to be much smaller, try looking in department stores; they often have a grocery section. In smaller towns and villages, particularly in the south, the traditional small meat, vegetable, bread, hard good, and even milk shops will be your source of groceries.

Italy is part of the EU and uses the euro. You should often be able to use your credit or debit card. Look for a sign saying Carta Si indicating acceptance of Visa and Master Charge. Many gas stations will accept cards, even American Express and Diners Club (very popular). Cash machines are common in cities and in tourist towns and we have not had any problems using them with our American debit cards.

THE TOUR – ITALY

TOUR 7 GATEWAY CITY – ROME (ROMA), ITALY
Population 3,900,000

All roads really don't lead to Rome these days, but many Italian autostradas do lead to the GRA autostrada, Rome's ring road. Once established on the GRA you have a number of campgrounds to choose from, many actually have signs right on the autostrada. You can easily drive directly to any of the three Rome campgrounds that we describe below without really getting involved with heavy Rome city traffic.

After you've checked into the campground and set up your camp it is time to see Rome. One good first day strategy is to head for the Piazza del Popolo which is situated at the north end of central Rome. From Camping Tiber or Camping Flaminio you can catch the north suburban rail metro line directly to the Piazza, from Camping Roma it is two busses and 45 minutes away.

Once at the **Piazza del Popolo** you have a choice. You can transfer to the metro line and go west toward (but not all the way to) the Vatican or you can head the opposite direction and get off at the Colosseum stop. Save those possibilities for later and just stroll south from the Piazza on Via del Corso. Many of the famous sights of Rome are located short distances to the left and right of this narrow city street. About 800 meters after leaving the Piazza you'll reach a cross street named Via Condotti. If you turn left here you'll be walking down a famous shopping street and soon reach the **Piazza di Spagna** and the **Spanish Steps**. Returning to Via del Corso and con-tinuing south you'll see signs directing you left to the **Trevi Fountain**, right to the **Pantheon** (and on its far side the **Piazza Navona**), and finally reach the **Piazza Venezia**. Facing you across it is the **Vittorio Emanuele Monument** with the **Capitoline Hill** just behind it. To the left is the **Forum** and if you walk down Mussolini's Via dei Fori Imperiali for about a kilometer you'll arrive at the **Colosseum**. Join the crowds to take a look and then catch the subway back to the Piazza Popolo. You've just taken a four-kilometer walk that passed right through the heart of Rome. You'll probably find yourself following variations of this path many times during your visit.

Rome is truly full of things to see. Besides the Roman excavations and land-marks you'll find dozens of churches (many with great masterpieces inside), hun-dreds of Renaissance and baroque architectural triumphs, and many piazzas full of fountains and tables where you can relax and enjoy the passing show.

The **Vatican City** is a venue which can easily occupy you for a day or days. You can walk there from the Piazza dei Popolo, or use the metro or bus system. Try attend-ing a mass in **St. Peter's**, be blessed by the Pope in the **Piazza San Pietro**, lose yourself in the **Vatican Museums** and the **Sistine Chapel**.

When you are temporarily overcome by monuments and museums sample the cafes and trattorias in the piazzas. Try the piazza in front of the Pantheon or the nearby Piazza Navona. After dark visit the Piazza di Spagna with its Spanish Steps or the Trevi Fountain. The **Trastevere district** on the far side of the Tiber is a good place to

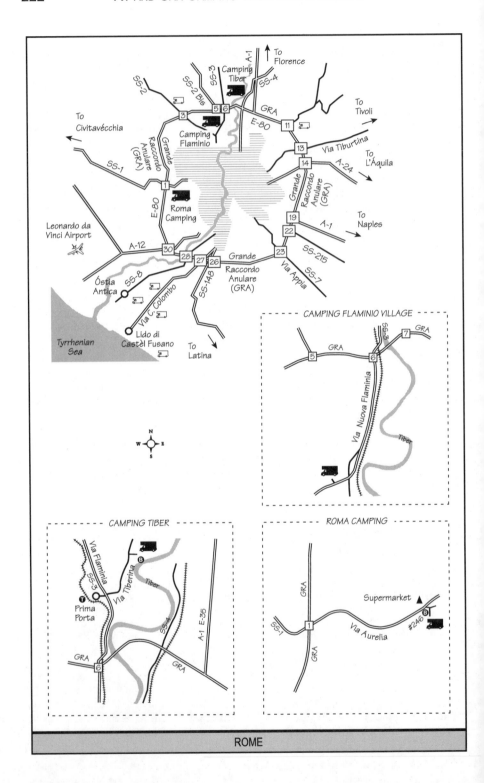

ROME

find reasonably priced restaurants and an active street scene.

Óstia Antica is an excavated Roman city which rivals Pompeii. It was the ancient seaport to Rome, gradually abandoned and covered by silt from the Tiber. It has now been excavated and covers a large area. Many people find it much like Pompeii and a lot easier to visit. To drive there take Exit 28 from the GRA on the west side of Rome and head for the coast on Via del Mare. Fourteen kilometers from the GRA you'll spot the sign for Ostia Antica, the site is on the right.

Tivoli, about 30 kilometers from the GRA on the northeast side of Rome, has two well-known attractions. The first is the excavations of the emperor **Hadrian's Villa**. These can be rewarding and uncrowded, particularly if you are visiting on a weekday outside the high season. Pick a good weather day. You will also find the **Villa d'Este** in Tivoli. It is famous for its gardens and hundreds of fountains. The Villa d' Este dates from a much later time than Hadrian's Villa, they were built by a Catholic cardinal in the sixteenth century. To reach Tivoli take the No. 13 exit from the GRA and follow Via Tiburtina (SS5) northeast. Approaching Tivoli you will see signs for Villa Adriana (Hadrian's Villa).

Rome Campgrounds

▲ CAMPING TIBER

Address:	Via Tibernia Km 1.4, I-00188
	Roma (Prima Porta)
Telephone:	06 33610733
Fax:	06 33612314
Website:	www.campingtiber.com
E-mail:	info@campingtiber.com
GPS:	N 42° 00' 37.9", E 012° 30' 08.2"

March 7 - Oct 30 (Varies)

Camping Tiber is a good choice as your first campground when visiting Rome. Its location on the outside of the GRA means you can easily park and avoid city traffic.

The campground is a large grassy field next to the Tiber River. There are very few permanent rigs, this is a tourist campground. Camping sites are not marked or assigned. Electrical boxes (Euro, 6 amp) are scattered but there are quite a few. The shower/toilet facilities are recently improved, there's a new restroom building. Hot water for showers (not adjustable) is free. The campground has a restaurant, bar, grocery shop, and swimming pool. There is a laundry room with coin-operated washer and room for hanging clothes to dry.

Access to Rome from this camping area is easy. The campground has its own bus, which during the high season, will deposit you at the Prima Porta metro station. Walking to the station is an easy twenty minutes, but why not ride, you'll walk plenty once you get in to town. The metro in to the center of the city runs every ten minutes or so, tickets are available at the station. The train runs above ground until just before reaching central Rome so you can get some idea of what the countryside looks like. This line runs only as far as the Roma-Viterbo station. The station is located just north of the Piazza di Popolo, you can walk down the Via Del Corso from here or catch the

A line of the subway. There are stalls at the station selling maps and guidebooks.

To find the campground take the first Exit 6 (assuming you are heading west), the one going north, not far west of where the A1 highway from the north intersects the GRA. You will be on a four lane highway (Via Flaminia) for about a 1.8 km (1.1 mile) and then exit to the right onto Via Tiberina. The campground is another 1.2 km (.7 mile) from the exit, you can follow the campground signs which actually start on the GRA itself.

▲ CAMPING FLAMINIO VILLAGE

Address:	Via Flaminia Nuova 821, I-00191 Roma
Telephone:	06-3332604
Fax:	06-3330653
Website:	www.villageflaminio.com
E-mail:	info@villageflaminio.com
GPS:	N 41° 57' 30.4", E 012° 28' 49.8"

March 15 - Dec 31

Camping Flaminio is an extremely large campground occupying a large south-sloping wooded hillside and the flat area below it. Camping sites are unnumbered and unassigned. Many trees provide quite a bit of shade. There are very few permanent residents at this campground. Electrical outlets (Euro, 3 amp) are provided for many of the sites. Facilities here have been run down for many years but some effort now seems to be underway to improve them. The shower/toilet building is older and not luxurious, hot showers (pushbutton, premixed) are free, as is hot water in bathroom basins. Dishwashing water is cold. Many of the toilets are continental. The campground has a restaurant, bar, and store together on a site on the hill, there is also a pool and playground. Laundry facilities with coin-operated machines are at the shower/toilet building. A new shopping center nearby provides a good place to get groceries. If you are a runner, bike rider, or just want to stretch your legs, there is a great bike path just on the far side of the nearby Due Ponte station. It runs along the river all the way to the center.

Access to downtown Rome from Campground Flaminio is similar to that from Campground Tiber. The same metro line runs just across the street from the campground, get instructions at the reception desk on how to walk to the station because it is really quite difficult to find. Ask how to safely cross the highway, don't attempt to sprint across, this is suicidal. The station, Due Ponti, is small and unattended. It is a request stop, heading out from Rome make sure to push the button to let the driver know that you want to stop. Heading in to town the train will stop when the driver sees you waiting. Campground Flaminio has decent bus service, you can also use it to get in to downtown Rome, it just will take longer than using the train. Bus tickets are available at the reception desk, you can't buy metro tickets at the campground but should be able to get day passes good on all public transportation.

To reach Campground Flaminio you take Exit 6 from the GRA on the north side of Rome, just as for Camping Tiber, but this time take the Exit 6 that leads south and head towards central Rome on the Via Flaminia Nuova. Follow the campground signs, in three kilometers (1.9 miles) the road splits with the right fork appearing to go into a tunnel (actually an underpass), you take the left fork, still following Via Flaminia

Nuova. It is easy to get stuck in the right lane so be alert. Immediately after this fork you will see the sign for the campground, it is located on the right side of the road.

▲ ROMA CAMPING

Address:	Via Aurélia 831, I-00165 Roma:
Telephone:	06 6623018
Fax:	06 66418147
GPS:	N 41° 53' 16.3", E 012° 24' 14.6"

Open All Year

The advantage that Camping Roma has over Camping Tiber and Camping Flaminio is that it is really easier to find. You don't have to negotiate the maze of off-ramps and camping signs on the GRA (ring road) in the vicinity of Exit No. 6. Camping Roma is also nice because it has a large supermarket just across the highway with a convenient pedestrian overpass.

This is a medium-size campground situated on a small hill above the Via Aurelia, which is really a four-lane autostrada at this point. Traffic noise is a fact of life here, you get used to it. Sites are on grass off gravel and dirt circular access roads, they are unmarked and unassigned. Many trees provide shade. Electricity (Euro, 3 amp) is available but you'll need a long cord for some sites. The shower/toilet buildings are very basic, hot water showers are provided but there is no hot water in bathroom basins or for dishwashing. There are just a few stool-type toilets, most are continental. The campground has a small grocery shop and a snack bar but shopping across the highway is much better.

Access to Rome from the campground is by bus. The Number 246 stops at the gate every 15 minutes and quickly drops you at the Largo Boccea where you switch to the 46, 49, or 490. These three busses will drop you just about anywhere in Rome that you could wish to visit. The time from the campground to Piazza del Popolo is about 45 minutes. In high season there's a shuttle to the nearest metro station.

To reach the campground take Exit 1 from the GRA ring road to the west of Rome. Head towards the city on Via Aurelia for about 2 kilometers (1.2 miles). When you see the big supermarket on the left take the off-ramp to the right, the campground entrance is on the right just after you exit the Via Aurelia. The entire route is well signed.

DRIVE 1 – ROME TO FLORENCE
260 Kilometers (161 Miles), 3 Hours

A long The Way – From Rome follow the A1DIR and A1 north to Florence. It's an easy drive on a good autostrada. In Italy the secondary roads can be really slow, particularly when passing through towns so count your blessings.

When you reach the Florence on the A1 autostrada take the Firenze Sud exit. Detailed instructions for driving to the Florence campgrounds are included in the campground descriptions below.

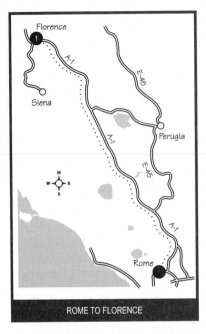

ROME TO FLORENCE

FLORENCE (FIRENZE), ITALY
Population 460,000

If you go to Italy, you must go to Florence. The city is synonymous with the Renaissance, definitely one of the top destinations in Italy, some would say the most important stop in the country. The whole old town is a virtual museum.

Florence is a pleasure to visit. Besides the well know sights the town has a good English-language book store and also an English-language movie house. Restaurants around the central walking streets are expensive, but only a few blocks away there are nice places with reasonable prices.

During the Renaissance the Medici family was such an active patron of the arts that the city became the ultimate center of artistic endeavors. On the must-see list is the **Uffizi Gallery** which contains one of the world's great collections of Italian Renaissance paintings. Nearby in the **Academy Gallery** the city's signature sculpture, Michelangelo's towering **David,** attracts legions of admirers. Florence also has a great Romanesque cathedral, known as the **Duomo**. It is the fourth largest in the world, and is known for its large dome, prototype for most of the others you'll see throughout Europe. The dome has unfortunately started cracking, and is being repaired. Don't let this stop you from climbing to the top and trying to spot your rig up in the campground. In front of the Duomo is the **baptistery** with its renown bronze doors. You can cross the mediaeval **Ponte Vecchio** to reach the **Pitti Palace** with its museum and the **Boboli Gardens**.

Florence Campgrounds

▲ CAMPEGGIO MICHELANGELO

Address:	Viale Michelangelo 80, I-50125 Firenze
Telephone:	055 681197
Fax:	055 689348
Website:	www.ecvacanze.it
E-mail:	Michelangelo@ecvacanze.it
GPS:	N 43° 45' 43.4", E 011° 16' 06.8"

Open All Year

Camping Michelangelo is one of the best-known and loved campgrounds in Europe. Don't even think of coming to Florence and staying anywhere else unless it is either full or closed. The campground sits just below the Piazzale Michelangelo, a parking plaza south of the Arno river overlooking the old section of Florence. The Piazzale is reputed to have one of the best views in Europe, and the campground has almost the same view. It is within two km of the centrally-located Ponte Vecchio so

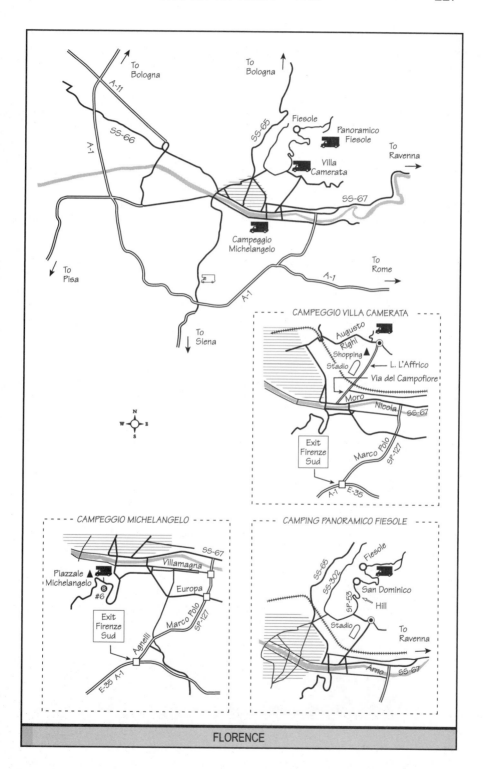

FLORENCE

most of the things you will want to see are within easy walking distance.

Camping sites are unmarked and unassigned. They are on grass and under olive trees on terraces scattered down the hill from the entrance. Sometimes it is difficult to find a good flat parking spot, especially when the site is crowded. The largest flat sites are near the bottom. Electrical outlets (Euro, 3 amp) are widely scattered. Hot showers are free, as is hot water for basins and dishwashing sinks. The campground has a grocery shop and a snack bar. Arrive early in the day, this is a popular campground. Bus service to and from the railroad station is via Number 6, the campground stop is know as Camping.

From the A1 autostrada take the Firenze Sud exit. After leaving the toll booth continue on the four lane highway north for 4 kilometers (2.5 miles) towards Florence until it terminates just after the Arno bridge. Turn left here and follow the Arno north bank for 2.0 kilometers (1.2 miles), then turn left and cross the bridge. Turn right

MICHELANGELO'S DAVID

immediately on the other side and drive west for .7 kilometers (.4 miles) to an inter-section. Here you want to turn left and go away from the river on Viale Michelangelo but local traffic flow engineering (one way streets) will make you jog a block to the left and then to the right before you can get on the Viala. Watch for the international camping sign and signs for Piazzale Michelangelo. Once on Viale Michelangelo you'll wind to the right and the campground will be on your right near the top of the hill, about 2 kilometers (1.2 miles) from where you left the river. An easy way to find Camping Michelangelo is to follow signs for Piazzale Michelangelo, the campground is on the right just before you reach the Piazzale.

▲ CAMPEGGIO VILLA CAMERATA

Address:	Viale Augusto Righi 2/4, I-50137 Firenze
Telephone:	055 601451
Fax:	055 610300
GPS:	N 43° 47' 05.4", E 011° 17' 34.7"

Open All Year

A good alternative to Camping Michelangelo is Camping Villa Camerata. The view is not as good but it is almost as convenient with good bus service (No. 17B to/from the railway station) or a 45-minute walk in to town.

This medium-sized campground is located on the grounds of a large hostel. It is a tourist campground with no permanent residents. There are three different camping areas: a tent-only area, a tent/RV area with sites on grass that is often closed when the campground is not full, and a gravel and grass parking area for RVs. Sites are marked but not assigned. Electrical outlets (Euro, 5 amp) are widely spaced. The shower/toilet buildings are old and it is sometimes possible to use the nicer ones inside the hostel building. The showers (premixed, pushbutton valves) are hot, water to basins is cold, and the toilets are not continental. There is a good supermarket about a kilometer from the campground in the direction of downtown Florence.

Camping Villa Camerata is located northeast of central Florence. From the A1 autostrada take the Firenze Sud exit. After leaving the toll booth continue on the four lane highway north for 4 kilometers (2.5 miles) towards Florence until it terminates just after the Arno bridge. Turn left here and follow the Arno north bank for 2.3 kilometers (1.4 miles), then turn right on Via del Campofiore following signs for Fiesole. Proceed north on this road (it soon changes names but continue straight ahead) for 2.6 kilometers (1.6 miles), you will see occasional campground signs. At 2.6 kilometers (1.6 miles) turn left at a small semi-roundabout and then almost immediately right into the campground/hostel driveway.

▲ CAMPING PANORAMICO FIESOLE

Address:	Via Peramonda 1, I-50014 Fiesole
Telephone:	055 599069
Fax:	055 59186
Website:	www.florencecamping.com
E-mail:	panoramico@florencecamping.com
GPS:	N 43° 48' 24.5", E 011° 18' 22.0"

Open All Year

Camping Panoramico is located in Fiesole, a mountaintop suburb about 7 kilometers from downtown Florence. There is frequent city bus service up to Fiesole. The town is thought to be even older than Florence. Inhabitants of this Etruscan village may have founded the city spread out below.

The campsite is located at the very crest of a hill some 1.5 kilometers beyond the village of Fiesole. The sites are arranged on terraces facing in all directions. The terraces are often narrow and might provide a maneuvering problem for caravans (trailers) or larger rigs. Many different species of trees provide shade and almost every site has a good view. Electricity (Euro, 3 amp) is available to most sites. The shower/toilet buildings are older but well maintained and clean. Free hot water is available for showers (adjustable), bathroom basins, and dishwashing sinks. The campground has a grocery shop, snack bar/bar, and dump station.

Bus transportation to Florence is from the square in Fiesole (Bus 7). Reaching it

FEEDING THE PIGEONS IN VENICE'S ST. MARK'S SQUARE IS ALWAYS FUN

requires a hike of about 1.5 kilometers (.9 miles). A minibus provides limited transportation to the bus during high season. Using a bike to get into Florence is not advisable unless you are in good shape, the hill on the way back wouldn't be much fun.

To reach the campground follow the instructions given for the campground at Villa Camerata above. After passing Villa Camerata continue to the stop sign, then turn right and proceed up the hill. After 4 km (2.5 miles) or so you'll pass through the village of Fiesole and in another kilometer you'll see the a campground sign pointing right up a small steep road. Follow this road for another half-kilometer as it winds up to the campground entrance. The combination of the steep access road and limited maneuvering room in the campground make this a poor choice for large trailers and large motorhomes.

DRIVE 2 – FLORENCE TO VENICE
260 Kilometers (161 Miles), 3 Hours

A long The Way – From Florence follow the A1 north to Bologna. The distance is about 100 kilometers (62 miles). **Bologna** is a great city to stop for a few hours to stretch your legs and look around.

Bologna has a convenient central location on the main autostrada between the north and Rome. This is a rich town famous for its food. Window-shop along its covered arcades and make a visit to a good restaurant. You can do some sightseeing in the neighborhood of the central **Piazza Maggiore**, make sure to see Bologna's leaning towers, the **Torre degli Asinelli** and the **Torre Garisenda**. They are similar to the ones in San Gimignano which you will see later in the tour. There were once almost 200 of them in Bologna. The **Pinacoteca Nazionale** art gallery has many paintings by Italian masters. Bologna was a leading university town in the Middle Ages, at one time over 10,000 pupils were registered.

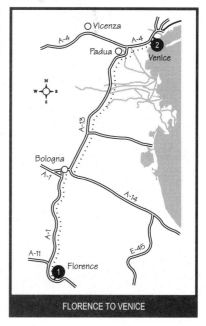

From Bologna continue northwest on A13 to Padua and then the A4 to Venice. The distance to Venice is 140 kilometers (91 miles).

The Venice campgrounds located below are widely separated. See the individual campground descriptions for driving directions.

VENICE (VENÉZIA), ITALY
Population 65,000

Venice really needs no introduction. Everyone knows the delights of the city of canals. What everyone doesn't know is that Venice is one of the best cities in Europe to visit as a camper. The city is surrounded by campgrounds, many with convenient boat transportation into town. We'll give you

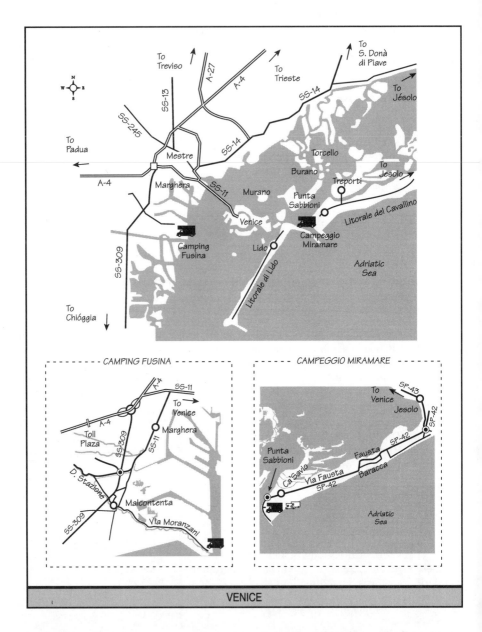

information about two of these, one on the mainland west of Venice and the other at Punta Sabbioni on the peninsula between Venice's lagoon and the ocean.

The real joy of Venice is the atmosphere. This is a town that has never known automobiles and for that reason it really is a city out of the past. While there are many things to see, the most enjoyable pastime is just wandering the streets. Keep a good map in hand but don't worry, getting lost is half the fun.

The most enduring image of Venice is probably the gondolas. You may not feel that a visit is complete until you have taken a ride in one. Be warned, they are very expensive! You do not have to worry about being stuck on shore, however. The busses of Venice are the vaporetti, covered boats that ply the canals. They're easy to use and convenient.

The countryside inland from Venice was used by her wealthier families for country villas. During the 16th century many were designed by Andrea Palladio in a style called Palladian. In the U.S. both Monticello and Mount Vernon have elements of this style. The town of **Vicenza** is the best place to see his work.

Venice Campgrounds

▲ CAMPING FUSINA

Address:	Via Moranzani 79, Fusina, I-30030, Venezia
Telephone:	041 5470055
Fax:	041 5470050
Website:	www.camping-fusina.com
E-mail:	info@camping-fusina.com
GPS:	N 45° 25' 10.0", E 012° 15' 21.5"

Open All Year

Fusina is a large campground located on the edge of the Venice lagoon near the industrial town of Marghera. There is a great view of Venice across the water and the

CAMPING WITH A VIEW OF VENICE AT THE FUSINA CAMPGROUND

only intrusion from the surroundings is the large ships passing directly in front of the campground in a ship channel not 50 meters from the shore. Free entertainment!

Campsites are on a grass field with quite a few shade trees and are not numbered or assigned. Electricity is available from widely scattered boxes (Euro, 6 amp). Toilet/shower facilities have improved over the past few years and now there is free hot water for showers, basins, and dishwashing. The campground has a restaurant, grocery shop, and also a dump station. There is a ferry service over to Venice, usually in small boats. Runs are made every hour or so and the trip takes about a half-hour. It is convenient but a little pricey.

The campground is well signed and easy to find from both the A4 autostrada and from Highway SS11. From the autostrada take the first off-ramp after the toll booth as you approach Venice and take the first right on the traffic circle under the autostrada. This should put you on SS309. At the next traffic circle in 2.5 km (1.5 miles) take the third exit (actually by doing this you continue straight). You should see the first campground sign about here and will find them at every turn until you reach the campground. After the circle continue for 0.9 km (.6 miles), turn left. In 0.5 kilometer (.3 miles) turn right at a T. In 1 km (.6 miles) turn left and in another 4.7 km (2.9 miles) you'll be at the campground.

▲ CAMPEGGIO MIRAMARE

Address:	Lungomare Dante Alighieri, 29,
	Punta Sabbioni, I-30010 Venezia
Telephone	
and Fax:	041 966150
Website:	www.camping-miramar.it
E-mail:	info@camping-miramar.it
GPS:	N 45° 26' 25.3", E 012° 25' 17.6"

March 29 - Nov 2 (Varies)

The Litorale del Cavallino, a long peninsula stretching from Jesolo to Punta Sabbioni, encloses a large part of Venice's lagoon. There are campgrounds standing shoulder to shoulder all along this beach for miles and miles. One of the smaller but most convenient of these is Camping Miramare with about 150 sites. Just to give you some idea, the Marina de Venezia just down the road has 3,000 sites. In August there is a three-day minimum stay at this campground.

Camping Miramare is the closest campground to the ferry, it sits separate from the others across from a small beach on the entrance to the lagoon, not the outer beach. Camping is on sandy grass, sites are separated by shrubs and trees. There are no permanent units here. Electricity (various plug types including Euro, 6 amp) is available to most sites. The shower/toilet buildings are the cleanest we've seen in Italy. Free hot water is provided for showers, bathroom basins, and dishwashing. There's a shop, laundry machines, a playground, and a dump station. A restaurant is located next door and the campground has a nice little supermarket. Across the street is a little beach and 2 km to the left when leaving the campground is the open ocean beach. In high season a shuttle will take you to the beach or to the ferry.

Transport to Venice is extremely convenient. The ferry dock is a half-kilometer from the campground, boats run every half-hour during daylight hours and every hour or so at night. The trip takes about forty minutes including a stop at the Lido. The dock in Venice is just east of St. Mark's square near the Bridge of Sighs. Take the Punta Sabbioni boat when leaving Venice for the campground.

Drive to the campground by continuing east past Venice on the A4 and then traveling around the east side of the lagoon through Jesolo and then following signs to Punta Sabbioni. Go all the way to the end of the peninsula where you'll find the ferry and bus terminal. Turn left along the water, you'll see the Miramare entrance in under a kilometer. The distance from the Venice off-ramp to Punta Sabbioni is about 75 km (47 miles).

DRIVE 3 – VENICE TO VERONA
125 Kilometers (78 Miles), 1.5 Hours

A long The Way – From Venice drive west on A4. This autostrada will take you directly to Verona.

Along the way, 20 kilometers (12 miles) east of Venice is **Padua**. One of Italy's oldest university towns, Padua's patron saint is St. Anthony. Since he's also the saint of lost things many pilgrims who have lost something of importance visit the city's **Basilica del Santo** for help. In addition to being a charming place to wander the streets Padua has the **Scrovegni Chapel** with frescoes by Giotto, it is one of Italy's top artistic attractions.

As you approach Verona continue on the A4 until it meets the A22. Turn north on the A22 and take the Verona Nord exit. Final driving instructions are in the campground description below.

VERONA, ITALY
Population 260,000

Verona, of course, is famous as the setting of Shakespeare's Romeo and Juliet. Some of the sights to see are from that period. **Juliet's home** is a tourist magnet, there is a statue of Juliet and you can take a picture of her balcony. We also found the 14th-

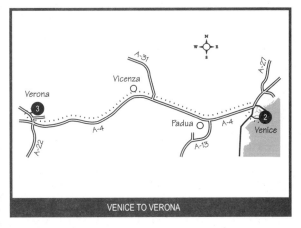

VENICE TO VERONA

century **Scaligeri Castle** and the **fortified bridge** over the Adige River to be interesting. The castle was the home of the Scaligeri family, the rulers of the town during the period in which Shakespeare set the play.

Verona was also an important Roman town. There is a huge **Roman amphitheater** now used for opera performances, and Roman ruins have been excavated in the old town near the **Piazza delle Erbe**. Tourist action centers around this piazza, near

Juliet's home, which has cafes with outside seating and vendor stalls set up in the middle of the square. The streets around the square form a pedestrian area with shops and restaurants.

Verona Campground

▲ Camping Romeo e Giulietta

Address:	Via Bresciana 54, I-37139 Verona
Phone:	045 8510243
E-mail:	camping_verona@tin.it
GPS:	N 45° 26' 49.5", E 010° 54' 45.2"

March 1 - Nov 30 (Varies)

This is a large campground totally devoted to tourist campers. Campsites are on grass and are divided by hedges. Electricity (Euro, 4-6 amp) is convenient to the sites. The shower/toilet building is modern and clean, hot water is provided for showers (pushbutton valves), bathroom basins, dish and clothes-washing sinks. The campground also has a swimming pool, a bar with snacks and a very small grocery shop. On the road toward town you'll find two large supermarkets with lots of parking.

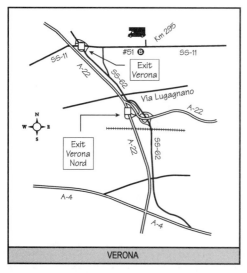

There is a bus stop just outside the campground with service to town. Busses run approximately every hour, you want the Number 51. The distance to town is 5 km (3.1 miles).

The campground is most easily reached from the Verona Nord exit of the autostrada that crosses the Brenner Pass, the A22. Upon exiting the toll plaza continue straight ahead so that you are driving north along the side road (SS62) next to the autostrada. After 2 km (1.2 miles) take the right onto SS11 toward Verona. The campground will be on your left in 1.7 km (1 mile) near the Km 295 marker.

If approaching on secondary roads from the direction of Verona take SS11 toward Peschiera. The campground is near Km 295 on the right.

Drive 4 – Verona to Levanto
288 Kilometers (179 Miles), 3 Hours

A long The Way – From Verona drive south on A22 until you reach theA1. The distance is 86 kilometers (53 miles).

On the A1 drive northwest for 53 kilometers (33miles) until you reach the A15.

On the A15 drive south to the intersection with the A12 near La Spezia. The distance is 99 kilometers (61 miles).

Follow the A12 northwest for 24 kilometers (15 miles) to the exit marked Carrodano and Levanto. Follow the signs down to the coast and Levanto. See the campground description below for final driving instructions.

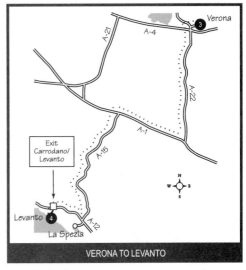

VERONA TO LEVANTO

LEVANTO AND THE CINQUE TERRE, ITALY

The Cinque Terre, a series of five tiny towns perched above the Gulf of Genoa, has become a top destination for travelers searching for an unique experience. The five villages: **Riomaggiore, Manarola, Corniglia, Vernazza, and Monterosso;** seem isolated but are in fact linked by walking trails, rail, and even narrow winding roads. The roads are virtually unnoticed because they approach from high above and

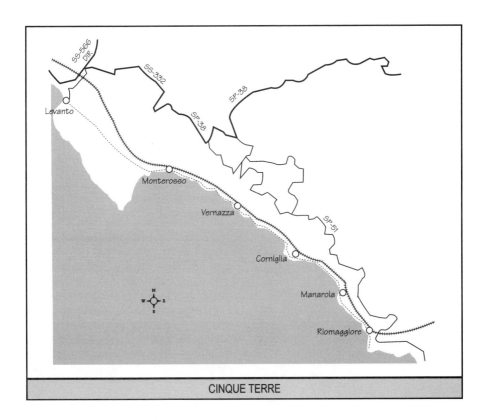

CINQUE TERRE

do not actually enter most of these towns. The rail is almost entirely inside the cliffs so it is equally unobtrusive. The tracks only make a fleeting appearance in each village and then disappear again into the tunnels. Visitors hike the breathtaking trails between the towns, pause for rest and refreshment when they wish, and use the frequent trains for cheap and convenient backup transportation. The usual strategy is to use the train to get to either Monterosso or Riomaggiore, walk until you are tired, and then hitch a train ride home.

The trail between the towns varies in difficulty. Riomaggiore to Manarola is a flat wide path that takes about 30 minutes. Manarola to Corniglia is a little more strenuous but still pretty easy, plan on about 45 minutes. Corniglia to Vernazza and Vernazza to Monterosso are both relatively difficult with lots of up and down sections. They will take from an hour and a half to two hours each. These are, of course, just average times. It is also possible to follow an even more difficult trail north to Levanto from Monterosso, but the route is not well marked. It takes at least two hours.

Cinque Terre Campground (Levanto)

▲ Camping Acqua Dolce

Addres:	Via Guido Semenza 5, I-19015 Lévanto
Telephone	
and Fax:	0187 808465
E-mail:	acquadolce@tin.it
GPS:	N 44° 09' 55.2", E 009° 36' 49.8"

March 1 - Nov 15

Levanto is not really part of the Cinque Terre, but it could easily be. It is the next town to the north and sits in a narrow valley fronted by a nice sandy beach. The train

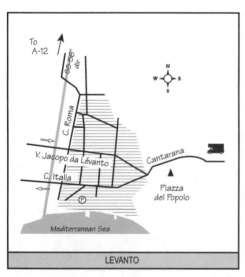

LEVANTO

blasts out of the mountain here for only a hundred meters or so just as it does in the Cinque Terre towns to the south. There are several campgrounds so Levanto is a great base for exploring. The Cinque Terre walking paths actually come as far as Lévanto or the local train can give you access to any Cinque Terre town in just minutes.

Acqua Dolce is a medium-sized campground set on terraces on the south side of Levanto. Olive trees on the terraces provide shade. The area can be crowded in the summer months but the extended opening dates of this campground give you a good opportunity to visit during the shoulder season when there is more room. Camping sites are numbered but not physically separated. Electricity (Euro, 6 amp) is near all of the wheeled-vehicle sites. There are also sites for tents. The shower/toilet building is simple but modern with hot showers requiring payment. Sinks for shaving, dish washing, and laundry all have free hot water. The campground has a bar/pizzeria and dump station. Restaurants, shopping (groceries and other), and the beach are all within easy walking distance.

Levanto itself is most easily reached by taking the Carrodano exit some 25 kilometers north of La Spezia on the A12 autostrada. Once you reach the town the fun has just begun. Although small, it is a maze of one-way streets and the campground signage is poor. Your best bet is to follow the main road (Corso Roma) all the way to the beach, turn around and head back looking for the first one-way road to the right. This is V. Jacopo da Levanto. Turn right here and drive to the end, two blocks, then bear right toward the beach and then left at a park to head inland along the tiny Piazza del Popolo and into Via Cantarana. The campground is just ahead on the left. You'll probably see some campground signs along the route. It is actually easier to drive than to explain.

DRIVE 5 – LEVANTO TO PISA
106 Kilometers (66 Miles), 1.25 Hours

A long The Way – From Levanto drive back up the hill to the A12 and head south. After 81 kilometers (50 miles) on the A12 take the Pisa Nord exit and head south on SS1. After 9.3 kilometers (5.8 miles) on SS1 turn left onto SS12, also called Viale delle Cascine. There is a campground sign at the corner, the campground is on the left just 300 meters down the road.

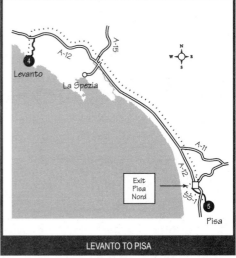

PISA, ITALY
Population 100,000

About 90 kilometers (56 miles) west from Florence is the town of Pisa. Known around the world for its **leaning tower**, Pisa is easy for campers to visit. Of course you must see the tower, and the town's other major sights, the **Duomo (cathedral)** and **Baptistery**, are right next door. All are located on the very large grassy **Field of Miracles (Campo dei Miracoli)**, not a 15-minute walk from the Torre Pendente (Leaning Tower) campground.

Pisa Campground

▲ CAMPEGGIO TORRE PENDENTE DI SIGNORINI MARCO

Address:	Viale delle Cascine 86, I-56122 Pisa
Telephone:	050 561704
Fax:	050 561734
Website:	www.campingtoscana.it/torrependente
E-mail:	torrepen@campingtoscana.it
GPS:	N 43° 43' 26.8", E 010° 22' 59.1"

Easter - Oct 15 (Varies)

You can see the leaning tower peeking around the corner of the Duomo from this campground's entrance so its name appears to be justified. This is a large campground set in a grassy field on the western edge of Pisa. Electricity (Euro, 5 amp) is available to most sites. There are free hot showers and the campground has a bar/restaurant, a small shop, a nice new pool, and a playground. The leaning tower is about 1 kilometer (.6 mile) from the campground, a 15-minute walk. There is also a convenient bus to central Pisa. Along the route to the tower, about 400 meters from the campground, is a nice supermarket.

Find the campground most easily from SS1, a secondary road which runs north and south on the western side of Pisa. Don't try to drive through the town, it is not worth it. Exactly 1.3 kilometers (.8 miles) north of the Arno bridge, at about kilometer 336.5 you'll see a campground sign pointing east down Viale delle Cascine. The campground is 0.3 km (.2 miles) down this road on the left.

DRIVE 6 – PISA TO SIENA
161 Kilometers (100 Miles), 2 Hours

A long The Way – From the campground drive south on the SS1 for 1.5 kilometers. You want to get onto the eastbound Strada de Grande Comunicazione Fi-Pi-Li but the entrance is convoluted and involves driving around a large square block. Make two right-hand turns and following signs for the Strada and you should find yourself at the on-ramp.

Drive east on the autostrada for 17 km (11 miles) to where it merges with SP31, then continue east another 2.4 km (1.5 miles) and take the exit for southbound SS439 (marked Pontedera and Ponsacco).

THE TOWER AND DUOMO IN PISA

Follow SP23, SS439 and then SP15 following signs for Volterra, a distance of 37 km (23 miles). **Volterra** was originally an Etruscan town. It's a walled city with parking outside the walls, you can easily walk in to the central square. The prime attraction here, other than the town itself, is probably the Etruscan museum, the **Museo Etrusco Guaranacci**.

Back on the road, take SS68 eastward for 16 miles and then follow SP47 north to **San Gimignano**. This is another Etruscan town, but it's best known for the 14 towers built during the 13th century. Again, park outside the center and walk in to see the sights.

From San Gimignano drive eastward on SP1 for 13 km (8 miles) (follow signs for Siena) and join the Superstrada Firenze Siena which will carry you the 22 kilometers (14 miles) south to Sienna. Take the Siena Nord exit and then see the driving instructions in the campground write-up below.

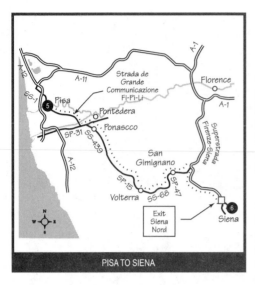

PISA TO SIENA

Siena, Italy
Population 60,000

How can you pass up the chance to visit a town that has a color named after it? A one-time rival to nearby Florence, Siena today is not as well known, which makes it a great place to visit. Today's Siena has only about a third the inhabitants that it did at the height of its power in the fourteenth century.

The life of the town revolves around the **Piazza del Campo**, a very large sloping plaza surrounded by cafes on the upper side and the Gothic **Palazzo Comunale** on the lower. Up the hill from the Campo is the **Duomo**, known as one of Italy's prettiest cathedrals with its black and white marble. The atmosphere in Siena is very quiet, particularly in the off season, you'll want to spend your time wandering the streets or sitting in a cafe on the Campo.

Siena Campground

▲ Siena Colleverde Camping

Address:	Strada Di Scacciapensieri 47, I-53100 Siena
Telephone:	0577 280044
Fax:	0577 333298
E-mail:	campingsiena@siena.turismo.toscana.it
GPS:	N 43° 20' 08.4", E 011° 19' 54.6"

March 28 - Nov 10 (Varies)

This is by far the most convenient campground for visiting Siena. It sits on a hillside about two kilometers northeast of town and offers fine views of the city across the intervening valley.

Camping Colleverde is a medium-sized campground on a sloping site, fortunately there are three large flat areas set aside for motorhomes and trailers. The wheeled vehicle sites are numbered, others are not. There are many nice tent sites here. Electricity is convenient to the wheeled vehicle sites (Euro, 3 amp). The shower/toilet buildings are clean and well maintained, hot showers (adjustable, pushbutton valves) are free in one of the buildings as is hot water in the bathroom wash basins and dishwashing sinks. The campground has a small shop and bar with some take-out food. There is a large swimming pool and also a dump station and laundry machines. Just down the hill from the campground is a good supermarket.

Bus transportation to central Siena is convenient. Bus 8 stops near the campground and will take you to the Piazza Gramsci. You can also easily walk or ride a bicycle to the center of town, the distance is about 3 km.

International camping signs or dump site signs are on all of the approaches to Siena, they direct you to this campground. It is located on the hillside on the northeast side of town, on the far side of the train station. The easiest route is from the Siena Nord exit from the Florence to Siena highway. At the end of the exit ramp turn right and almost immediately (0.2 km, .1 mile) you will come to a traffic circle where you should turn left. In another 1.1 km (.7 mile) turn left again. After 0.8 kilometer (.5 mile) at the roundabout turn left and cross the railroad tracks. In just 0.2 km (.1 mile), turn right at the next roundabout. In another 0.5 km (.3 mile) turn left at another roundabout and proceed up the hill for 1 km (.05 mile) and

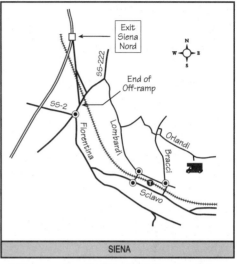

SIENA

turn right. The road will curve around toward Siena and at the T in 0.2 kilometer (.1 mile) turn left. The campground is on the right in 0.8 kilometer (.5 mile). While this sounds complicated the route is well signed at the various turns and should present no problems. Traffic is not overly heavy as you never really get near the center of town.

DRIVE 7 – SIENA TO ROME
225 Kilometers (140 Miles), 2.5 Hours

A long The Way – From Siena follow SS73, also called E78, east for 20 kilometers (12 miles) and then the SS326 another 28 kilometers (17 miles) east to the A1 autopista. Now turn south and follow the A1 for 145 kilometers (90 miles) and then the A1Dir for another 21 kilometers (13 miles) to Rome's GRA ring road.

Information Resources

See our Internet site at www.rollinghomes.com for many links to information sources.

Italian Government Tourist Board, 630 Fifth Avenue, Suite 1565, New York, NY 10111 (212 245-4822). In Canada the address is Suite 907, South Tower, 17 Bloor Street East, Toronto, Ontario M4W 3R8 (416 925-4882).

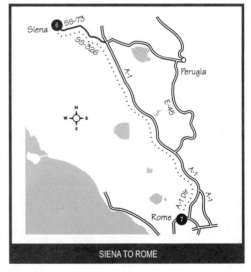

SIENA TO ROME

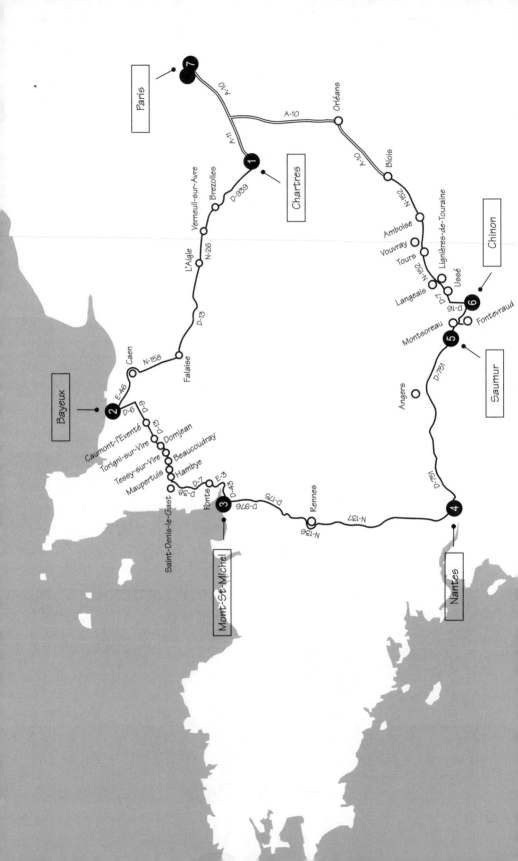

Chapter 11

Tour 8

France 1

Top Attractions

- ❖ Paris
- ❖ Chartres Cathedral
- ❖ Bayeux Tapestry
- ❖ WWII Invasion Beaches
- ❖ Mont-St-Michel
- ❖ Loire Valley

General Description

France is so big, is in such a central location, and has so many attractions that you could spend more time camping here than in any other country in Europe. With the magical city of Paris, a lush countryside, world-famous wine regions, a variety of coastlines, the Alps, and tons of art, architecture, history, and food you'll find much more to see and do than you'll ever have time for. Best of all, France is an excellent place to camp, there are good convenient campgrounds virtually anywhere you would want to go.

The tour outlined here is the first of two French tours in this book and covers 1,077 kilometers (668 miles). It makes a circle in northwest France with great overnight stops in Normandy and the Loire Valley. Several of the driving days are quite short, none are extremely long. Most driving is done on the pleasant secondary roads rather than the autoroutes. Most of the campgrounds are municipal ones, municipal campgrounds are a wonderful feature of French camping.

The campgrounds listed in this tour would allow camping from the middle of April until the end of September. Not coincidentally, any time during this period would be a great time to do this tour using either a tent or RV. Tenters might appreciate the better weather from late May onwards.

The gateway city for this tour is Paris, one of the world's great cities. It has excellent air access of course, and is a good location for picking up a rental automobile or RV.

The first driving day is a short drive to the west to Chartres, best known for its famous cathedral. The campground here is a good municipal one, there's a streamside path from the campground in to town.

The second drive takes you northwest to Bayeux, home of the famous Bayeux tapestry and also an excellent location for side trips to visit the World War II D-day beaches.

The third driving day goes westward to Mont-St-Michel on the coast. It's a great place for photos and you have a choice of dry camping in the parking lot next to the island or staying in an excellent campground at the foot of the peninsula.

On the following drive you leave the coast and travel south to the Loire Valley. Nantes is known for it's **Château des Ducs de Bretagne** and has a good municipal campground.

The route for the fifth drive heads east up the Loire Valley. The destination is Saumur, you camp on an island in the river with great views in the evening of the flood-lit château from your campsite.

Drive six is a very short one which gives you a chance to explore some of the many châteaux nearby. The night is spent at Chinon which has its own famous castle.

Drive seven, the final one, means heading back to Paris. You follow the Loire eastward as far as Blois, then join the autoroute to speed back and turn in your vehicle or find a campground to stay in while you spend more time enjoying Paris.

Roads and Driving

The roads in France rate second only to Germany. There is an extensive system of autoroutes or freeways. Unfortunately these are toll roads and the tolls mount up quickly. Fortunately, there is a great road system of "N" and "D" roads also, and they are free. In most places you can make good time on secondary roads. They may be a better alternative to freeways in France than in any other country in Europe. On maps autoroutes are designated as "A" roads, Routes National (red) as "N" roads, Routes Departmental (yellow) as "D" roads, and small local roads (also usually yellow) as "C" roads. It pays to use the autoroutes through major towns, you can pass through quickly and usually there are no tolls on the urban sections.

The autoroute toll rates are not all the same, but they are uniformly expensive. There are four classes of vehicles for purposes of tolls on the autoroutes. Class 1, the cheapest, is basically cars. Class 2 is motorhomes up to 3.5 metric tons (3,500 kilograms) and cars pulling caravans. Class 3 is motorhomes of 3.5 metric tons and over (generally they have duals on the back). Class 4 is motorhomes with three or more axles. Class 1 vehicles get the cheapest rates, Class 2 rates are approximately 50% higher, Class 3 rates approximately 100% higher than Class 1, and Class 4 about 150-

200% higher than Class 1. Class 1 rates vary from about 0.05 euro per kilometer to 0.10 euro per kilometer depending upon the highway, they are privately run and rates vary. During the summer holiday season, from July to September on Tuesdays, Wednesdays, and Thursdays, on some highways, special rates apply. These are reduced rates for cars with caravans and motorhomes under 3.5 metric tons.

Tolls are generally collected when you leave the autoroute although there are some collection stops en route. Credit cards are accepted at the toll booths.

French drivers can generally be characterized as good but aggressive. They are notorious speeders, but less so now that automated speed-cameras are becoming common. They are accustomed to sluggish motor homes, we've never had any unpleasant experiences with French drivers. Although not as much a problem as in the past you should be aware than many French intersections have no traffic-control signs, the person on the right has the right-of-way. This is called *priorité à droite*. You must be alert to this. Major roads and arterials usually have *passage protegé* or right-of-way. This is indicated by either a small yellow white-bordered diamond-shaped sign or a pyramid-shaped, red-bordered, white sign with an upward pointing arrow posted frequently along the road. Don't assume you have the right of way over entering vehicles unless you see these signs. Defensive driving is essential.

While touring France you may notice route signs carrying the word Bis. This stands for *Bison Futé*, these are routes to be used during peak traffic periods like the end of August when everyone in the country seems to be driving back to Paris after the holidays. Actually you can expect the roads to be full of holiday drivers at the beginning and end of July and August and also on the 14th, 15th and 16th of those months.

Bicycles are very popular in France and drivers are accustomed to dealing with them. Dedicated bicycle paths are not really as common as in some other countries but the extensive secondary road system offers some of the best bicycle touring possibilities in Europe.

Breakdown help on the autoroutes is organized by the police, motoring organizations are not allowed to respond first. The emergency number for the police is 17, fire is 18, and ambulance is 15.

Camping and Campgrounds

France is reported to have more than 10,000 campgrounds. This may be true, almost every village seems to have a municipal campground of some kind. These municipal campgrounds are one of the treasures of France, they are often inexpensive and comfortable without unnecessary facilities to drive up prices, and they are invariably in convenient locations often with good public transportation nearby.

French tourist and information offices, even in smaller towns, almost always have free information about campgrounds in the surrounding region, often in the form of attractive high-quality booklets.

Free camping is very popular in France. When in doubt about whether free camping is allowed you should always ask permission. Many towns in France provide low-cost or free parking areas for camping-cars (motorhomes), most have no facilities but some have dump stations, restrooms, and even low-amp electrical hookups. They are called "aires de camping" or "etapes de camping" and are listed in guidebooks published by the Fédération Francaise de Camping et de Caravaning (FFCC) and others. They can be found in many bookstores and larger newsstands in France.

Many campers like to use the autoroute rest areas as campgrounds, in fact they are sometimes listed in the guides mentioned above. Note that free camping in autoroute rest areas in southern France is definitely not recommended. Very frequently RVers in southern rest areas are gassed while they sleep (sleeping gas is introduced through vents) and wake with massive headaches and missing valuables. We have personally met a number of RVers who have had this experience, this is not an empty warning!

Camping International Cards are not required in France but are helpful. They will usually be accepted in lieu of a passport as security for payment and can also be used instead of your passport to establish your identification, something that is required each time you check into a French campground.

Practical Tips

Even by European standards France is a relatively expensive country. Taxes are high and France, until recently, tended towards being a "hard" money member of the European Community. The euro is used here. There are, however, offsetting money-saving strategies that you can use.

France is famous for her hypermarkets or hypermarches, huge supermarkets selling almost everything. If you shop in the hypermarkets you'll find that you have the best selection at the best prices. You can also often buy gasoline at hypermarkets, many have their own stations in the parking lots with much lower prices than those along the autoroutes. Note that hypermarket gas stations are often closed for a few hours for lunch.

The small food shops in France are one of the country's biggest attractions. You will want to do some shopping in them even if the things you buy cost you a little more. A boulangerie is a bread store, fresh batches of bread are baked twice a day, morning and early afternoon. French bread is delicious but doesn't keep long so you'll often see people along the road with a fresh baguette (called a French stick by the English) under their arm. Patisseries are often co-located with boulangeries, they sell delicious pastries. For picnic and camping treats try a charcuterie selling prepared meats like hams, sausages, terrines and pâtés, as well as delicious salads. There are also often cooked dishes like cassoulets. A butcher shop is a boucherie.

Credit cards are widely used in France and become more popular each year. Most hypermarkets and gas stations accept cards, Visa seems to be the most popular. Cash machines are everywhere, most hypermarkets have a machine.

THE TOUR – FRANCE 1

TOUR 11 GATEWAY CITY – PARIS AND THE ILE DE FRANCE, FRANCE
Population 9,400,000

Many people think that Paris is the most fascinating city in the world. You could easily spend a year visiting Paris and still not see and do everything. Long before you were finished you'd be ready to start over.

The sights of Paris are well documented elsewhere, the listing here is very incomplete. We will try to give you a mental picture of the region's arrangement and an idea of where you might camp and how you can get around. There are many guides to the city available, you'll definitely need one of them as well as a good map.

Paris is a giant city, the greater Paris area, called the Ile de France, has over 9 million people. There is a 35-kilometer ring road around the center of Paris, the Ville, which has over 2 million inhabitants. You'll probably have no reason to drive inside the ring road which is good since traffic is terrible. All of our campgrounds are located outside it. Paris has a wonderful subway or Metro system, it is said that no point inside the ring road is more than half of a kilometer from a Metro station.

The Seine River winds its way through the Ile de France and the city. It provides

THE PYRAMID ENTRANCE TO THE MUSÉE DU LOUVRE IN PARIS

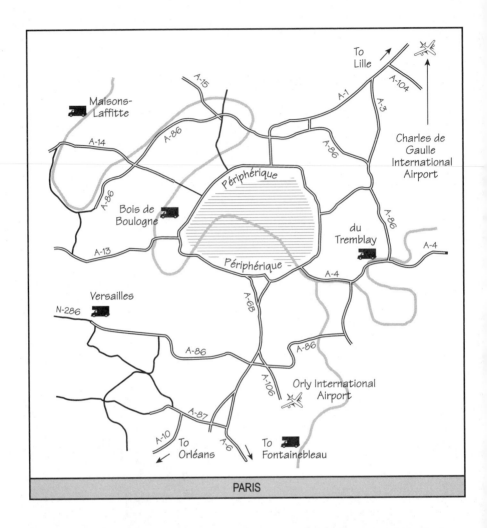

PARIS

a reference for keeping track of where you are. The geographic center of the city is an island, the **Ile de la Cité**. On this small island you will find several important tourist sites: **Notre Dame Cathedral**, **Sainte-Chapelle**, the **Conciergerie** and the **Crypte Archéologique**.

The **Left Bank** of the Seine (facing downstream of course) near the Ile de la Cité is the student quarter, the **Sorbonne** is located here. The **St-Germain-des-Prés** quarter, and the **Luxembourg Gardens** are nearby. As you move downstream along the river you'll pass the **Musée d'Orsay**, **Les Invalides**, and the **Eiffel Tower**.

On the right bank near the Ile de la Cité are the **Marais** and **Beauborg** quarters where you'll find the **Pompidou Center**, and the **Musée Picasso**. Downstream is the **Musée du Louvre,** probably the world's most complete and impressive art museum. From the Louvre you can pass through the **Jardin des Tuileries** and across the **Place**

de la Concorde to the head of the **Champs-Elysées**. Strolling up the boulevard you'll eventually reach the **Arc de Triomphe** and be able to see **La Défense** in the distance at the far end outside the ring road.

Everything mentioned above except La Défense is in a fairly compact central area. Farther afield but still inside the ring road are the **Sacré-Coeur** and **Montmartre**, **Montparnasse** and the **Cimetière du Père Lachaise** and the **Cité des Sciences** museum.

To go even farther afield, outside the ring road, you can still use public transportation. The RER (suburban rail lines) and the SNCF (national railroad) are well integrated with the metro subway system. RER tickets can be purchased from easy-to-understand machines and ticket windows and will take you well outside the city. In fact, three of the four campgrounds we describe below are conveniently tied to the metro stations of central Paris by the RER.

The Bois de Boulogne campground is the closest to Paris. See **Paris Campground No. 1 - Paris** below. Also close and more convenient if you approach from the south or west is Champigny, see **Paris Campground No. 2 - Near Paris** below.

VERSAILLES

When you visit Paris it is not really necessary to camp in Paris itself. You will find that use of the RER (suburban rail line) makes Versailles just as convenient as the Bois de Boulogne. Here you have the added convenience of being close to the most impressive château and gardens in France. See **Paris Campground No. 3 - Versailles** below.

The **Versailles Château** is huge, when it was built it was so admired by other European monarchs that you will find it the model for similar palaces throughout Europe. It is the most popular destination in France outside Paris and the crowds can be terrible. If you camp nearby you can get there early or late to avoid long lines. Don't miss the huge gardens.

FONTAINEBLEAU

Historically **Fontainebleau Château** preceded that at Versailles. Many kings made contributions to the château but today it reflects mostly those of Françoise I and Napoléon. Smaller than Versailles and not quite so over-the-top, the château and surrounding gardens are a pleasure to visit. It is also usually not nearly as crowded as Versailles. The campground here is less convenient, but it's also a more secluded place in a quiet location. See **Paris Campground No. 4 - Fontainebleau area** below.

MAISONS-LAFFITTE

The small prosperous town of Maisons-Laffitte is located next to the Seine to the northwest of Paris. It has shops and restaurants and makes a very pleasant base for your Paris visits. An added bonus is the town's **Maisons-Laffitte Château.** It was built by the architect Mansard (you've seen his roofs) and finished in 1651 during Louis XIV's reign. The town also has a horse-racing track. The campground here is listed as **Paris Campground No. 5 - Maisons Laffitte.**

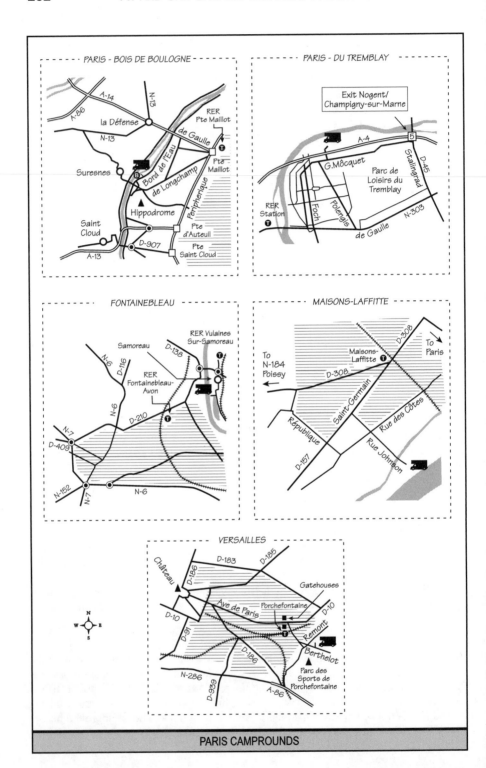

PARIS CAMPROUNDS

Paris Campground No. 1 - Paris

▲ CAMPING DU BOIS DE BOULOGNE

Address:	2, Allée du Bord de l'Eau, F-75016 Paris
Telephone:	01 45243081
Fax:	01 42244295
Website:	http://www.abccamping.com/boulogneuk.htm
E-mail:	resa@mobilhome-paris.com
GPS:	N 48° 52' 08.0", E 002° 14' 03.8"

Open All Year

Camping du Bois de Boulogne is probably most people's first choice for a stay in Paris. You should give it at least one visit. It is located in the Bois de Boulogne just outside the Paris ring road and is really the only campground actually in Paris. It is set right on the bank of the Seine River, is large, and is usually crowded. Sites have been being upgraded lately, almost all now are separated by hedges and most have convenient electricity (Euro, 10 amp), water, and gray-water drains. Grass is scarce, most sites are gravel or dirt. You probably won't spend much time in your rig or tent however, Paris beckons. The shower/toilet buildings are old but serviceable, they have hot showers and hot water for dishes and are heated in cooler weather. The campground offers a good grocery store and a bar/café as well as take-out food in the summer.

Access to the city is convenient. During the summer there is a shuttle bus from the campground to the Port Maillot metro station, at other times city bus service (RAPT #244) also offers access to Port Maillot. The walk to the subway line is not impossible, in forty minutes you can walk across the park to the Port Maillot station or, more easily, down the river to the Pont de Neuilly station which is quite a bit closer.

Finding the campground is not a difficult challenge if you have some notion of where it is. Take the Port Maillot Exit from the ring road and then follow the campground signs. Bear in mind that the campground is on the far side of the Bois de Boulogne from the freeway exit, at some points the signs are a little confusing but there are so many routes through and around the park that you'll eventually be successful. Probably the worst traffic is on a sunny weekend afternoon in the spring when every person in Paris seems to be in the Bois.

Paris Campground No. 2 - Near Paris

▲ CAMPING DU TREMBLAY

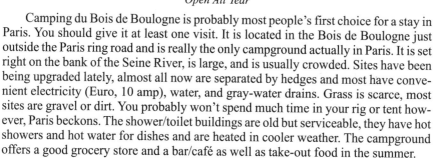

Address:	Boulevard des Alliés,
	F-94507 Champigny, Marne Cedex
Telephone:	01 43974397
Fax:	01 48890794
Website:	www.abccamping.com/tremblay.htm
E-mail:	receptcc@stereau.fr
GPS:	N 48° 49' 45.6", E 002° 28' 35.6"

Open All Year

Located southwest of the city and outside the ring road, Campng Du Tremblay has decent RER service to Paris and a nice riverside location.

The sites here are grassy back-ins with hedges separating them. Electricity (French, 10 amp) can require a long cord. Restroom buildings are older and nothing fancy but decently maintained and have hot water for showers. There is a trail along the river (the Marne), by heading downstream you can reach the Joinville-le-Pont RER station in 1.6 km and from there you can be in Paris in just a quarter-hour or so. There also is a bus from the RER station to the campground.

Easiest access is from the A4 heading westbound. Take Exit 5 and in 0.3 km (.2 miles) turn left onto D45 (Avenue de Stalingrad) heading south. You will pass along the side of a park and after 0.8 km (.5 miles) should turn right onto N303. After 1.1 km (.7 miles) a campground sign will point you right onto Boulevard de Polengis. This puts you in a residential area, after another 0.9 km (.6 miles) you'll be pointed right again and signs will take you under the freeway to the campground.

Paris Campground No. 3 - Versailles

▲ Camping International Versailles

Address:	31 Rue Berthelot, F-Porchefontaine, 78000 Versailles	
Telephone:	01 39512361	
Fax:	01 39536829	
Website:	www.campint.com	
E-mail:	CI.versailles@free.fr	
GPS:	N 48° 47' 39.6", E 002° 09' 40.2"	

April 1 - Oct 31

The campground sits in a grove of trees that slopes downwards towards Porchefontaine, a Versailles suburb. The campground is large and people park pretty much where they please in an attempt to find a flat space. There are few of these so you will need some kind of chocks to level your rig, tenters seem to have a little better luck although they too have problems. Electricity (Euro, 6 amp) is available but boxes are widely spaced. Small toilet buildings are scattered around the campground, a modern building with adjustable hot showers and areas for dish and clothes washing (hot water provided for both) is at the foot of the slope near the entrance. There is a sports facility next door with swimming pool and running track and a forest above the campground with hiking paths. Restaurants and stores are within easy walking distance.

Public transportation to Versailles and to Paris are conveniently located near the campground. RER train service to Paris is accessible at the Porchefontaine station only a half-kilometer from the campground and a bus (to the chateau) runs frequently along Avenue de Paris which is slightly farther away. The walk to the château is about 3.5 kilometers.

The campground has good signage making it easy to find. It is off Avenue de Paris which is the large boulevard which starts at the château and heads east, eventually becoming D10 to Paris. If you start at the château and drive east on Avenue de Paris you'll want to turn right after about 2 kilometers just after the two gatehouses. You'll drive past the Porchefontaine RER station, under the tracks, and up the hill following signs for Camping Parc des Sports de Porchefontaine or Camping International.

Paris Campground No. 4 - Fontainebleau area

▲ CAMPING MUNICIPAL LA GRANGE AU DIMES

Address: F-77210 Samoreau
Telephone: 01 64237225
GPS: N 48° 25' 19.5", E 002° 44' 56.5"

March 15 - Sept 30

There are several smaller campgrounds on the banks of the Seine to the east of Fontainebleau. This one is friendly and well-run.

This Samoreau municipal campground is a grassy field that slopes to the banks of the Seine. The river is pretty quiet but it's nice to watch the occasional barge pass. Sites are in two fields separated by a hedge, both sides have electricity (French, 10 amp). The shower/toilet area is older but adequate, hot showers are provided, as is hot water for dishes. This small town has a few restaurants and shops, most of the action is in Fontainebleau, about 6 kilometers (4 miles) to the west.

The local bus is infrequent, you'll have to plan your trips carefully if you wish to use it. There is a train station about 3 kilometers (1.9 miles) in the direction of Fontainebleau for trips in to Paris.

To find the campground examine your Fontainebleau area map carefully and find the Seine. Samoreau is one of the small towns along the river, once you reach it you can't miss the campground.

Paris Campground No. 5 - Maisons-Laffitte

▲ CAMPING INTERNATIONAL MAISONS LAFFITTE

Address: Ile de la Commune, 1 Rue Johnson,
                F-78600 Maisons-Laffitte
Telephone: 01 39122191
Fax: 01 39127050
Website: www.campint.com
E-mail: ci.mlaffitte@wanadoo.fr
GPS: N 48° 56' 23.0", E 002° 08' 45.9"

April 1 - Oct 15

Camping International is another popular base for exploring Paris. Located on the bank of the Seine some 15 kilometers (9 miles) outside the ring road it has the advantage of being in a relaxed small town with all services and having very convenient public transportation to Paris. In the off season it is often possible to get a site right on the bank of the Seine with no fence between you and the river.

The large campground occupies flat ground that is actually an island. Sites are large and mostly separated by small hedges, surfaces are grass or packed dirt, many trees provide quite a bit of shade. There are many rental mobile homes here, they occupy about a third of the sites. Electricity (Euro, 4 or 10 amp) is available but outlets are widely spaced. The shower/toilet buildings are older but clean, premixed hot water is piped to pushbutton valves in showers, bathroom basins, dishwashing sinks, and laundry tubs. The shower water was only tepid when we last visited. Facilities really don't seem to be able to keep up with the demand when this campground is full. The campground has a bar/pizzeria/restaurant and grocery shop on the bank of the river. Other amenities include a playground and laundry facilities. An outside kiosk provides internet access. The campground is a ten minute walk from central Maisons-Laffitte with its train station and shops. The trip to Paris on RER trains is reasonably priced and connects you directly with the subways. There are supermarkets near the train station in Maisons-Laffitte and the château is about five minutes on the far side of the train station.

Easiest access to the campground is from the east on D308. If you zero your odometer as you leave N184 and head east on D308 you will enter Maissons-Laffitte at 2.6 km and see a campground sign pointed right at 3.0 km. Turn right here and then left following signs onto La République. You are in a quiet neighborhood with crowded streets since parked cars create one-lane bottlenecks. Now continue straight for 0.4 kilometers to a T. Watch for stop signs since most cross streets have the right a way. Now turn left and in 0.2 km turn right on Rue Johnson, the campground is just ahead.

DRIVE 1 – PARIS TO CHARTRES
82 Kilometers (51 Miles), 1.5 Hours

Along The Way – From Paris drive southeast on the A10 autoroute. Not far from Paris the autoroute splits with A10 heading south and A11 continuing west. Take the A11 following signs to Chartres. In another 90 kilometers (56 miles) leave the autoroute at Exit 2. Follow the N123 south along the west side of the autoroute for just 3 kilometers (2 miles) through several roundabouts and turn toward town on N154. See the instructions in the campground write-up to find Camping Municipal.

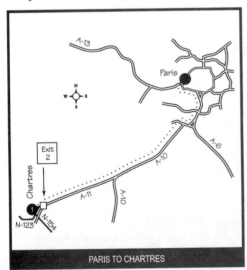

PARIS TO CHARTRES

CHARTRES, FRANCE
Population 40,000

When most folks think of Chartres they're really thinking of its early Gothic cathedral, the **Cathédrale de Notre Dame**. As you approach Chartres the spires of the cathedral are visible from miles away, and once there they dominate the town itself. This cathedral was a true 13th-century building project, it was finished in only a quarter century. Many cathedrals you'll see in Europe have been under construction for centuries and aren't finished yet. When you tour the cathedral note the mostly original "Chartres blue" stained glass windows, they're awesome!

Chartres Campground

▲ CAMPING MUNICIPAL DES BORDS DE L'EURE

Address: 9, Rue de Launay, F-28000 Chartres
Telephone: 02 37287943
Fax: 02 37287943
E-mail: camping-roussel-chartres@wanadoo.fr
GPS: N 48° 26' 05.9", E 001° 29' 59.3"

April 13 - Nov 15 (Varies)

Bords de l'Eure is a pleasant medium-sized municipal campground with a great location. Chartres is near enough to Paris that it is possible to take day trips to the big city by train if you wish. It is a pleasant river-side walk to the cathedral in the center of town, 30 minutes (3.5 km) or so to the cathedral and a few more to the gare or train

ONE OF THE STAINED GLASS WINDOWS IN CATHÉDRAL DE NOTRE DAME IN CHARTRES

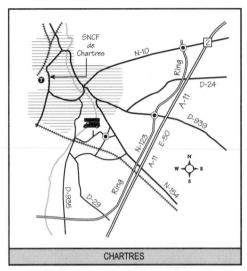

CHARTRES

station. There is also bus service around Chartres but it does not run to the campground.

Camping sites are back-ins on grass with a few hedges for separation. Electricity (French, 6 amp) is available to about 30 sites, there are at least that many more RV sites and also a large tent field. Sanitary facilities include free hot showers and hot water for dishes. A supermarket is only a half-kilometer distant. There is one coin-operated washing machine.

You'll find that the route to the campground is well signed from N154, the highway running southeast towards Orléans. From the intersection of N154 and the ring road (N123) head toward the center of town, proceed 0.9 km and then turn left at a stoplight. In 0.2 km at a traffic circle take the second exit to the right and follow the road down the hill for another 0.4 km, the campground is on the right.

DRIVE 2 – CHARTRES TO BAYEUX
219 Kilometers (136 Miles), 2.75 Hours

Along The Way – Today's route picks it's way across the French countryside. While there are no outstanding stops along the way you'll have a chance to see what rural France is really like. You'll also get lot of practice negotiating French roundabouts.

From Chartres follow D939 northwest to Brezolles and Verneuil-sur-Avre, a distance of 50 kilometers (31 miles). Now follow N26 to the west to L'Aigle and D13 to Falaise a distance of 80 kilometers (50 miles). In Falaise turn northward on N158 to Caen, 50 kilometers (31 miles). Circle around Caen and drive northwest on E46 to Bayeaux, a distance of 32 kilometers (20 miles). Turn right to circle around Bayeaux on the

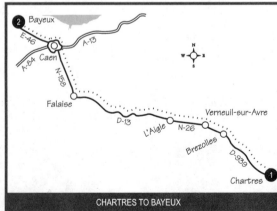

CHARTRES TO BAYEUX

N13 which forms a ring road here. See the campground write-up for instructions on finding the campground.

BAYEUX, FRANCE
Population 15,000

Bayeux's small size belies the interest it holds for visitors. First, the town is the location of the **Bayeux Tapestry** which depicts the story of the Norman invasion of England in 1066. You shouldn't miss the opportunity to examine it, assisted by a running commentary through a set of headphones. Second, Bayeux is a great base for touring the **Allied invasion beaches of World War II**. They are all just a few miles away, and Bayeux has a museum and information to orient you properly. You'll need to use your vehicle or take an organized tour, public transportation is just too inconvenient. There are several other campgrounds along the ocean nearby.

Bayeux Campground

▲ BAYEUX-CAMPING MUNICIPAL

Address: Bd. Périphérique d'Eindhoven,
F-14400 Bayeux
Telephone
and Fax: 02 31920842
GPS: N 49° 17' 02.3", W 000° 41' 52.0"

May 1 - Sept 30

Bayeux's attractive campground has all the features you want in a city campground: great location, nearby shopping, good facilities, and extreme cleanliness. This makes it a popular place. English campers throng to the coastal region.

Bayeux-Camping Municipal has curbed gravel driveways and neatly-clipped grass sites. The few trees are mostly ornamental. It is a fairly large place. Parking is on paved back-in spaces or on grass. Electrical boxes (Euro, 5 amp) are widely spaced and may require a long cord. The modern shower/toilet buildings are very clean. They have hot water showers. There is a municipal swimming pool next door and a supermarket across the street. A small kiosk sells limited supplies and food in the campground during the height of the season. Central Bayeux is a fifteen-minute walk or bike ride.

The campground is located north of town on Bd. Périphérique d'Eindhoven, also called N13 and E46, it is a portion of the small ring road that runs all the way around the town. There are several signs, the campground is just across the street from the Champion supermarket.

DRIVE 3 – BAYEUX TO MONT-ST-MICHEL
130 Kilometers (80 Miles), 1.75 Hours

A long The Way – From Bayeux drive south on D6 for 13 kilometers (8 miles). When you reach the D9 turn west and follow this highway to Caumont-l'Eventé, and then D13 onward through Torigni-sur-Vire, Domjean, Tessy-sur-Vire, Beaucoudray, Maupertuis, and Hambye. The distance is 61 kilometers (38 miles). Just before reaching Saint-Denis-le-Gast turn south on D38 which soon becomes D7. At Ponts pick up the E3 for 9 kilometers (6 miles) until the D43 cuts off to the right. Follow D43 west to Mont-Saint-Michel.

BAYEUX TO MONT-ST-MICHEL

MONT-ST-MICHEL, FRANCE

If you decide to visit **Mont-St-Michel**, and you should, don't do it on a weekend or holiday. This world-famous abbey and cathedral, situated on an offshore

CAMPING THE PARKING LOT AT MONT-ST-MICHEL

rock, attracts so many people that the line of cars sometimes runs across the causeway to the mainland and then five kilometers inland. You can beat the crowds and enjoy the site by picking the time for your visit and by doing something that the majority of the tourists can't do. You can spend the night just outside the walls of the island village.

Mont-St-Michel Campgrounds

▲ MONT-ST-MICHEL PARKING LOT   [€]

    GPS: N 48° 37' 47.3", W 001° 30' 26.2"

Open All Year

    There is a public parking area along the causeway just outside the city entrance. A large area is set aside for camping-cars (motorhomes). There is a daily parking fee that allows you to spend the night. We call it "almost-free camping", the cost was 8 Euros last time we visited. There are no facilities except a public toilet just inside the city gate (small fee). Things slow down considerably when the tour busses leave in the evening. This isn't a great place to stay when the weather is bad since it's so exposed. Also, watch where you park. The incoming tides here are known for their height and speed.

▲ CAMPING DU MONT-ST-MICHEL

    Address: Route du Mont-Saint-Michel,
                       F-50170 Le Mont-Saint-Michel
    Telephone: 02 33602210
    Fax: 02 33602002
    GPS: N 48° 36' 51.9", W 001° 30' 31.4"

Feb 15 - Oct 31

    This large campground has excellent facilities and is located just 2.5 kilometers (1.6 miles) from Mont-Saint-Michel. It is at the base of the causeway out to the island and you can walk or bike out easily from the campground, many people do.

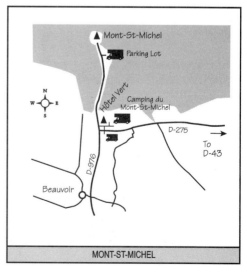

    The campground is located behind the Hôtel Vert in the northeast quadrant of the intersection of D275 and D976. Half of the campground is on the far side of D275 so there are really two campgrounds, each with it's own restroom facilities. Parking is in back-in sites on grass, the very wide sites are separated by hedges. Electrical boxes are widely-spaced (both Euro and French, 10 amp). Restrooms are modern and have adjustable hot showers, hot water to bathroom basins, and hot water for washing dishes. There is a mini-golf course and bicycles are available for rental. Sev-

MONT-ST-MICHEL

eral decent restaurants are in the cluster of tourist-oriented businesses (of which this is one) at the base of the causeway, they cater to tourist busses but offer a less-expensive alternate to the many restaurants on the Mont itself.

DRIVE 4 – MONT-ST-MICHEL TO NANTES
171 Kilometers (106 Miles), 2.25 Hours

A long The Way – From Mont-St-Michel drive south on D976 which quickly turns into D175. After 60 kilometers (37 miles) you'll reach the suburbs of Rennes. Follow the ring route around the west side of town, the highway is N136. From Rennes drive south on N137 directly to Nantes, the distance is 97 kilometers (60 miles). See the campground write-up for the final directions for finding Camping du Petit Port.

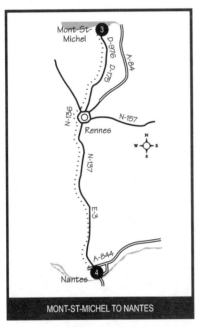

MONT-ST-MICHEL TO NANTES

NANTES, FRANCE
Population 495,000

Astride the Loire River but west of the area generally known as the Loire Valley is the city of Nantes. While it is large, Nantes has a relaxed pace, a very good municipal campground and a medieval district next to the river. Historically Nantes was part of Brittany but today the city is the capital of Pays de la Loire and is a major inland seaport.

The massive **Château des Ducs de Bretagne** seems more castle than château. You can walk the walls and visit the **Musée des Salorges**, a naval museum that deals primarily with the slave trade, Nantes shippers were heavily involved in it. The nearby **Cathédrale St-Pierre** is late Gothic and contains the tomb of Françoise II, the Duke who was largely responsible for building the Château des Ducs in its present form.

The Erdre and Sèvre Rivers enter the Loire at Nantes and boats cruise the rivers which have many châteaux along the shores. This is also Muscadet wine country.

Nantes Campground

▲ CAMPING DU PETIT PORT

Address:	21 Boulevard du Petit-Port, F-44300 Nantes
Telephone:	02 40744794
Fax:	02 40742306
Website:	www.nge-nantes.fr
E-mail:	camping-petit-port@nge-nantes.fr
GPS:	N 47° 14' 33.0", W 001° 33' 26.9"

Open All Year

This is a large above-average municipal campground, and in France that is saying a lot. It is only 3 kilometers (1.9 miles) from the city's center, by far the most convenient campground in Nantes.

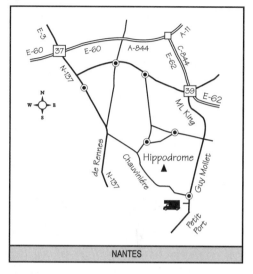

The campground sites are arranged along two long parallel driveways. The sites for wheeled vehicles are separated from each other by hedges and shrubs. There are now many permanent resident rigs, some apparently in storage and others rental mobile units. Tent sites are in a separate area. Electricity (6 or 10 amp) is available to most wheeled-vehicle sites, as is water and a drain. The shower/toilet buildings are well maintained and have hot water for showers, basins, and dishes. The campground has a small shop in the office. There is a nice walking path along a small stream (the Cens) that passes the campground and a swimming pool, restaurant, and shops are nearby. Tram service to the center of town is just outside the campground gate, the nearest stop is Morrhonnière on the #2 (red) line.

Since this is a municipal campground it is well signed. Easiest access is from the north. Take Exit 37 from the north ring road (E60). Proceed south toward the city center for 1.5 kilometers (.9 miles) and turn left onto Boulevard de la Chauvinière following the campground sign. This street curves around the south side of the Hippodrome and after another 1.9 kilometers (1.2 miles) comes to a large traffic circle. Turn right here onto Boulevard du Petit Port and the campground will be on your right almost immediately.

DRIVE 5 – NANTES TO SAUMUR
140 Kilometers (87 Miles), 2 Hours

Along The Way – While it would be possible to follow an autoroute east to Saumur it's a lot more interesting, and also less expensive, to use secondary roads. D751 follows the south bank of the Loire all the way east to Saumur.

Along the way you will pass the town of **Angers**. It lies about 95 kilometers (59 miles) upstream from Nantes and 45 kilometers (28 miles) downstream from Saumur and is a bustling town with a population of over 150,000. Angers has its own famous château, a 13th-century fortress which contains the medieval **Apocalypse Tapestry**.

SAUMUR AND THE LOIRE VALLEY, FRANCE
Population Saumur 35,000

One hundred kilometers southwest of Paris by autoroute you will find one of

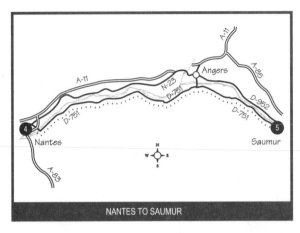

NANTES TO SAUMUR

France's best-loved regions. The Loire Valley has it all: beautiful countryside, history, wine, and food, and of course the châteaux.

The Loire Valley is probably best known for the dozens of châteaux built here throughout French history. The oldest are really military castles. Later the valley's proximity to Paris made it a popular place for the rich and powerful to build their country homes. You'll find that there are quite a variety of different types of châteaux: some are isolated and almost deserted, others are crowded with busloads of visitors; some have museums and others are completely unfurnished. You'll probably find yourself trying to visit as many as possible. You'll probably also find yourself studying some French

RVERS VISITING THE CHÂTEAU DE SAUMUR

history, trying to see how all of these places fit into it. Several Loire châteaux have sound-and-light shows in the evening. The shows are popular and easy to enjoy if you're camped nearby. In the Loire, unless you happen to be actually camped in a town with a chateau, you'll travel around in your vehicle. While there is some public transportation available it's not easy to use it to visit many of the sights.

Visiting the Loire is more than visiting the châteaux. There are pleasant and historical towns like Tours, Saumur, and Chinon. This is also wine country so you'll have lots of opportunities for tastings. Of course, like all wine areas the Loire has great food.

Saumur is a popular tourist destination and very camper-friendly. The municipal campground has great views of the château and a pleasant island location.

The **Château de Saumur** is impressive from below, particularly from the campground. It is one of the best châteaux along the Loire for pictures. The old town below the château has shops and restaurants. Saumur is home to the French cavalry academy and also the **École Nationale d'Équitation** with its **Cadre Noir** which puts on equestrian shows for visitors. Saumur is also a center for sparkling wine and for mushrooms, you can taste the wine and visit fascinating caves where mushrooms are grown.

Saumur Campground

▲ CAMPING L'ILE D'OFFARD

Address:	Rue de Verden, F-49400 Saumur	
Telephone:	02 41403000	
Fax:	02 41673781	
Website:	www.CVTLOISIRS.com	
E-mail:	iledoffard@wanadoo.fr	
GPS:	N 47° 15' 35.5", W 000° 03' 53.4"	

March 1 - Oct 31

Camping Municipal is a four-star campground and the place to stay to be within walking distance of Saumur's restaurants and tourist sites. It is located on an island in the Loire and has a great view of the very photogenic Saumur Chateau. The 1-km walk along the bank to the bridge over to town is very pleasant.

The campground occupies a point of land on the east (upstream) end of the island. It is fenced so there is no direct access to the river although the location is very scenic. Grassy sites (and a few gravel-surfaced ones near the entrance) have quite a bit of shrubbery and shade. Electricity (Euro, 16 amp) and water are available throughout but outlets are scattered. Sanitary facilities are good with hot water

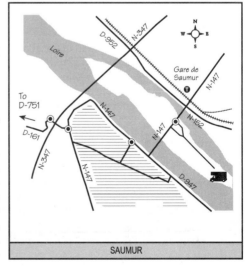

showers available. There is a restaurant/bar and small store at the campground, a municipal swimming pool is located next door as are municipal tennis courts. There are a lot of rental tents and rental caravans at the campground, the location makes this a popular place.

To reach the campground follow signs from downtown Saumur across the river to the island and then east on the island itself to it's eastern end.

DRIVE 6 – SAUMUR TO CHINON
35 Kilometers (22 Miles), .75 Hour

A long The Way – You may be perfectly happy to stay two nights in Saumur. On the other hand, Chinon, nearby, is a pleasant little town with it's own attractions.

From Saumur head east to Montsoreau. Turn inland on D947 and follow signs to **Fontevraud-l'Abbaye**. This is really a quick stop, but worthwhile. You'll find that Richard the Lionhearted and his mother, Eleanor of Aquitaine, two of most famous characters of the Middle Ages, are entombed here.

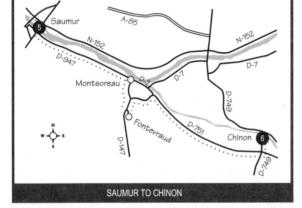
SAUMUR TO CHINON

Upon leaving the Abbey follow D751 and D749 southeast to Chinon.

CHINON, FRANCE
Population 9,000

Chinon is an enchanting town on the banks of the Vienne River. The medieval streets of the village along the river are overlooked by the **château**, really more of a fortress. Chinon's golden age was earlier than many châteaux in the Loire, Richard the Lionhearted died in the town of Chinon in 1189. Joan of Arc was presented to the Dauphin here for the first time in 1429, this is where she picked the disguised Dauphin out of the crowd although she had never met him before. Most of the château has been dismantled over the years but the Royal Apartments of Charles VII and Joan of Arc's time remain.

Besides the château Chinon has a very good **wine museum**, the **States General House** where Richard the Lionhearted died also has a museum of local history.

About 12 kilometers (7 miles) north of Chinon is **Ussé Château**. About 14 kilometers (9 miles) beyond, on the north bank of the Loire is **Langeais**. The first castle was built on this location in the 10th century but Louis XI finished the one that stands there today in 1469. It is unusually well preserved and a good château for a tour.

On the south side of the Loire again, near the confluence with the Cher, is

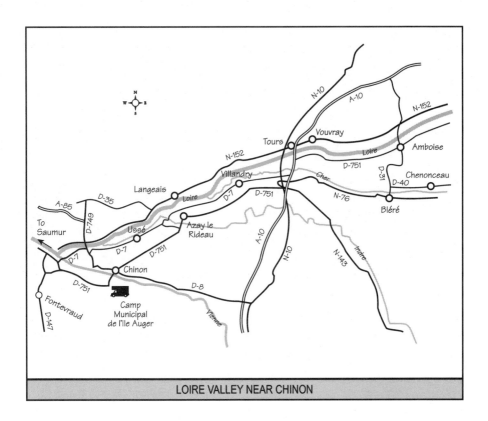

LOIRE VALLEY NEAR CHINON

Villandry. This château is known for its extensive gardens, including an unusual kitchen garden.

Probably the most-loved of all the Loire Châteaux is **Chenonceau**. To get there from Villandry drive upstream along the Cher River on N76 to Bléré. Cross the river heading northward and turn right on D40. There are lots of signs, you'll soon arrive at the Chateau.

Heading back toward Chinon, **Azay-le Rideau** is 21 kilometers (13 miles) northeast of Chinon and near the Indre River. The small fairy-tale château is surrounded by water, it's very photogenic.

Chinon Campground

▲ CAMP MUNICIPAL DE L'ILE AUGER

Address:	Quay Danton, F-37500 Chinon	
Telephone:	02 47930835	
GPS:	N 47° 09' 52.8", E 000° 14' 08.1"	

March 15 - Oct 15

CHENONCEAU IS EVERYONE'S FAVORITE CHÂTEAU

When you visit the Chinon area there's no better place to stay than the town's municipal campground. It is on the banks of the Vienne River, just across from the château. The view is great!

The medium-sized campground is a grassy area on the river bank but with no direct access to the river, there is a fence. It is divided into several clusters of sites by low shrubs. Electricity (Euro; 4, 8, or 12 amp, your choice) is available. The clean shower/toilet facilities have hot showers. There is a playground in the campground and a boules-playing area. Stores, restaurants, and the château are a five to ten minute walk across the bridge. There's a swimming pool next to the campground.

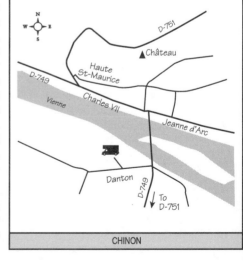

To find the campground just look across the river from old Chinon below the château. Signs direct you across the bridge and then right to the gate.

DRIVE 7 – CHINON TO PARIS
300 Kilometers (186 Miles), 3.5 Hours

A long The Way – Today's route again follows the Loire, switching from one shore to the other. At Blois it's time to head for the autoroute and make better time on the way back to Paris.

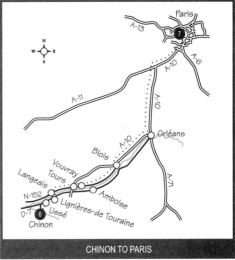

CHINON TO PARIS

From Chinon drive north on D16 to D7. Turn east and follow it as far as Lignières-de-Touraine. You'll pass right by the chateau of Ussé so if you didn't visit it while camped at Saumur or Chinon you can do so today. Turn north and cross the Loire to Langeais, another chateau stop if you haven't seen it already.

From here follow the north bank on N152 east. You'll pass through the outskirts of Tours and perhaps stop to taste a little wine in Vouvray. You'll also pass opposite Amboise. Amboise has a château as well as being a very engaging little town.

You'll soon arrive at Blois. Follow signs around town to the onramp for the A10 autoroute. The A10 will take you all the way to Paris.

Information Resources

See our Internet site at www.rollinghomes.com for many links to information sources.

French Government Tourist Office, 444 Madison Avenue, 16th Floor, New York, NY 10022-6903 (212 838-7800). In Canada the address is 1981 McGill College Ave, Suite 490, Montreal, Quebec H3A 2W9 (514 288-4264).

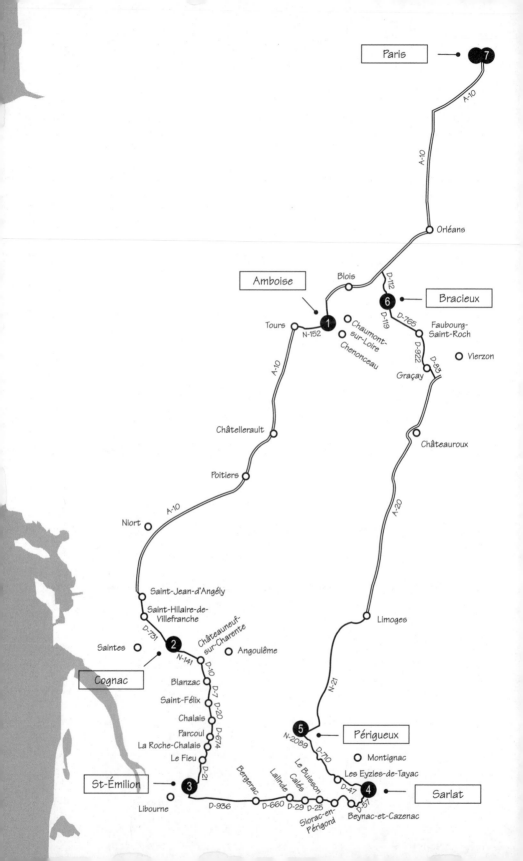

Paris

7

A-10

A-10

Orléans

Amboise

Blois

D-112

Bracieux

6

Tours

N-152

1

Chaumont-
sur-Loire

Chenonceau

D-119

D-765

D-922

D-83

Faubourg-
Saint-Roch

Vierzon

Graçay

A-10

Châtellerault

Châteauroux

Poitiers

A-20

Niort

A-10

Saint-Jean-d'Angély

Saint-Hilaire-de-
Villefranche

Limoges

D-731

Saintes

2

Châteauneuf-
sur-Charente

Angoulême

N-141

Cognac

Blanzac

D-10

Saint-Félix

D-7

D-20

N-21

Chalais

Parcoul

D-674

5

Périgueux

La Roche-Chalais

N-2089

Le Fieu

D-21

Bergerac

Le Buisson

D-710

Montignac

St-Émilion

3

Lalinde

Calès

Les Eyzies-de-Tayac

4

Sarlat

Libourne

D-936

D-660

D-29

D-25

Siorac-en-
Périgord

D-47

D-57

Beynac-et-Cazenac

Chapter 12

Tour 9

France 2

Top Attractions

- ❖ Paris
- ❖ Loire Valley
- ❖ Cognac Houses
- ❖ St-Émilion wine village
- ❖ Dordogne Valley
- ❖ Saumur
- ❖ Périgueux

General Description

This is the second of two tours outlined in this book for travel in France. The first is described in Chapter 11. The route for that tour circles Normandy, this tour travels through an area of western France to the south of the area covered by the first tour. For a longer tour it would be easy to combine the routes outlined in these two chapters.

Like the first tour this one uses Paris as the gateway city. Rather than duplicate the Paris information here we refer you to the previous chapter. The total distance of this tour is 1,291 kilometers (801 miles).

Campground openings would allow you to follow this route from about the first of May until the end of September. Any time during this period would be a fine time to take this trip.

The first driving day you travel southwest from Paris to the Loire Valley. The campground in Amboise is on an island in the middle of the Loire River, it offers fine views of the city's château overlooking the town from the south bank.

Drive two takes you farther south, this time to the home of cognac. The municipal campground here is a fine one, and the town's cognac houses offer tours and samples of their products.

Drive three takes you to the eastern reaches of the Bordeaux wine region to the town of St Émilion. Here you can visit tasting caves in town or ride the wine train to visit several of the local vineyards.

On the fourth driving day you'll travel eastward through Bergerac and into the Dordogne Valley. The day's destination is Sarlat, a charming town that is the center of the Dordogne region.

The next drive is short but interesting. While traveling north to Périgueux you'll have a chance to stop and see the pre-historic sites around Les Eyzies. These include a full-scale replica of the most famous cave paintings in the world, those of **Lascaux**. Périgueux itself is best known for it's food, regional delicacies including foie gras, truffles, and canard.

Drive six takes you north again to the Loire Valley. The evening stop is at Bracieux, a small town near one of the Loire's most famous château, Chambord.

The final day's drive takes you back to Paris.

Roads and Driving

See previous chapter.

Camping and Campgrounds

See previous chapter.

Practical Tips

See previous chapter.

THE TOUR – FRANCE 2

TOUR 9 GATEWAY CITY – PARIS, FRANCE

See previous chapter.

DRIVE 1 – PARIS TO AMBOISE
218 Kilometers (135 Miles), 2.25 Hours

Along The Way – From Paris drive southwest on the A10 autoroute. About 200 kilometers (124 miles) from the Paris ring road exit from the autoroute at the Angers/Château-Renault/Amboise exit and continue south on D31. When you reach the Loire riverbank, after 14 kilometers (9 miles), turn right and in 2.6 kilometers you'll be in Amboise. See the campground description for the final directions to Camping L'Ile d'Or.

AMBOISE, FRANCE

The château in Amboise is a royal castle, its golden age was the fifteenth century

A VEIW OF THE AMBOISE ROYAL CASTLE AT NIGHT FROM THE CAMPGROUND

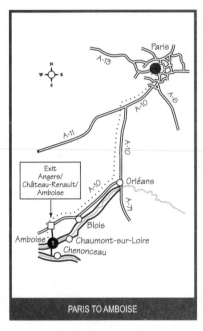

PARIS TO AMBOISE

under Charles VIII. Leonardo da Vinci spent time here as the guest of King Francis I, you'll find a museum containing models of some of his inventions.

The very nicely-located campground is on an island in the river and convenient for visiting Amboise as well as the surrounding area.

Chaumont-sur-Loire Château sits above the Loire about 16 km northeast of Amboise. This is the château that Catherine de'Medici acquired and forced Diane de Poitiers to accept in exchange for Chenonceau.

The château of **Chenonceau** is probably most people's Loire favorite. This is the château that is actually built out over the Cher and forms a bridge. It is a popular destination so you may find it more enjoyable to visit either early or late in the day, especially on weekends. It's located about 15 kilometers (9 miles) south of Amboise along the Cher River.

Also, see the previous chapter for more Loire Valley sights.

Amboise Campground

▲ CAMP MUNICIPAL L'ILE D'OR

Address: F-37400 Amboise
Telephone: 02 47234723 or (April 1 to Sept 30) 02 47572337
GPS: N 47° 25' 00.1",
                        W 000° 59' 14.6"

Easter - Sept 24 (Varies)

This is a municipal campground conveniently located about a half-kilometer from the chateau in Amboise. It's on an island in the middle of the Loire, much like the campground in Saumur visited in the first France tour.

This is a large campground with parking on grass. Electrical boxes are widely spaced (French, 10 amp) and spaces not delineated although folks park in an orderly fashion since the layout is fairly geometrical. Some sites are in large treeless fields and other are under trees in the shade. Restrooms have hot showers and there is hot water for washing dishes. Out-

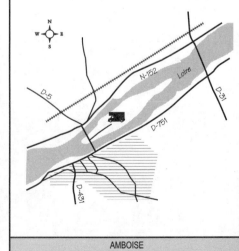

AMBOISE

side the gate and behind the office is a restaurant and central Amboise is so convenient that you'll be tempted to walk in for your croissants and coffee in the morning. The view of the floodlit chateau at night from just outside the entrance gate is excellent.

Easiest access is along the north bank of the Loire from the D31 to the east. When you reach the bridge just turn south across it and turn to the east on the island at the campground sign, the campground is at the east end of the island.

DRIVE 2 – AMBOISE TO COGNAC
270 Kilometers (167 Miles), 3 Hours

A long The Way – From Amboise travel west on the N152 on the north bank of the Loire to Tours and follow signs to get on the A10 autoroute southbound. Follow the A10 southbound for 208 kilometers (129 miles) and exit at the Échangeur de Saint-Jean-d'Angély. Following signs for Cognac travel south on N150 for 13 kilometers (8 miles) to Saint-Hilaire-de-Villefranche and then turn southeast on D731. In 22 kilometers (14 miles) you'll enter Cognac. See the campground description below for final directions to Cognac Municipal Campground.

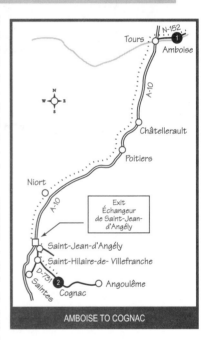

COGNAC, FRANCE
Population 20,000

If it's not from the Cognac region it's not cognac - it's brandy. If you like cognac, or if you're just interested, this is a fun little town to visit. Many of the most important brands have cellars in town and offer tours and tastings including Camus, Hennessey, Martell, and Otard. Others are near town including Rémy Martin. There's also a **Musée de Cognac**.

Cognac Campground

▲ CAMPING DE COGNAC

Address:	Boulevard de Châtenay, Route de Ste Sévère, F-16100 Cognac
Telephone:	05 45321332
Fax:	05 45365529
E-mail:	ccdc-camping @wanadoo.fr
GPS:	N 45° 42' 31.2", W 000° 18' 47.3"

May 1 - Oct 15

MANY OF THE IMPORTANT COGNAC NAMES OFFER TOURS OF THEIR CELLARS

This is a beautifully maintained large municipal campground about a kilometer outside the town of Cognac. It sits in an island in the Charente river and is within a 20-minute walk of the Cognac houses.

Parking here is on grass off paved drives. Sites are divided by hedges and electrical boxes (French or Euro, 6 amp) and are widely scattered. Restrooms have hot water for showers and dishes. There is a very nice swimming pool and trails for walking in a park nearby.

The campground is located along the D24 north of town. This is the road toward Sainte-Sèvére. Campground signs will lead you to the campground from most approaches to the city. They lead you through the town, there is not a good ring road around the norh side of Cognac.

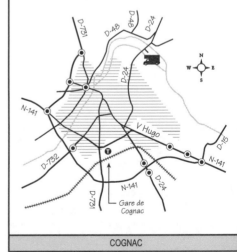

DRIVE 3 – COGNAC TO ST-ÉMILION
121 Kilometers (75 Miles), 1,75 Hours

A long The Way – Rather than travel the autoroute today we'll take the direct and less expensive route through the French countryside.

From Cognac travel southeast on N141 and then D10 through Châteauneuf-sur-Charente for 11 kilometers (7 miles). Near Blanzac switch to the D7 and continue south for 30 kilometers (19 miles). Near Saint-Félix switch to D20 and continue south to Chalais, 14 kilometers (9 miles). In Chalias switch to D674 and again continue south through Parcoul, and La Roche-Chalais, 32 kilometers (20 miles). Now, about 4 kilometers south of La Roche-Chalais take the right fork onto D21 toward Le Fieu. In 24 kilometers (115 miles) turn west on D244. Follow D244 for 5 kilometers (3 miles) and then turn south on D122. In 2 kilometers follow the camping sign left for Camping La Barbanne.

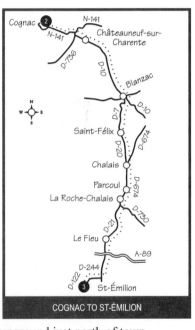

COGNAC TO ST-ÉMILION

ST-ÉMILION, FRANCE
Population 400

This beautiful little town is everything that you would expect in a Bordeaux wine village. It has old stone houses and vineyards surrounding it on all sides. There are lots of wine shops and restaurants. The fact that the town is frequented by tourists is good, not bad. You can enjoy the atmosphere and avoid the high prices by staying at the great campground just north of town.

You can take a ride on the wine train through some of the nearby vineyards. One of the best, **Château Ausone,** is just outside town. Check at the tourist office for vineyards open for guests. The town also has an underground church called the **Eglise Monolithe** and a castle built by Henry III of England, the **Château du Roi.**

St-Émilion Campground

 DOMAINE DE LA BARBANNE

Address:	Route de Montagne, F-33330 Saint-Émilion
Telephone:	05 57247580
Fax:	05 57246968
Website:	www.camping.saint-emilion.com
E-mail:	BARBANNE@wanadoo.fr
GPS:	N 44° 55' 02.8", W 000° 08' 27.3"

April 1 - Sept 22

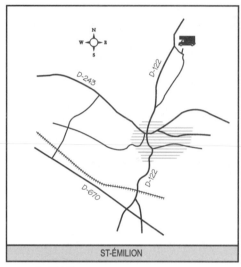

ST-ÉMILION

The campground is large, about 150 sites. They are back-in sites separated by hedges with parking on grass except for about 10 reserved for traveling camping-cars, these are gravel-surfaced. Electrical boxes are widely spaced (French, 6 amp). There are no permanently situated caravans. A small lake is adjacent to the campground and some of the nicer sites are facing it. Hot water is provided for showers (adjustable) and bathroom basins. There is a nice restaurant and a grocery shop in the reception office offering a good selection of local wines. Other facilities include two swimming pools, fishing in the small lake, tennis courts, mini golf and bicycle hire. There's a nice walking path around the lake although the distance is only about a half-kilometer.

St-Émilion is about 2.5 kilometers (1.6 miles) south of the campground along a country road. You can easily ride a bicycle or walk to town, there is no bus but the campground provides a shuttle.

OUTDOOR RESTAURANTS FILL THE SQUARES IN THE TOWN OF ST-ÉMILION

St-Émilion is located just east of Libourne. The campground is about 2.5 kilometers (1.6 miles) north of St-Émilion just off Highway D122 to Montagne and Lussac.

DRIVE 4 – ST-ÉMILION TO SARLAT
132 Kilometers (82 Miles), 2 Hours

A long The Way – From the south side of St-Émilion drive south for 1 kilometer (.6 mile) to join D936. Turn east and follow this highway as it joins the Dordogne River and arrives in the town of Bergerac, the distance is 50 kilometers (31 miles).

Bergerac is a good place to stop and look around. The town is known for its wine and, amazingly, tobacco. You may also be familiar with the town's namesake, Cyrano de Bergerac. The **Musée du Tabac** covers the tobacco industry, a drive 8 kilometers (5 miles) south to **Chateau Monbazillac**, home of the region's most famous wine, might round out your visit.

From Bergerac continue east, this time on the north side of the river on D660. At Lalinde, 18 kilometers (11 miles) east you must cross the river again and join the D29 as you continue eastward. In just 3 kilometers at Calès switch to D28 and then D29 as you follow signs for Le Buisson. In Le Buisson continue along the south bank of the river on D25 and at Siorac-en-Périgord the road becomes D703 and crosses the river to pass through Beynac-et-Cazenac. Just east of Beynac take the left fork and follow D57 northeast to Sarlat-la Canéda. See the campground description for final instructions for finding Camping Les Pereires.

SARLAT-LA-CANÉDA, FRANCE
Population 11,000

Sarlat-la-Canéda is located at the geographic center of the Dordogne region and is a good town to use as a base for your explorations. Sarlat itself has many attractions, it also is the best place to buy supplies in the valley.

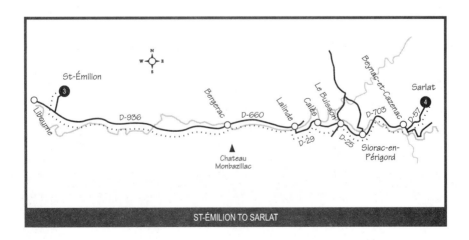

ST-ÉMILION TO SARLAT

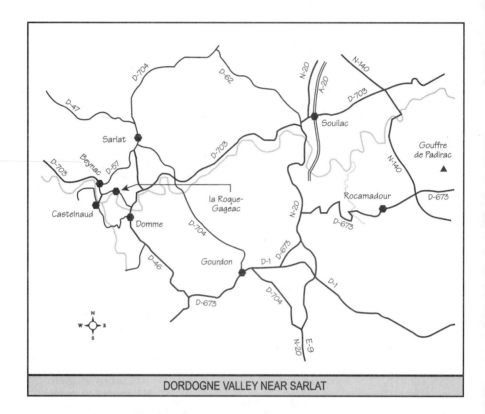

DORDOGNE VALLEY NEAR SARLAT

Sarlat is said to have a higher concentration of Medieval, Renaissance and 17th-century building facades than any town in France, today they are protected by law. The center of activities in Sarlat is the **Place de la Liberté**, a square in the center of a district of walking streets. Each Saturday a street market famous throughout France is held in the square.

Adjoining the Place de la Liberté is the **Cathédrale St-Sacerdos**, known for its organ. Another much-visited monument in Sarlat is the **Lanterne des Morts**, a conical-capped tower in the cemetery.

You'll find two small museums in town. **L'Homo Sapiens** has information about prehistoric man and the **Aquarium** spotlights the surprisingly large number of varieties of fish in the Dordogne River.

Sarlat's immediate vicinity holds many attractions. Just 10 kilometers south-west of Sarlat two 13th century castles face each other from outcroppings on opposite sides of the river, just as they did during the 100 Years War. The French were in **Beynac**, which is restored and must be toured with a guide, and the English in **Castelnaud**, with its own self-guided tour. There's also an exhibit of medieval siege weapons.

You can follow the north bank of the Dordogne less than 5 kilometers east from Beynac to **la Roque-Gageac**, a small village on the riverside beneath an overhanging cliff. Here you can catch a boat for a ride on the river. If you drive a short distance on across the river the road climbs a small mountain to the hilltop bastide village of **Domme**. Domme is justifiably famous in literature for its views (Henry Miller) and is also known for the caves beneath the town, they can be reached by elevator from the central square.

South of Sarlat at the eastern border of the region are two entirely different attractions. **Rocamadour** is a medieval pilgrimage town impressively situated on a cliff side. See if you can find Durandal, Roland's sword, plunged into the rock wall. **Gouffre de Padirac** (Padirac Chasm) is a giant series of limestone caves where visitors actually ride in a boat to view some of the more remote caverns. The underground regions are floodlit and elevators make access easy, these caves are some of Europe's finest. A driving tour from Sarlat to Rocamadour and then Gouffre de Padirac would be about 125 kilometers (78 miles) round trip.

Sarlat Campground

▲ CAMPING LES PÉRIÈRES

Address:	Rte. Ste Nathalène, F-24203 Sarlat
Telephone:	05 53590584
Fax:	05 53285751
Website:	www.campings-dordogne.com/les-perieres
E-mail:	LES-PERIERS@wanadoo.fr
GPS:	N 44° 53' 35.3", E 001° 13' 45.7"

April 1 - Sept 30

There are at least 35 campgrounds within a 20 kilometer radius of Sarlat, les

THE WEEKLY OUTDOOR MARKET IN SARLAT IS FAMOUS THROUGHOUT FRANCE

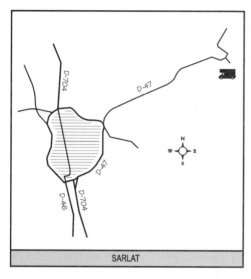

Périères is the closest to town and the only one allowing you to stroll in on foot. The distance to town is about one kilometer.

Campsites are arranged on spacious terraces in a semicircle overlooking the swimming pool and main buildings. All sites are covered with well-tended grass and most have convenient electrical (both Euro and French, 6 amp) and water connections. The five shower/toilet buildings are clean and well kept, hot water is provided for showers (adjustable), bathroom basins, and dishwashing. There are two beautiful swimming pools, one indoor. Other amenities include tennis courts, a bar and snack bar, terrace restaurant, small shop, and library. Many restaurants and shops are within walking distance in the old town.

To find the campground follow D47 toward Proissans and Ste. Nathalène. This small highway leaves Sarlat towards the northeast. You'll see the campground just a short distance up the hill from the old town.

Drive 5 – Sarlat to Périgueux
63 Kilometers (39 Miles), 1 Hour

Along **The Way** – From Sarlat head north on D47. The winding road will bring you to Les Eyzies-de-Tayac at 20 kilometers (12 miles).

Les Eyzies is a good stop on such a short mileage day. It occupies the Vézère River valley, sometimes called the "cradle of mankind". In dozens of caves along this valley archeologists have discovered prehistoric cave paintings and living sites. The **Musée National de la Préhistoire** will introduce you to the subject, the **Abri Pataud** nearby is an actual cave dwelling. Three kilometers away is the **Grotte du Grand Roc** area where you'll find cave dwellings, limestone caverns, and even the **Musée de Spéléologie** which covers cave exploration. Twenty-five kilometers up the Vézère near Montignac is **Lascaux** where some of the world's most impressive cave

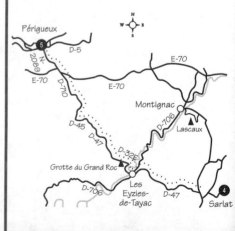

paintings were discovered in 1940. The original caves have been closed to visitors because bacteria and algae introduced by the visitor traffic were destroying the paintings but a replica cave has been constructed and is well worth a visit. The replica is called **Lascaux II**.

From Les Eyzies continue northwest on D31, D32E, D47, D45, D710, and N2089 always following signs for Périgueux. The distance is 41 kilometers (25 miles). See the campground description for final directions for finding Camping Barnabé.

PÉRIGUEUX, FRANCE

The town is know for its part Romanesque, part Byzantine **Cathédrale Saint-Front**. The **Musée du Périgord** will introduce you to the town's Roman ruins. Best of all is the Saturday street market, you'll be amazed by the nicest vegetables you've ever seen. And then there's the foie-gras.

THE CATHÉDRALE SAINT-FRONT IN PÉRIGUEUX

Périgueux Campground

▲ CAMPING DE BARNABÉ

Address: Rue des Bains, F-24750
                Boulazac-Périgueux
Telephone: 05 53534145
Fax: 05 53541662
GPS: N 45° 11' 13.0", E 000° 44' 31.1"

Open All Year

Camping Barnabé is an older but pleasant and unique place. There are sites on both sides of the Isle River, and a gondola-like hand-cranked cable ferry to carry you across. The campground is also easily within walking distance of the city.

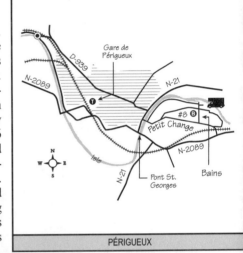

There are several camping areas here. One is behind the main building, one across the road, primarily for larger rigs and storage, and another across the river. The sites behind the office are good, parking is on grass with separating hedges in several places. Electrical boxes are widely separated (French and a few Euro, 4 or 6 amp). Restrooms are old but clean and some have been retiled, hot water is provided for showers and for dishwashing. The bar/restaurant overlooks the river and there are also mini-golf and Ping-Pong tables. The campground is 1.5 kilometers (.9 miles) from the bridge leading across to the old city, there is also bus service. Catch the Line 8 bus, the campground stop is Rue des Baines.

The campground is located in a residential area east of the city. It is well signed off N2089, the road eastward to Brive. Coming from town, about 2 kilometers (1.2 miles) east of the point where the N2089 leaves the city across the Pont St. Georges, turn left on Blvd. de Petit Change. After 0.5 kilometers (.3 miles) turn right on Rue des Bains, the campground is at the end, another 0.4 kilometers (.2 miles).

DRIVE 6 – PÉRIGUEUX TO BRACIEUX
325 Kilometers (201 Miles), 3.5 Hours

A long The Way – From Périgueux drive east on N21. This highway will lead you 100 kilometers (62 miles) northeast to the A20 autoroute at Limoges.

Drive north on the A20 for 159 kilometers (98 miles) to Exit 9, marked Graçay-St-Outrille. From the exit drive north on D83 to Graçay and D922 to Faubourg-Saint-Roch, a distance of 32 kilometers (20 miles). From Faubourg-Saint-Roch follow

D765 northwest for 10 kilometers (6 miles) to the intersection with D119, then turn north on D119 which will take you directly to Bracieux. The campground is on the north side of town, see the campground write-up for final directions.

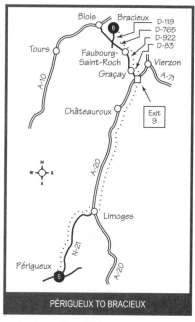

BRACIEUX, FRANCE

This is a municipal campground perfectly located in a quiet little town and convenient for sightseeing, particularly for a visit to Chambord. The eastern Loire around Bracieux has many châteaux but the three best known are Chambord, Cheverny, and Chaumont. **Chambord**, seven kilometers (4 miles) to the north of Bracieux and about five kilometers south of the Loire is the largest and probably most impressive of the Loire's châteaux. It is a royal château, building was started by Françoise I in 1519, it was actually finished by Louis XIV. The Château has an isolated location and visitors come in cars and busses. On occasion we've had the whole place to ourselves with no other visitors. Leonardo da Vinci is said to have worked on the design, he was a

TENT CAMPING IN THE LOIRE VALLEY

visitor to the Loire at that time, and died in the valley.

Cheverny is located 10 kilometers (6 miles) southeast of Bracieux. It was finished in 1634 and is a luxurious country residence. The château is known for it's perfect classical-era design, the interior is beautifully furnished.

Bracieux Campground

▲ CAMPING MUNICIPAL DES CHATEAUX

Address:	11 Rue Roger Brun, F-41250 Bracieux
Telephone:	02 54464184
Fax:	02 54460915
GPS:	N 47° 33' 05.4", E 001° 32' 20.0"

April 1 - Oct 15

CHAMBORD IS THE LOIRE'S LARGEST AND MOST IMPRESSIVE CHÂTEAU

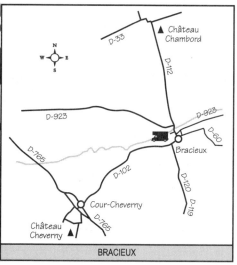

This municipal campground is located on the northern edge of the town of Bracieux. It is a good place to stay while visiting the chateaux upstream from Tours, especially Chambord and Cheverny. Bracieux is less tourist-oriented than some towns and campgrounds in the area and in a way that's a relief.

This is a large campground with parking on grass off gravel drives. Electrical boxes (French, 3 amp) are widely scattered. Restrooms are modern and clean with hot water for showers and dishes. Amenities include a pool and tennis courts and the village offers basic shopping and restaurants.

Bracieux is small and the campground is well signed. It is located on D112, the road toward Chambord to the north.

DRIVE 7 – BRACIEUX TO PARIS
162 Kilometers (100 Miles), 1.75 Hours

A long The Way – From Bracieux follow the D112 north past Chambord and across the Loire to the entrance for the A10, 20 kilometers (12 miles). Then follow A10 all the way to Paris, a distance of 140 kilometers (87 miles).

Information Resources

See our Internet site at www.rollinghomes.com for many links to information sources.

French Government Tourist Office, 444 Madison Avenue, 16th Floor, New York, NY 10022-6903 (212 838-7800). In Canada the address is 1981 McGill College Ave, Suite 490, Montreal, Quebec H3A 2W9 (514 288-4264).

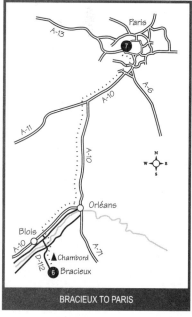

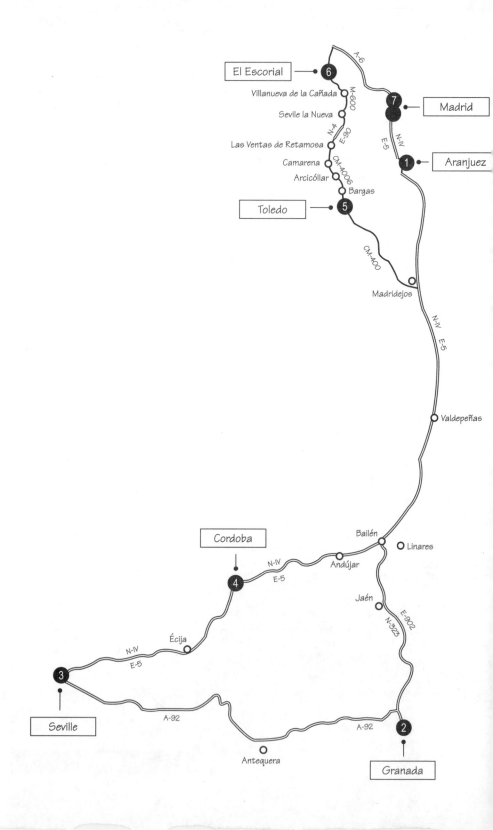

El Escorial

Villanueva de la Cañada

Sevile la Nueva

Las Ventas de Retamosa

Camarena

Arcicóllar

Bargas

Toledo

Madridejos

Valdepeñas

Cordoba

Bailén

Linares

Andújar

Jaén

Écija

Seville

Antequera

Granada

Madrid

Aranjuez

A-6

M-600

N-4

E-90

CM-4006

CM-400

N-IV

E-5

N-IV

E-5

N-IV

E-5

A-92

A-92

N-IV

E-5

N-323

E-902

Chapter 13
Tour 10

Spain

Top Attractions

- ❖ Madrid
- ❖ Palacio Real Aranjuez
- ❖ Granada
- ❖ Seville
- ❖ Mezquita in Cordoba
- ❖ Toledo
- ❖ El Escorial
- ❖ Valley of the Fallen

General Description

Spain is reported to be the second most popular tourist destination in Europe with only France having more visitors. By following the tour in this chapter you'll visit many of the most popular cities in the country.

This tour covers a total of 1,308 kilometers or 811 miles. There are three long driving days, one medium one, and three with distances of less than 100 kilometers. The long driving days are on autopistas so with an early start any of them can be finished early in the afternoon allowing you sightseeing time in the destination city.

Campground opening dates would allow you to make this tour any time of year but you should be aware that temperatures in the interior of Spain, particularly in the Madrid area, can be very cool in the winter. The best time to do this tour is between April 1 and October 31.

The gateway city for this tour is the capital of Spain, Madrid. It has the country's best air connections, and, like all of our gateway cities, offers automobile and RV rentals.

THE PRADO IN MADRID HOUSES SOME OF EUROPE'S TOP MASTERPIECES

The first driving day is a very short one, a good way to get familiar with your vehicle and with the camping scene. Aranjuez is just 40 kilometers or so south of Madrid and has plenty to see and do including a palace to tour and a big hypermarket for stocking up on supplies.

Get an early start for the second day of driving because this is the tour's longest driving day – 370 kilometers (229 miles), about 4 hours on excellent roads. Granada is rich in atmosphere and sights, you'll be busy well into the evening.

The third drive takes you west to Sevilla. The most popular sight is the cathedral, the world's third largest.

On drive four you'll head back east, your destination is Cordoba. The attraction here is the Mezquita, and also the old city streets in the central area.

The following driving day you'll head back for the region around Madrid. Toledo is just 60 kilometers (37 miles) south of the city, but you must spend the night there so you can visit the old city after the tourist busses have gone home.

The final night is spent west of Madrid near the town of San Lorenzo de Escorial. This was the center of power of Spain's most powerful king, Philip II. His huge El Escorial monastery is often called the first government office complex, but there was and is much more to the building than that.

The final drive is another short one, just 50 kilometers (31 miles) on good roads, less than an hour to get you back into Madrid.

If you would like to modify this tour you might consider staying in the Madrid region. You would visit four of the seven destinations listed here and spend very little time actually driving. There are many additional Spanish destinations and campgrounds listed in our second Europe book – ***Traveler's Guide to European Camping***.

Roads and Driving

Roads are generally pretty good in Spain. The system is improving as the country builds autopistas (expressways) and many miles of them are open. The major secondary roads that are the alternative to the toll roads are for the most part decent. Many, especially in central Spain outside the immediate vicinity of Madrid, don't have much traffic and you can move right along. Others, particularly along the Mediterranean can be terribly crowded, you'll count yourself lucky to have the toll autopista handy.

The quality of Spanish driving is just fine (it has improved in recent years). The only difference you'll notice from North America is a slightly more aggressive technique, just as in the rest of Europe.

The national number for emergencies in Spain is 112.

Camping and Campgrounds

Spain has quite a few campgrounds. They've been developed with sun-seeking tourists from the rest of Europe in mind. In the last decade or so many Iberian residents have begun to buy campers to take advantage of the camping facilities. Some

AN INTERESTING MOTORHOME IN THE GRANADA CAMPGROUND

leave their rigs in the campgrounds so there are increased numbers of semi permanent resident campers in some campgrounds, especially near larger cities.

Winter camping is not very practical in the interior of Spain. While campgrounds may be open the weather can be very cool. Often campground amenities, like restaurants and stores, are closed for the winter.

You'll find a grab bag of electrical connectors in use here. Some newer campgrounds use the Euro (CEE17) outlet, but many more have older German-style outlets.

A Camping Card International is usually not required in Spain but is helpful if you wish to avoid handing over your passport to the reception desk.

Practical Tips

Spain is a member of the European Union (the EU) and uses the Euro. Now that Spain is part of the EU the prices are really not much different from those in the rest of Europe. Gas and groceries are cheaper but campgrounds are consistently more expensive. Hypermarkets are common in cities and even smaller towns have medium-sized supermarkets.

Credit cards are easy to use in Spain. You can almost always buy gas and groceries with credit card. Cash machines are ubiquitous.

DISPLAY OF DISHES AT A TAPAS BAR NEAR THE PLAZA MAYOR

THE TOUR – SPAIN

TOUR 10 GATEWAY CITY – MADRID, SPAIN
Population 3,200,000

Madrid is one of the lesser-visited European capitals and is known mostly for its museums. Don't let the lack of monuments keep you away. Once you are in Madrid you will find that the street, cafe, and bar scene is the real attraction, and there are many good day trips into the surrounding countryside. The central city is relatively compact and accessible. If you don't feel like walking there is a good subway system.

Most visitors to Madrid would be surprised to learn that the city was little more than a country town when Philip II decided to make it his capital in 1561. Even after that he spent much of his energy building El Escorial nearby, and in 1588 the defeat of the Spanish Armada signaled the end of Spain's glory years and imposed limits on the city's growth and wealth. Only the Plaza Mayor was actually planned as a plaza, the others grew from crossroads.

Number one on most visitor's reasons for coming to Madrid is probably the **Prado Museum**. It is one of the top two or three museums in the world and houses an enormous collection of paintings collected over the centuries by Spanish royalty. Nearby you'll also find the **Centro de Arte Reina Sofía** which houses **Guernica**, one of Picasso's most famous paintings. Also nearby are the **Museo Thyssen-Bornemiza** and several other museums including the **Archaeological Museum (Museo Arqueológico)** which has an underground replica of the Altamira cave paintings.

You can have a good look at central Madrid with a walking tour that connects its plazas. Start at the **Plaza de Oriente** on the western edge of the central area and work your way east. The Plaza de Oriente is bordered by the **Royal Palace** and is the site where Franco gave many of his speeches. The Royal Palace is enormous and well worth touring. To the southeast the **Plaza Mayor** is one of the largest town squares in Europe, it is surrounded by arcades and dates from 1620. Around the Plaza Mayor is the older section of Madrid, especially just to the west. There are narrow streets and small plazas to explore. The **Puerta del Sol** to the northeast of the Plaza Mayor is the center of traffic in town. It is the zero kilometer point for Spain's highways and has the central metro station underneath. The **Plaza Cánovas del Castillo** has a statue of Neptune in the center of a traffic circle with the Paseo del Prado boulevard stretching north and south. The Prado Museum is on one side of this plaza and the Museo Thyssen-Bornemisza on the other. North of this is the **Plaza de la Cibeles** with the well-loved statue of Sybil in the center of another traffic circle. Even farther north is **Plaza de Colón** with a statue of Columbus in the center. Finally, just down the top shopping street in town, **Calle de Serrano**, is the **Plaza de la Independencia** and the entrance to the **Parque del Retiro**.

Madrid is known for its late dinner hour and late night partying. No one would think of going to a restaurant before nine o'clock, ten is better. Before dinner you can visit the tapas bars of **Cava de San Miguel**, just west of the Plaza Mayor. After dinner try the **Malasaña district** near the Plaza dos de Mayo which is near the Noviciado (line 2), Bilbao, and Tribunal (line 1) metro stops just north of central Madrid.

Madrid Campgrounds

▲ CAMPING OSUNA

Address:	Avda. de Logroño S/N, E-28042
	Barejas (Madrid)
Telephone:	917 410510
Fax:	913 206365
E-mail:	camping.osuna.Madrid@microgest.es
GPS:	N 40° 27' 13.6", W 003° 36' 12.0"

Open All Year

Preferred by visitors to Madrid largely because its easy metro access lets you reach the center of the city easily, Camping Osuna is located just off the M-40 ring road on the eastern side of the city. Across the street is the very large and virtually treeless Parque Juan Carlos I with miles of walking trails and many other attractions. Camping is in two areas. One is demarcated by short hedges near the entrance and has shade trees, the other is a large grassy area without separations between sites. Electrical boxes are very widely spaced and low-amp (German, 3 amp). Facilities are old but kept fairly clean. Hot water is provided for showers (twist valves, adjustable) and dishwashing. The Canillejas metro station at the eastern end of the green line is about a kilometer distant.

To reach the campground southbound on M-40 take Exit 8 which is marked Avda de Logroño. Go left at the roundabout at the foot of the ramp to pass under the freeway and railroad tracks, and take the first right beyond, the campground entrance is on the left just after the turn. Heading north on M-40 there is no exit so you must go to Exit 7 and reverse direction, then follow the directions above.

▲ CAMPING ALPHA

Address:	Carretera N-1V, Km. 12.4,
	E-28906 Getafe (Madrid)
Telephone:	916 958069
Fax:	916 831659
E-mail:	bungalows@alpha.e.telefonica.net
GPS:	N 40° 19' 02.0", W 003° 41' 19.9"

Open All Year

Camping Alpha is a large campground with many permanent resident trailers. Space for tourists is limited but generally available, especially in the off season. Sites are dirt, mud is a problem if it is raining. Electricity (Euro and German, medium amp) is available at all sites, water and gray-water drains are also available at many. The shower/toilet building is modern and clean with hot showers but water in bathroom basins, dishwashing sinks, and laundry sinks is cold. The bar/restaurant and grocery shop remain open all winter. Transportation to Madrid is by a combination of bus and subway. A fifteen-minute bus ride will bring you to the Legazpi subway station on Line 3, the central Sol station is five stops away.

Camping Alpha is situated near the N-IV freeway south of the city in an indus-

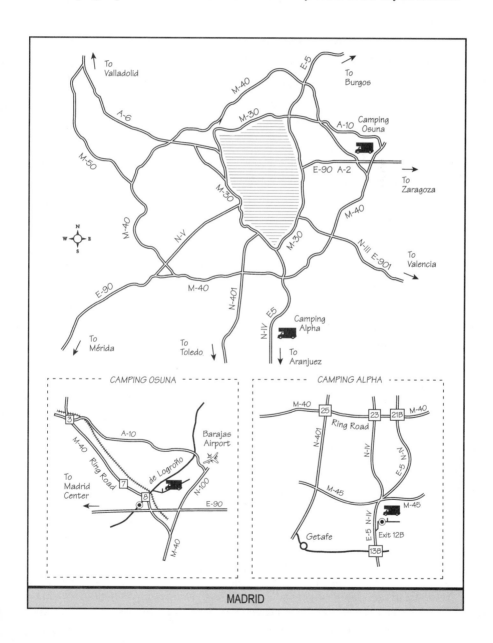

trial subdivision. You can only enter the campground if you are traveling north on the freeway, use the Getafe off-ramp (No.13b) to turn around if you are heading south. The turn-around route is simple and has campground signs to lead you around. Heading north there is an off-ramp just north of the No.13 exit, take it and at the 12.4 km point a sign for the campground points right into the entrance for the industrial area, drive to the roundabout, the campground entrance is on the left on the far side.

DRIVE 1 – MADRID TO ARANJUEZ
40 Kilometers (25 Miles), .75 Hour

Along The Way – From Madrid drive south on the N-IV, also sometimes called the E-5. 30 miles (19 kilometers) south of Madrid take Exit 37 and drive southeast on M-305. See the campground write-up for final directions to Camping Soto del Castillo.

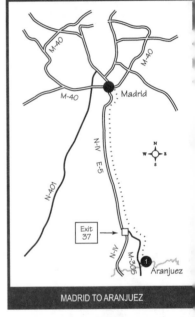

ARANJUEZ, SPAIN
Population 39,000

The equivalent of Versailles for the 18th-century Spanish Bourbons was Aranjuez. It is located about 40 kilometers northeast of Toledo and about the same distance south of Madrid. The small town is on the banks of the Tagus River and is one of the greenest places in the interior of Spain as a result. The **Palacio Real** is Versailles-style and there are extensive gardens. The **Casa del Labrador**, located nearby, is a smaller palace well worth a tour to see the interior.

MADRID TO ARANJUEZ

Aranjuez Campground

▲ CAMPING SOTO DEL CASTILLO

Address:	Soto del Rebollo S/N,
	E-28300 Aranjuez (Madrid)
Telephone:	918 911395
Fax:	918 914797
Website:	www.aranjuez.com
GPS:	N 40° 02' 30.8", W 003° 35' 58.1"

Open All Year

This campground is popular in winter as a convenient and inexpensive stopover for folks headed south to the Costa del Sol. The nearby gardens and palace will make you want to stay another night and it is also possible to use this campground as a base for exploring Madrid since there is good train service.

It is a municipal campground but has good facilities. Parking is on grass, sites are

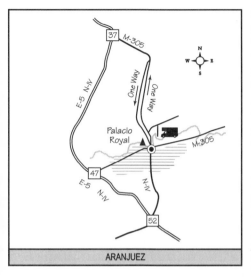

ARANJUEZ

not marked or separated and long cords (6 amp) may be necessary. Even in winter there is usually some service available in the bar/restaurant although the pool is closed. There's a heated bathroom and hot water in showers and dishwashing sinks. Just downstream along the river a pedestrian bridge will take you across the river into the gardens and then it's an easy walk to the Palacio Real and town.

The campground is easy to find if you keep in mind that it is located on the north side of the river to the east of town. Follow the road on the north side of the river eastward from the bridge near the Palacio Royal for about a half-kilometer and you'll spot the campground sign pointing right to the campground.

DRIVE 2 – ARANJUEZ TO GRANADA
370 Kilometers (229 Miles), 4.25 Hours

A long The Way – This is a long day's drive by European standards. From Aranjuez drive south to join the N-IV at Exit 52. Then follow N-IV (E-5) and N-323 (E-902) all the way south to Granada. See the campground write-up for final directions to the Granada campgrounds.

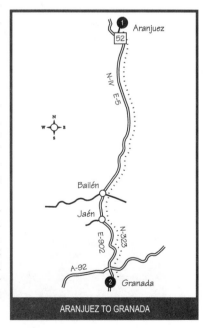

ARANJUEZ TO GRANADA

GRANADA, SPAIN
Population 240,000

Granada, like Cordoba, has a rich Moorish history, but Granada's golden age was later than Cordova's. To evoke the period of Moorish splendor during the 13th, 14th, and 15th centuries try reading *Tales of the Alhambra* by Washington Irving, which is also the best introduction to the **Alhambra**, Granada's most important attraction. Sitting high on the mountainside above Granada the Alhambra has palaces, towers and gardens with names you've heard all your life: Generalife, Alcazaba, and Court of the Lions. You'll also want to explore the city's old quarter or **Albaicín** and drive up the **Camino del Sacromonte** past gypsy cave houses to the monastery near the top of the mountain.

Granada Campgrounds

▲ CAMPING REINA ISABEL

Address:	Laurel de la Reina No 15,	
	E-18140 La Zubia (Granada)	
Telephone:	958 590041	
Fax:	958 591191	
Website:	www.campingreinaisabel.com	
E-mail:	granada@campingreinaisabel.com	
GPS:	N 37° 07' 28.7", W 003° 35' 09.2"	

Open All Year

This campground is located in the quiet Granada suburb of La Zubia, an easy 15-minute bus trip from the center of town. Buses run every 20 minute or so, very convenient.

The campground has about 40 back-in sites. They are separated by hedges, electricity (mostly Euro, 6 amp, some German, 5 amp) is available, sometimes requiring long cords. The restroom building is modern and clean and has hot showers but cold water to bathroom basins. The dishwashing area has one warm water tap. The restaurant here is very good, it gets a lot of trade from outside the campground.

To find the campground from the N-323 that runs west of Granada take Exit 135 for the Ronda Sur highway, then very soon take Exit 2 for La Zubia. From the large roundabout under the freeway go south toward La Zubia, you'll see the campground on the right in 2.9 kilometers (1.8 miles).

LOOKING UP AT THE DOME INSIDE THE CATHEDRAL IN GRANADA

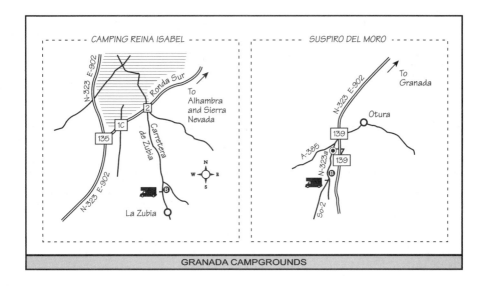

GRANADA CAMPGROUNDS

▲ SUSPIRO DEL MORO

Address:	Autovia Bailér-Motril Km 139,
	E-18630 Otura (Granada)
Telephone:	958 555411
Fax:	958 555105
E-mail:	suspirodelmoroo@eresmas.com
GPS:	N 37° 04' 06.3", W 003° 39' 07.6"

Open All Year

Suspiro del Moro is located along the road from the coast about 14 kilometers (9 miles) outside Granada. In the summer you'll appreciate the slightly cooler temperatures that this campground in the Sierra Nevada foothills offers.

The campground is located on a flat shelf with a large pool area and restaurant between it and the highway. Campsites are on gravel and sparse grass with some shade trees. The sites are numbered and hedges provide some separation between small groups of sites. Electricity (German, medium amp) is available at widely-spaced cement vaults that service groups of sites, about half of the sites can use electricity at one time. There are two clean and well maintained shower/toilet buildings, they have hot showers (premixed pushbutton valve), and cold water for bathroom basins, dishwashing sinks and laundry tubs. The large pool on a terrace between the roadside restaurant and the campground is the social center of the campground, there is also a small grocery shop.

Bus service to Granada is on pretty much an hourly schedule, you'll want to try to catch an express as they takes only about 20 minutes to make the run versus three times that for the others. The reception desk has the details as well as lots of visitor information about Granada.

The campground is along the old N-323a, now a modern autopista running along-side is used by most travelers from the coast. To get to the campground take Exit 139 from the autopista which is signed as being to La Malahá and Otura, then follow N-323a along the west side of the autopista. The campground is on the right 1.8 kilometers (1.1 miles) from the junction at the point where there is a Y with a road splitting off for Almuñécar.

DRIVE 3 – GRANADA TO SEVILLE
258 Kilometers (160 Miles), 2.5 Hours

A long The Way – From Granada follow A-92 eastward through Andalucia to Seville. See the campground write-ups for final directions to the Seville camp-grounds.

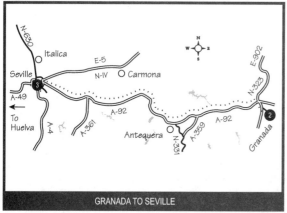

GRANADA TO SEVILLE

SEVILLE (SEVILLA), SPAIN
Population 700,000

Always a great city to visit, Seville is looking good after be-ing spruced up for EXPO 92. Im-provements include new high-ways, a new bus and train sta-tion, and a new riverfront prom-enade. However, the real attrac-tions continue to be the historic buildings, vivacious people, and old neighborhoods or barrios sur-rounding the city center.

The most important buildings are clustered a short distance from the Guadalquivir River. Seville's **cathedral**, quickly built in just over 100 years, is the largest in Spain and the third largest church in the world (after Rome's St. Peter's and London's St. Paul's). Next door is the **Giralda Tower**, originally a Moorish mosque's minaret and now the cathedral's bell tower. The tower affords great views of the cathedral's gargoyles. Nearby is the **Alcázar**, a Moorish-style palace actually built by the Christian king Pedro I in the 14th century. It has a delightful garden.

Just north of the Alcázar is the **Barrio de Santa Cruz**, today rather upscale. Here you'll catch glimpses of flower-filled patios behind wrought-iron gates. The **Calle de las Sierpes** is a favorite shopping and strolling street.

From Seville you can drive some 25 kilometers (15 miles) east to **Carmona**, a very old walled hillside village. Take a look at the **Roman Necropolis** and the town's fortifications. There is a Parador here in the ruins of the **Alcázar de Arriba**.

Just north of Seville on N-630 is **Italica**, an ancient Roman city that is being excavated. This is no Pompeii but there is a large **amphitheater**. The town may not look like much now but three important Roman emperors were born here: Trajan, Hadrian, and Theodosius.

The **Parque Nacional de Doñana** is Spain's largest national park and very popular with bird watchers and nature lovers. Drive west on A-49 toward Huelva and then south at Exit 10 toward Almonte. Near the coast you'll find the Reception and Interpretation Center, starting point for very popular jeep tours of the park. Total distance from Seville is about 100 kilometers.

You can drive west along the coast from the park to see the point where Columbus departed on his first voyage to America near Huelva. The actual point of departure is **Palos de la Frontera** but the monastery of **La Rábida** is known to Spaniards as the "birthplace of America" because Columbus used it as a base and received much of his political support from the friars here.

Seville Campgrounds

▲ CAMPING VILLSOM

Address: Camping Villsom, Ctra. Madrid-Cádiz N-IV
              Km 554.8, E-41700 Dos Hermanas (Sevilla)
Telephone: 954 720828
GPS: N 37° 16' 39.3", W 005° 56' 11.3"

Open All Year

This campground has been a popular place to stay when visiting Seville for many years. The many orange trees shading the sites make it very pleasant. Sites are back-ins (German, 7 amp), rigs over about 25 feet will find few places to park. Restrooms offer hot adjustable showers and there are some hot water faucets in the dishwashing room, bathroom sinks have cold water only. Breakfast is served in summer and there is a nice pool as well as a mini-golf course. The bus to Sevilla (No. 132 Dos Hermanas-Sevilla) is about a half-kilometer distant and there are Carrefour and Lidl supermarkets within a kilometer.

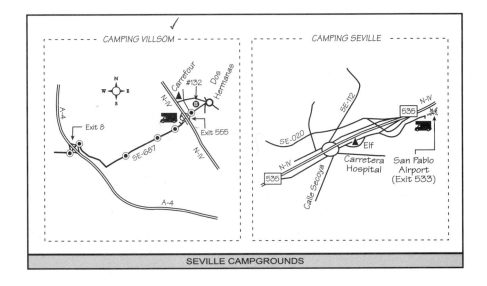

SEVILLE CAMPGROUNDS

To most easily reach the campground take Exit 8 from the A-4 Highway south of Seville. Follow signs for Dos Hermanas. You will find the campground on your left at 3.5 km from the highway just before you reach the overpass over the N-IV highway. From the N-IV you can take Exit 555, the campground is on the west side of N-IV.

▲ CAMPING SEVILLA

Address:	Ctra National N IV (Madrid-Cádiz)
	Km 534, E-41007 Sevilla
Telephone:	954 514379
GPS:	N 37° 25' 04.6", W 005° 55' 04.7"

Open All Year

Camping Sevilla is a medium-sized campground located next to the N-IV (E-5) Cádiz-Madrid freeway east of Sevilla near the airport (at the end of the runway). It is a flat field with packed sand and grass sites. A few trees provide some shade. Most sites have convenient electricity (German, 6 amp). The shower/toilet buildings are older but well maintained, there are free hot showers (adjustable) and cold water for bathroom basins and dishwashing sinks. The campground also has a swimming pool, a bar/restaurant, and a grocery shop. The airport next door has jet traffic and is noisy during takeoffs. Bus transportation to Sevilla (about 10 kilometers (6 miles) to the west) is frequent but you must walk about a kilometer to the stop if it is not summer when there is a bus from the campground. Check at the reception desk for details.

A FUN WAY TO SEE THE SIGHTS IN SEVILLE

Access to the campground is from a side road next to the freeway. While the campground is at kilometer 534 you must exit the freeway at the exit at Km 535 (west of the campground). There is a traffic circle under the freeway at this exit, the side access road leads east from this circle along the south side of the freeway. Follow it 0.7 kilometer (.4 mile) past the back of the Elf station to the campground. There are campground signs pointing (a little ambiguously) at the proper exit from the traffic circle.

DRIVE 4 – SEVILLE TO CORDOBA
139 Kilometers (86 Miles), 1.75 Hours

A long The Way – From Seville follow N-IV (E-5) east to Cordoba. See the camground write-up for the final directions to Campamento Municipal El Brillante.

CORDOVA (CÓRDOBA), SPAIN
Population 300,000

Cordova's glory days were during the tenth century when the Moorish city was one of the world's greatest. Today Cordova is about a third the size that it was then and a much less important player on the world's stage. Cordova remains one of Spain's most-visited tourist cities. People come to see the **Mezquita**, the large mosque that was later con-

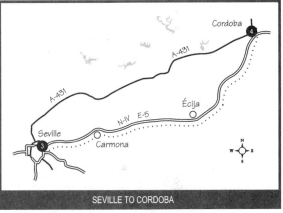

verted to a church. You'll also enjoy the narrow streets and squares of the old city near the Guadalquivir River.

Cordova Campground

▲ CAMPAMENTO MUNICIPAL EL BRILLANTE

Address:	Avda. del Brillante No. 50, E-14012 Córdoba
Telephone:	957 282165
Website:	www.campingelbrillante.com
E-mail:	elbrillante@campings.net
GPS:	N 37° 54' 02.1", W 004° 47' 14.5"

Open All Year

Long an institution in Cordova, Campamento Municipal has recently been upgraded with modernized restrooms and even some new sites with electricity, water, and sewer. Expect hot weather if you're here in the summer, the pool is very popular.

This is a medium-sized campground with sites on packed dirt under trees, some are olive trees. There are also some frames and netting for artificial shade. Electricity

(German and Euro, 10 amp) is convenient to many of the sites. The shower/toilet buildings are recently renovated, they have free hot showers, hot water in bathroom basins, and hot water for dishwashing sinks. There is a beautiful swimming pool at the campground which is also open to people not camping here, it has a separate entrance for them. There is also a restaurant and a small grocery shop. A brand new large shopping center with a huge Carrefour supermarket is about 1 kilometer from the campground.

City busses #10 and #11 run from a stop in front of the campground to the El Corte Ingles store in the center of town and run frequently. You can also walk through town toward the river to the old town, the distance is about 3 kilometers and the walk takes about 40 minutes.

Easiest access is from the N-IV (E-5) highway running southeast of town. Take Exit 399 and zero your odometer. At first follow signs for Badajoz. At 1.1 kilometers (.7 miles) on your odometer the road splits, go straight toward Córdoba Norte (not

THE INTERIOR OF THE MESQUITA IN CORDOBA

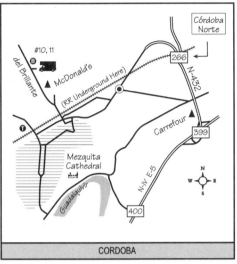

CORDOBA

toward Badajoz). Pass though several stop-lights and at 3.8 kilometers (2.4 miles) on your odometer the road climbs up and over some railroad tracks. Continue passing straight through a traffic circle and through many more stoplights. At 5.4 kilometers (3.4 miles) on your odometer you'll see an old tower on the left and a sign on the right seemingly telling you to turn right for the campground. Don't do it. Continue another 0.2 kilometer (.1 mile), 5.6 kilometers (3.5 miles) from where you zeroed your odometer, and turn right. Don't turn more than 90 degrees, you are actually in a big traffic circle that straddles a large park and want to pass through and into Ave. del Brillante on the far side. You'll see the campground on the right 1.2 kilometers (.7 miles) from the turn, 6.8 kilometers (4.2 miles) from where you originally zeroed your odometer.

DRIVE 5 – CORDOBA TO TOLEDO
356 Kilometers (221 Miles), 3.75 Hours

A long The Way – From Cordoba follow N-IV (E-5) northeast. After 270 kilometers (167 miles) exit from the highway near Madridejos onto CM-400 and follow the highway northeast for 69 kilometers (43 miles) to Toledo. See the campground write-up for the final directions to Camping "El Greco".

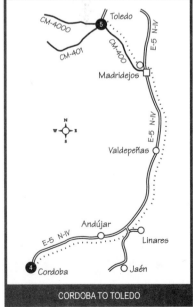

CORDOBA TO TOLEDO

TOLEDO, SPAIN
Population 67,000

The first thing to do when you arrive in Toledo is to drive the **Carretera de Circunvalección** which follows the Rio Tajo around the south side of the city. There are several places where you can park and take advantage of memorable views of the city across the river gorge. You'll be able to see most of the important monuments in the town and appreciate the military advantages of Toledo's site.

The city has justifiably been designated a national monument. It is a well-preserved medieval town and as such is probably best enjoyed by wandering the narrow streets in the morning before the tour busses arrive or in the evening after they leave. This is a good reason to spend several days at the campground here. The tourist sights include the **Cathedral**, the **House and Museum of El Greco**, **El Alcázar**, and **Santo Tome**, which houses El Greco's *The Burial of Count Orgaz* in a chapel with its own entrance.

Toledo Campground

▲ Camping "El Greco"

Address:	Ctra. CM-4000 Km 0.7, 45004 Toledo
Telephone:	925 220090
E-mail:	elgreco@ratemail.es
GPS:	N 39° 51' 54.7", W 004° 02' 49.4"

Open All Year

✓ El Greco is an excellent medium to large campground situated on the bank of the Tagus River about 2 kilometers (1.2 miles) west of Toledo's old town. Camping sites are on packed dirt under a grove of trees, shade is important here in the summer and you may wish the trees were bigger. Hedges separate about half the sites. Electricity (Euro, 10 amp) is available but outlets are widely spaced. The shower/toilet buildings

GATES OF THE WALLED CITY OF TOLEDO

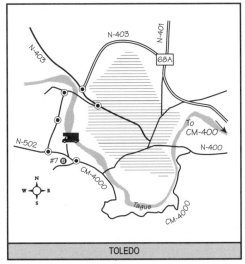

TOLEDO

are modern and have hot showers with push button valves (not adjustable) and cold water for bathroom basins. There is adjustable hot water for dishwashing and laundry tubs and a coin-operated washer and dryer. The campground has a nice swimming pool. The restaurant and bar and a grocery shop are open all year.

You can walk to the foot of the old town in 20 minutes from the campground or take a bus. The Number 7 stops just outside the gate and runs hourly. It will take you right to the central square in the old town.

The campground entrance is on Highway CM-4000 (Toledo's ring road) to the west of Toledo and it is well signed once you get to the west side of town.

DRIVE 6 – TOLEDO TO EL ESCORIAL
95 Kilometers (59 Miles), 1.75 Hours

A long The Way – From Toledo follow N-401 just a few kilometers north to Exit 65. From there follow CM-4006 north through Bargas, Arcicóllar, Camarena, and Las Ventas de Retamosa to meet N-V (E-90). Travel north on E-90 just 7 kilometers (4 miles) and leave the highway at Exit 32 to continue north on M-600. M-600 will take you through Sevila la Nueva, and Villanueva de la Cañada to El Escorial.

TOLEDO TO EL ESCORIAL

SAN LORENZO DE EL ESCORIAL, SPAIN
Population 11,000

There are two important sights in the neighborhood of this small town. The first is **El Escorial** itself, a huge combination monastery and palace built in 1584 by Philip II. Some historians consider it the first massive government office building. Inside the enormous pile you'll find tombs, an important art collection, a library, royal apartments and a massive basilica. About 10 kilometers from El Escorial (on the opposite side of the campground) is the **Valley of the Fallen (Valle de los Caidos)** with its 485-foot-high cross and a crypt and basilica hollowed out of the mountainside. It is a monument to the people killed during the Spanish Civil War.

San Lorenzo de El Escorial Campground

▲ Camping Caravanning "El Escorial"

€€	€€€	⛺	♿	🍴	🛒

Address: Ado de Correos No. 8, Carretera de
Guadarrama a El Escorial Km. 3.5,
E-28280 El Escorial, Madrid
Telephone: 918 902412
Fax: 918 961062
Website: www.campingescorial.com
E-mail: info@campingelescorial.com
GPS: N 40° 37' 33.0", W 004° 06' 00.1"

Open All Year

This is an enormous campground located about 6 kilometers from the town of San Lorenzo de El Escorial. It makes a good base for exploring the region and the city of Madrid

The campground has over a thousand sites. There are a large number of permanently located rigs but they are in an area isolated from the tourist sites and are not really a factor, except that they justify the large variety of amenities in the campground. Tourist sites are on sparse grass and are numbered but not separated by vegetation. Many have shade in the form of a metal frame with mesh cover. There is also a large grassy field for overflow and tent sites. Electricity (German, 5 amp) is available to most sites but there are enough sockets for about half the sites and the boxes are widely spaced. Shower/toilet buildings are modern and well maintained, heated

VALLEY OF THE FALLEN

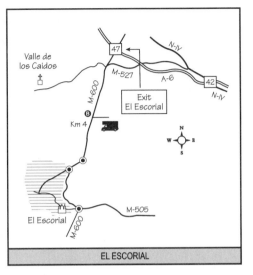

EL ESCORIAL

when necessary, and have free hot water for showers (adjustable, push button valve), bathroom basins and dishwashing. There are a limited number, considering the campground size, of coin-operated washers. Other amenities include a large grocery shop, restaurant/bar, disco, tennis courts, three swimming pools, and lighted basketball and soccer areas. There is a supermarket near the entrance to the town of El Escorial about 6 kilometers (3.7 miles) from the campground.

Both Madrid and San Lorenzo de El Escorial are serviced by a bus which stops at the campground entrance. The bus runs from near the El Escorial monastery to the Moncloa metro station in Madrid and stops at the campground en route so you can reach either one with it. Madrid is about an hour away.

You will find the campground on Highway M-600 about 6 kilometers (3.7 miles) north of San Lorenzo de El Escorial, near the 4-km marker. Coming from Madrid take the exit marked El Escorial from Highway A6 and follow signs for El Escorial. The campground will be on your left from this direction.

DRIVE 7– EL ESCORIAL TO MADRID
50 Kilometers (31 Miles), .75 Hour

A long The Way – From the camp ground follow M-600 north to the A-6 autopista and then the A-6 eastward to Madrid.

Information Resources

See our Internet site at www.rollinghomes.com for many links to information sources.

Spanish National Tourist Office, 666 Fifth Avenue, New York, NY 10103 (212 265-8822). In Canada the address is 2 Bloor Street West, 34th Floor, Toronto, Ontario M4W 3E2. (416 961 3131).

EL ESCORIAL TO MADRID

Index

ABOUT THE AUTHORS

For the last twelve years Terri and Mike Church have traveled in Mexico, Alaska, Europe, Canada, and the western U.S. Most of this travel has been in RVs, a form of travel they love. It's affordable and comfortable; the perfect way to see interesting places.

Over the years they discovered that few guidebooks were available with the essential day-to-day information that camping travelers need when they are in unfamiliar surroundings. *RV and Car Camping Vacations in Europe, Traveler's Guide to European Camping, Traveler's Guide to Mexican Camping, Traveler's Guide to Camping Mexico's Baja, Traveler's Guide to Alaskan Camping,* and *RV Adventures in the Pacific Northwest* are designed to be the guidebooks that the authors tried to find when they first traveled to these places.

Terri and Mike now live full-time in an RV: traveling, writing new books, and working to keep these guidebooks as up-to-date as possible. The books are written and prepared for printing using laptop computers while on the road.

Traveler's Guide To European Camping
6" x 9" Paperback, 640 Pages, Over 400 Maps
ISBN 0-9652968-8-1

Over 350 campgrounds including at least one in virtually every important European city are described in detail, directions are given for finding them, and in many cases information about convenient shopping, entertainment and sports opportunities is included.

Traveler's Guide To European Camping will tell you how to rent, lease, or buy a rig in Europe or ship your own from home. It contains the answers to questions about the myriad details of living, driving, and camping in Europe.

In addition to camping and campground information *Traveler's Guide To European Camping* gives you invaluable details about the history and sights you will encounter. This information will help you plan your itinerary and enjoy yourself more when you are on the road.

Use the information in this book to travel Europe like a native. Enjoy the food, sights, and people of Europe. Go for a week, a month, a year. Europe can fill your RV or camping vacation seasons for many years to come!

Traveler's Guide To Camping Mexico's Baja
6" x 9" Paperback, 224 Pages, Over 65 Maps
ISBN 0-9749471-0-5

Sun, sand, and clear blue water are just three of the many reasons more and more RVers are choosing Mexico's Baja as a winter destination. The Baja is fun, easy, and the perfect RVing getaway.

With the right information crossing the border onto the Baja is a snap. Only a few miles south you'll find many camping opportunities—some on beaches where you'll park your vehicle just feet from the water.

Traveler's Guide To Camping Mexico's Baja starts by giving you the Baja-related infromation from our popular book *Traveler's Guide To Mexican Camping*. It also covers nearby Puerto Peñasco. We've added more campgrounds, expanded the border-crossing section, and given even more information about towns, roads, and recreational opportunities. Like all our books, this one features easy-to-follow maps showing exactly how to find every campground listed.

RV Adventures in the Pacific Northwest
6" x 9" Paperback, 224 Pages, Over 75 Maps
ISBN 0-9652968-4-9

There are many reasons why the Pacific Northwest is considered an RVers paradise. It offers everything an RV vacationer could desire: seashores, snow-topped mountains, old-growth forests, visitor-friendly cities, and national parks. In fact, the Pacific Northwest is one of the most popular RVing destinations in North America.

RV Adventures in the Pacific Northwest provides eight exciting and interesting 1-week itineraries from the Northwest gateway cities of Seattle, Portland, and Vancouver. Maps and written descriptions guide you along scenic easy-to-negotiate tours. Each day's drive leads to an interesting destination. The book includes descriptions of the local attractions and activities as well as maps showing good local RV campgrounds.

Traveler's Guide To Mexican Camping
6" x 9" Paperback, 448 Pages, Over 250 Maps
ISBN 0-9652968-6-5

Mexico, one of the world's most interesting and least expensive travel destinations, is just across the southern U.S. border. It offers warm sunny weather all winter long, beautiful beaches, colonial cities, and excellent food. Best of all, you can easily and economically visit Mexico in your own car or RV.

The second edition of *Traveler's Guide To Mexican Camping* is now even better! It has become the bible for Mexican campers. With this book you will cross the border and travel Mexico like a veteran. It is designed to make your trip as simple and trouble-free as possible. In additon to camping and campground information the guide also includes information about important cities, tourist destinations, roads and driving, trip preparation, vehicle care, shopping, entertainment and sports opportunities. It will help you plan your itinerary and enjoy yourself more while you are on the road. Some of the features the second edition offers are:

❑ Instructions for crossing the border. New in this edition is detailed information about every important crossing and recommendations for the best places to cross with large RVs.

❑ There are now detailed descriptions of over three hundred Mexican camp-grounds, over sixty of them not in the previous edition.

❑ The new edition has information about camping in Belize including border-crossing details and campground descriptions.

❑ A new index map and formatting makes this edition very user friendly.

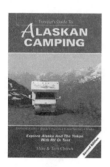

Traveler's Guide To Alaskan Camping
6" x 9" Paperback, 416 Pages, Over 100 Maps
ISBN 0-9652968-7-3

Alaska, the dream trip of a lifetime! Be prepared for something spec-tacular. Alaska is one fifth the size of the entire United States, it has 17 of the 20 highest peaks in the U.S., 33,904 miles of shoreline, and has more active glaciers and ice fields than the rest of the inhabited world.

In addition to some of the most magnificent scenery the world has to offer, Alaska is chock full of an amazing variety of woldife. Fishing, hiking, canoeing, rafting, hunting, and wildlife viewing are only a few of the many activities which will keep you outside during the long summer days.

Traveler's Guide To Alaskan Camping makes this dream trip to Alaska as easy as camping in the "Lower 48". It includes:

❑ Almost 500 campgrounds throughout Alaska and on the roads north in Canada with full campground descriptions and maps showing the exact location of each campground.

❑ Complete coverage of the routes north, including the Alaska Highway, the Cassiar High-way, and the Alaska Marine Highway.

❑ RV rental information for both Alaska and Canada.

❑ Things to do throughout your trip, including suggested fishing holes, hiking trails, canoe trips, wildlife viewing opportunities, and much more. There's even a full chapter on off-road camping trips for those who want to venture away from the beaten path!

To order complete the following and send to:

Rolling Homes Press
161 Rainbow Dr., #6157
Livingston, TX 77399-1061

Name_____

Address_____

City_____State_____Zip_____

Telephone_____

Description	Qty	Price	Subtotal
Traveler's Guide To Alaskan Camping	_____	$21.95	_____
Traveler's Guide To Mexican Camping	_____	$19.95	_____
Traveler's Guide To Camping Mexico's Baja	_____	$14.95	_____
Traveler's Guide To European Camping	_____	$24.95	_____
RV and Car Camping Vacations in Europe	_____	$16.95	_____
RV Adventures in the Pacific Northwest	_____	$14.95	_____

Subtract - Multiple Title Discounts

3 Book Set (3 Different Titles Shown Above)		**-10.00**	_____
4 Book Set (4 Different Titles Shown Above)		**-15.00**	_____
5 Book Set (5 Different Titles Shown Above)		**-20.00**	_____
6 Book Set (All 6 Titles)		**-25.00**	_____

Method of Payment	Order total	_____
❏ Check	Shipping:	5.00 *
❏ Visa	Total:	
❏ Mastercard		_____

Credit Card #   Exp. date
_____

Signature
_____

To order by phone call (425) 822-7846
Have your VISA or MC ready
U.S. Dollars or MC/VISA only for non-U.S. orders
Rolling Homes Press is not responsible for taxes or duty on books shipped
outside the U.S.

*$5 shipping regardless of quantity ordered for all orders sent to the same address in
the U.S. or Canada. Actual cost for multiple books shipped to other destnations.

Visit our web site at **www.rollinghomes.com**

For mail orders allow approximately 1 month for delivery